Husbands & Wives

Husbands & Wives

The Dynamics of Married Living

By

Robert O. Blood, Jr.

and

Donald M. Wolfe

The Free Press of Glencoe

PREFACE

MARRIAGE IS ONE of the most significant of human relationships. Yet surprisingly little is known about how ordinary husbands and wives get along with each other. Most previous studies have dealt with fragmentary or specialized groups of marriages. This book is one of the first ever to describe a cross-section sample of an entire community (metropolitan Detroit) and to provide comparative data from a representative sample of farm families. It is designed to give the intelligent layman as well as the professional student a picture of how American marriages operate.

This book is in part a report of the findings gained through interviews with 731 city families and 178 farm families. The interview materials provide a wealth of information about American husband-wife relationships, clearing up misconceptions that have existed and confirming other propositions about married life. In addition, this book contains a series of treatises on key aspects of marriage; it goes beyond the raw facts to interpret the dynamics of marriage relationships in meaningful terms. It is both a source of factual information about contemporary marriage patterns and a thoughtful stimulus to further understanding of American marriages, as they have evolved from the past and are changing in the present.

The urban interviews were gathered through the facilities of the Detroit Area Study, a research-training facility of the University of Michigan. The staff members responsible for the administrative work involved include Harry Sharp, Director; David Goldberg, Ruth Searles, John Takeshita, and David Varley. Special mention should be made of the collaboration of Ruth Searles with the authors, in the theoretical design of the analysis. Ronald Freedman provided the initial impetus and encouragement for undertaking the project.

Graduate students who participated in the formulation of the interview schedules, the interviewing itself, and the coding of the responses were Mickey Aiken, Robert Barnes, Albert Boswell, Richard

Burlingame, Donna Buse, Russell Chappell, Remi Clignet, Eleanor Cochrane, Theodore Curtis, Donald Dorfman, David Feuerfile, Martin Gold, Mae Guyer, Ellen Heyman, Beryl Hutchison, Toshio Kumabe, John Kunkel, Donald Nagler, Robert Richardson, Victor Schneider, Eileen Schulak, John Scott, David Sirota, Carol Slater, Charles Smith, Dietrick Snoek, Howard Wolowitz, and William Zeller.

To secure the farm interviews, a special research team was mobilized under the direction of Ann Blalock with Popie Mohring as sampler, and Marie Baker, Carter Pate, Adelaide Suits, Maxine Thompson, and William Zeller as interviewers.

The farm project was financed by a grant from the Horace H. Rackham Fund, by the Board of Governors of the Horace H. Rackham School of Graduate Studies of the University of Michigan. A second grant from the same source made possible the analysis of the Detroit data.

The analysis staff included Egon Gross, Heinz Kohler, Janice Longone, Bette and Joseph Rubinstein, Donald Walker, Donald Warren, and Roman Yoder.

To all these people the authors owe their thanks for indispensable assistance in a very large undertaking.

Finally, the roles of the two authors may be explained. Robert Blood was the principal investigator and drafted the manuscript of this book. Donald Wolfe carried the entire administrative responsibility for the complex analysis of the data over the years from 1955 to 1959, shared in revising the manuscript, and wrote the story of the interviewing. The two authors shared equally in the discussion and interpretation of the findings.

This book is therefore the joint product of many participants, not least of whom are the 909 families who generously gave of their time, in order that others might better understand the meaning of marriage in modern America.

Robert O. Blood, Jr.
Donald M. Wolfe

January 1, 1960

CONTENTS

Part Two

Family Functions

Part Three

The Evaluation of American Marriage

LIST OF TABLES

Chapter Three

Chapter Four

Chapter Eight

Chapter Nine

Appendix A

Chapter Nine

INTRODUCTION: A STUDY
OF MARRIAGE

THE QUESTION IS often asked in newspapers and magazines, "What is happening to American marriages?" The answer often comes in pessimistic terms. One impressive (and depressing) fact is the steady rise in the American divorce rate from as far back as there are any statistics at all. At the present time, between twenty and twenty-five divorces are granted each year for every one hundred couples married in the preceding year. Whether this rate will continue to rise is difficult to predict—and beyond the scope of this study. However, the interpretation of the causes of this divorce rate and of its implications for our changing ways of family living is of vital concern in this book.

Some writers think the American family is headed toward total collapse. They describe the American home as little more than a boarding house where husbands and children come to eat and sleep. They accuse the commercial services in the modern city of undermining the stability of the family and depriving it of its usefulness. Ogburn (1938) points out how the family function of economic production has been transferred to the factory, education to the school, religion to the church, protection to the police, and recreation to the movies, leaving little for the family to do except bearing children and providing affection.

Zimmerman (1948) fears that the contemporary urban family is becoming "atomistic" as a result of this loss of functions, meaning that family members put their individual welfare above the collective welfare. Such individualism, he thinks, is incompatible with the survival of the family. City dwellers are supposedly becoming indifferent to their family responsibilities and vulnerable to the competitive lures of teen-age peer groups and adult pals and lovers. Urban life, from this point of view, is anonymous and fragmentary, with each man knowing only a part of his fellows' personalities and deprived of those primary-group ties which used to make life meaningful.

To summarize, such writers feel that the American family is crumbling in decay. Insofar as it continues to exist at all, the family appears to be an increasingly meaningless hangover from the past. Such, in deliberate caricature, is the gloomy interpretation today.

THE CHANGING AMERICAN FAMILY

No one contests the fact that family life in America has undergone tremendous changes in recent years. In the "good old days" most Americans lived on farms, whereas only about one family in eight does now. If we go back far enough we come to a pioneer phase of American life, when individualism was penalized through bachelor taxes, and belonging to a family unit was a matter of sheer physical necessity. Husbands, wives, and children worked together in the fields, or separately in woods and cabin, to eke out an often bare subsistence. The husband protected his wife and children from marauding Indians and wild animals. Churches and schools were rare, leaving most religious and educational activity in the home.

Under these urgent circumstances, nobody worried about what was happening to the American family. There wasn't time to worry, and, if there had been, it would have been obvious that the family was a strict economic and social necessity in a precarious world.

Nobody questioned much about the role of women either—a

man could hardly get along without a wife to cook and sew and produce assistants for him. She, in turn, was even more dependent on him for protection and sustenance. Under the circumstances, his authority was as unquestioned as that of a military officer—and for the same desperate reasons.

Then came the industrial revolution. Its most important consequence was to separate the place where a man worked from his home. As a result, the members of the family no longer worked together and, as child-labor laws were passed, children became an economic liability instead of an asset. The husband's disciplinary role was impaired by his physical separation from the family and by the termination of his role as boss of the family work crew. (Homans, 1950.)

The further development of modern industry includes increasing mechanization of tasks, intricacy of assembly (as in electronics), paper-work co-ordination, and proliferation of skills. These trends have produced increasing job opportunities for women, until one-third of the total American labor force now consists of women.

The availability of jobs means that women no longer necessarily depend on a husband (or father) for support. No longer is marriage an economic necessity, nor is divorce economically impossible. Jobs are available today not only to single and divorced women but to married women as well. By 1950, for the first time in American history, a majority of all working women were married. (Myrdal and Klein, 1956.)

What does it do to the husband-wife relationship for both partners to be employed? (Detailed evidence from this study will be given in subsequent chapters.) There is a world of difference between a wife who works on the farm under her husband's leadership and the kind of independence gained by working for someone else. Certainly, the American husband's diminishing authority is due in great part to this steadily increasing proportion of wives who work outside the home.

Many other factors have altered the relationship between husbands and wives—wars, education for women, the development of contraception, etc. Regardless of the causes, the fact remains that families are different today from what they once were—except nobody seems to know exactly how they are different.

The spectrum of guesses includes the picture of disintegration to which we referred and numerous accusations of "momism" hurled against the supposedly domineering American wife and the submissive American husband. It also includes happier forecasts of new styles of family life. For example, Burgess and Locke (1953) coined a famous phrase about the historical change in the American family, "from institution to companionship." Such authors believe American marriages have not so much deteriorated as changed. Throughout this book, we will be aware of the context of change within which American families live today.

THE GOALS OF THIS BOOK

Our primary purpose is to understand the dynamics of American marriage, by systematically analyzing our empirical evidence. The general question is: what factors determine how husbands and wives interact and what are the effects of varying interaction patterns on the general welfare of the husband, the wife, and the family as a whole?

In order to find meaningful answers to this question, we shall delve into the impact, on the husband-wife relationship, of various characteristics of the nuclear family (such as, number of children and stage in the family-life cycle); the effects of the family's position and experience in the larger society (the church, the occupational system, etc.); the effects of their past experience and training (education, nationality background, social mobility, etc.); and, at times, the role of the personal needs and desires of the husband and wife.

However, before we can know what happens to the husband-wife relationship under varying circumstances, we must first know something about what American marriages are like in general. Hence, each chapter begins with a look at one characteristic of our entire sample of families. How do husbands generally treat their wives, and vice versa? What does each aspect of marriage mean to the participants? Answers to such questions bear on the controversial question with which we began this chapter: what's happening to the American family?

We are not interested in just any families. Many of the theories we have discussed about family life refer primarily to the effects of living in a city—a big city. It is the urban family which is primarily at issue today—and rightly so. The city is the new environment to which family patterns must adapt, and this new style of family will shape the future in an increasingly urbanized world. Hence one goal of this study is to examine city families in particular.

One can never understand anything well, without having a standard of comparison. For city families, that standard is partly provided by general impressions of what family life was like in the old days. A more precise comparison can be made with the way in which farm families live at the present time. The final objective of this study is to provide such a comparison between city families and farm families. This will test the impact of the urban environment as such, as distinguished from the educational, technological, and cultural changes which have affected both city and farm families.[1]

When we have done all this, we should understand much better what families are like today and how they got to be that way. At least, that understanding is our aim.

THE METHODS OF THIS STUDY

While our over-all approach throughout this book is to provide a general and theoretical discussion of family structure and process, of the problems families face and the services they perform for their members, it is essential to base this discussion on empirical evidence. Thus, this book is also a report of a major research project on the modern American family.

---

1. Such a comparison of city and farm families provides one possible basis for predicting the shape of things to come. If city families are different from farm families, perhaps they show the direction in which families are moving. But contemporary farm families don't really represent the past, since they are influenced by modern conditions. Nor do old families. If old couples don't talk to each other as often as young couples, is this an historical change in marriage patterns from one generation to another or is this a life cycle development which will be repeated as today's young couples get older? We will speculate about such interpretations as best we can, but the only way to be really sure would be to restudy today's young couples as they do get older.

The data presented in the tables and text come from a systematic probability-sample survey of families in the Detroit metropolitan area and from a comparable survey of farm families in southeastern Michigan. Structured and controlled interviews, lasting more than an hour each, were conducted with 731 urban and suburban wives and with 178 farm wives. Where comparable data are available, these data match very well the findings of the 1950 U.S. Census for the same geographical areas; the samples seem to be quite representative of the populations from which they were drawn. (For the interested reader, Appendix A contains a discussion of the sample as compared to Census material and of the sampling, interviewing, and analysis procedures followed in this study. The interview schedule is reproduced in Appendix B.)

It may seem strange that in a study of marriage only one partner should be interviewed. However, many previous studies have shown a close correlation between what husbands and wives say about their marriages, making it possible to rely on one partner's responses. There are undoubtedly individual cases where the husband would have given a different picture from the one the wife gave us, but these differences tend to get lost in the shuffle when large numbers of cases are considered.

Wives, in general, probably look at marriage somewhat differently from husbands. Hence, it should be remembered that this is a wife's-eye view of marriage. But we assume that when we make comparisons between groups of wives—as between middle-class wives and working-class wives—the sex bias cancels out and the differences which emerge are real differences between families.

The selection of wives instead of husbands was largely a question of productivity. Wives are more easily located at home so that more interviews can be obtained from them. In addition, to the extent that wives invest more time and effort in family matters, they may provide more complete and useful data. Although unavailable at present, a comparable study based on interviews with husbands would nevertheless add valuable detail.

To a large extent, this research is more exploratory than definitive, more hypothesis-generating than hypothesis-testing. Therefore, there has been a greater concentration on the theoretical importance than on the statistical significance of the findings. For this reason, and for reasons of maximum data presentation within reasonable cost, we have not reported confidence levels for many of the findings. This does not mean that the likelihood that small differences between small subsamples might be due to chance has been disregarded. Indeed, we have tried at all times to insert the proper cautions throughout the discussion. (In Appendix A, a number of tables are presented which show the estimated minimum percentage and mean differences between two groups necessary to assure finding similar differences 95 times in 100 repeated studies of similar samples from the same population, i.e., differences which reach the .05 level of statistical significance.) It should be noted that there are times when differences below the reliable minimum are suggestive of possible new understandings about family life. Such cases seem worth discussing if the proper cautiousness is taken.

We have looked not simply for isolated differences between groups but for patterns of relationships which can be interpreted meaningfully. In part, this means that we have looked for progressive regularities in the relationship of the same two variables. For example, we are impressed by the way husbands tend to make more decisions the higher their social status. Such tendencies in the direction of a relationship give added confidence beyond a simple comparison of two proportions.

Most importantly, however, we have searched for larger generalizations than can be derived from relating just two variables at a time. It is in these higher-order concepts and configurations that the meaning of marriage to husbands and wives can best be captured.

PREVIEW

We will begin our report about the 909 families by examining the structure of husband-wife relationships in terms of both the relative dominance of the two partners in decision-making and the participation of each in household tasks.

Then we will discuss the functions that marriage performs for its members—both the traditional ones of economic sustenance and childbearing, and the modern emphasis on companionship, emotional support, and love and affection.

In all these chapters, we will assess the vitality of marriage in contemporary America. Is it a last-gasping survival of ancient forms or a dynamic adaptation to new circumstances which serves useful purposes in the present? What are the various adaptations which marriages make to varying contemporary circumstances?

The concluding chapter pinpoints some of the major stresses in contemporary marriage patterns and summarizes the satisfaction which most husbands and wives find in their life together.

Part One

FAMILY STRUCTURE

THE SOCIAL STRUCTURE of a family consists of the positions which the members occupy in relation to each other. The most important aspect of family structure is the power positions of the members (see Chapter Two). Power may be divided equally between the husband and wife or wielded predominantly by one partner over the other.

The second aspect of structure is the division of labor (Chapter Three). This involves a pattern of roles in which the husband does some tasks, the wife others, and they do some together.

In combination, the power structure and the division of labor are the most basic things we can say about a family. They are affected by the family's position in the community and in turn provide the framework within which the family functions (Part Two).

THE POWER TO MAKE DECISIONS

NO CHANGE in the American family is mentioned more often than the shift from one-sided male authority to the sharing of power by husband and wife. Perhaps no change is more significant, either. The balance of power between husband and wife is a sensitive reflection of the roles they play in marriage—and, in turn, has many repercussions on other aspects of their relationship.

Power and Authority. Power may be defined as the potential ability of one partner to influence the other's behavior. Power is manifested in the ability to make decisions affecting the life of the family.

Authority is closely related to power. Authority is legitimate power, i.e., power held by one partner because both partners feel it is proper for him to do so. The family authority pattern is prescribed by the society at large in such forms as: "the man should be the head of the house"—or "husbands should not dictate to their wives."

Power, on the other hand, refers to the way in which husbands and wives actually deal with each other. Caspar Milquetoast, as a man, may be supposed to have considerable authority, but in practice he exercises very little power. Power and authority do not necessarily coincide.

TWO THEORIES ABOUT THE SOURCES OF POWER

The power to make decisions is influenced by the prescribed authority pattern. In a patriarchal system both the husband and the wife will ordinarily take for granted that the husband should make most of the decisions. He derives a measure of assertiveness from the social norm, and she, a corresponding measure of deference. But even in a tradition-bound society, there are variations between couples. Indeed, the whole conception of a hen-pecked husband implies a norm that is being violated.

The existence of such discrepancies suggests that there must be other sources of marital power beside authority. In the world at large, the illegitimate seizure of power usually rests on military might. But husbands and wives do not ordinarily point guns at each other. Even rolling pins and fists are more often preludes to the disintegration of marriage than the basis on which a balance of power is worked out.

The sources of power in so intimate a relationship as marriage must be sought in the comparative resources which the husband and wife bring to the marriage, rather than in brute force. A resource may be defined as anything that one partner may make available to the other, helping the latter satisfy his needs or attain his goals. The balance of power will be on the side of that partner who contributes the greater resources to the marriage.

Marriage itself may be thought of as an institution designed to meet certain vital needs of the participants. People get married because they believe that they will find sexual fulfilment, emotional response, companionship, and the new experience of parenthood, in living together. Both partners hope to attain these goals through the same marriage. Insofar as both partners contribute to each others' satisfaction in life, they build up a mutual respect that expresses itself naturally in mutual consultation. As one partner is able to contribute more than his share to the marriage, he acquires the basis for a more than fifty-fifty say in decisions. This is seldom a conscious process of weighing the balance. It is an automatic readjustment which occurs as the contributing partner discovers that he has a lot to offer to the marriage, while the receiving partner feels indebted for what has already been given and dependent upon what he hopes to receive in the future. Control over future resources is especially crucial, since decision-making involves the allocation of resources within the family. The partner who may provide or withhold resources is in a strategic position for influencing their disposition. Hence, power accrues spontaneously to the partner who has the greater resources at his disposal.

A second factor is closely related to resources. Anyone who is able to make a contribution is, almost by definition, a competent person—i.e., someone with special skills. To possess a skill enables the individual to make a contribution; in addition, it implies special competence in decision-making as such. Thus, a wife may not only depend on her husband for "bringing home the bacon" but recognize that in his work he becomes familiar with some of the complexities of life outside the home. Therefore, she may defer to his superior knowledge in decisions about politics, taxes, and cars.

The chief objective of this chapter is to look at the comparative competence of the two partners and their relative contributions to marriage, as explanations for the variations which occur between couples' balance of power. According to this hypothesis, Caspar is hen-pecked because he is incompetent and makes very little contribution to the life-satisfactions of his wife.

Culture or Competence?

If authority patterns and personal resources both influence the balance of power, are they equally important? There are two different theories: according to one, families do what the culture tells them to do; the other states that they do what their own characteristics dictate. In a stable society, the two sources of power will coincide. American society, however, has not been stable. Everybody knows that the balance of power between men and women has been changing. Has it changed because our ideas about how men and women ought to treat each other have changed? Or has it changed because the comparative resources of American men and women have changed?

The answer is not likely to be completely one or the other— since changes in one are bound to affect the other sooner or later. If husbands become infected with democratic ideas and start giving their wives more freedom, the wives will gain more competence. On the other hand, if wives gain increased resources, old patriarchal notions are not likely to remain unaffected for very long.

Despite this interdependence of ideological and pragmatic sources of power, there may still be an important difference in their potency. Historical analyses may show that one changes first and the other follows after. Contemporary analysis may show patriarchal norms continuing to influence the balance of power under changing circumstances, or it may show families adapting rapidly to new conditions no matter their ideological training.

The ideological theory will be tested first by looking for patriarchal subcultures in the Detroit area. If culture is more than just a rationalization of existing circumstances, Detroit families should be more traditional if they grew up on farms, or in "the old country," or in "the old days." This search will prove fruitless; the alternative pragmatic theory of the basis of power will have to be tested to show its usefulness. The evidence from Detroit in support of competence as the chief basis for power will be cumulatively impressive.

According to the resource theory, statements about patriarchal authority patterns or equalitarian ones are chiefly rationalizations of existing practice—like codifications of the common law. As people grow up under a husband-dominant family system, they come to take that balance of power for granted—and even to feel that it is right. Henceforward, the idea of patriarchy acquires momentum and influence in its own right, shaping generations to come until it is undermined by new conditions. At first, only the innovators in society see the handwriting on the wall and begin talking about new beliefs to fit new circumstances. For the rest of society, the old system hangs on by a kind of cultural lag, although increasingly paid only lip service. Finally, the social change is consolidated, and new ideas about marriage spread through the society to all but the most conservative.

From this analysis, it is clear that culture is not a sufficient explanation for power. It is not enough to say that wives used to be submissive to their husbands because they lived under a patriarchal system, or because that was the custom. The search must be pushed further into why the patriarchal system arose in the first place. The same search for "basic" causes will be necessary if we are to understand the modern pattern of decision-making.

THE HISTORY OF POWER IN AMERICAN MARRIAGES

The present is better understood if we look first at the past. In terms of the world-wide experience of the human race, we have clearly come from a patriarchal background. Murdock's (1949) comprehensive examination of 250 primitive and historic societies shows that far more societies have operated under husband-dominance than under any other system (such as wife-dominance or equality). There is similarly clear evidence on every hand that we Americans stem from patriarchal forebears, too. Why has patriarchy been so popular?

The dominance of men in marriage is often attributed to physical strength. While men do have more muscle power, any factor which operates purely in a biological fashion would be expected to have a universal effect. If superior musculature were the only reason for male dominance, we would expect men to dominate everywhere and in all times. The fact that they do not suggests that other factors must, at least, contribute to the picture.

Probably the most important of these additional factors is the economic role of men and women in different times and places (Ogburn and Nimkoff, 1955). For instance, hunting societies depend on the men for their food resources. The fact that men rather than women do the hunting reflects the great exertion required which only men can take. Meanwhile since women are childbearers and child-sucklers, they must stay behind by the fire (Scheinfeld, 1943). These are circumstances under which male dominance tends to prevail since the women depend on male prowess for sustenance. Under hoe culture, on the other hand, women have the necessary strength to perform productive work without having to stray far from home—

hence they tend to assume a more influential role in the family. The domestication of large animals brings man back into the forefront because of the strength required to handle them and the wandering necessary to pasture them. The replacement of the hoe by the plow (whether drawn by horse, mule, or bullock) similarly enhances the role of the male.

That partner is most powerful who is the instrumental leader, who gets those things done which most urgently need doing if the family is to survive (Parsons and Bales, 1955). Such a leader is not only economically productive himself but functions as the organizer and administrator of other family members in the task of economic production.

Our Patriarchal Forebears

Against this background it is possible to see why our American forebears were patriarchal. Under pioneer conditions, rugged masculinity was at a premium. Women had to be rugged, too, in order to endure the hardships of hunger and cold—but it was the men who wrested a living from the wilderness with axe and rifle. (Annie Oakley was a curiosity precisely because the rifle was so masculine a weapon.) A widow could hardly survive in the woods without grown sons to support her. It took a man to kill a bear, to fight off the Indians, to fell the trees and erect the cabin. (It is still men who build houses but the psychological impact is not the same when it is *other* men, and not the husband, who do the building.) In general, the more stark the conditions for survival, the more crucial the family decisions which must be made, so the more unchallenged the authority-figure is likely to be. Disobedience to the husband-father in the wilderness was like mutiny on a ship at sea, when all hands might be lost under inexperienced leadership.

As Americans shifted from hunting to agriculture, the conditions of life moderated, and the dominance of the male lost some of its stringent urgency. On the other hand, the farm homestead required the wife and children to pitch into many tasks of farming under the man's leadership. His position of economic leadership gave the man a dominant position in the family, which was strengthened by the periodic helpless dependence of the wife in childbirth and the obviously superior competence of the veteran farmer over his inex-

perienced children. The transition from forest to farm may have
changed the precise basis of the man's authority but it hardly altered
the extent of it.

Throughout the nineteenth century, a large share of Americans
lived on farms. But even in the cities, marriage was still largely
patriarchal. City life required the husband to go off to work away
from home, but wives seldom followed. It was chiefly single women
who worked in the early textile mills, according to Ogburn and
Nimkoff. With few exceptions, factories in those days were noisier,
dirtier, more dangerous, and less mechanized than they are now.
Much of the work still required brute strength. So women—single
or married—preferred not to work in them.

As for married women, the large number of children borne and
cared for, and the lack of labor-saving devices made the housewife
and mother too busy to work outside the home. Once again in the
history of mankind, the man became the sole source of support for
his dependents. And since the wife was one of these dependents, her
position continued subordinate as before.

Not all city workers were factory hands. In small businesses,
some wives did work with their husbands—but in a subordinate role
comparable to the wife on the farm. The gradual increase in the pro-
fessions required higher education which at first was closed to
women, increasing the gap between educated husbands and their
uneducated wives.

Through the Victorian era, the American family system remained
patriarchal, challenged only by a few exceptionally educated and
talented feminists. Since that time the picture has changed markedly.

The Rise of Women

The employment of women in appreciable numbers began with
World War I and continued into the booming 1920's. Not enough
men were available to fill all the jobs needed by the nation. Moreover, industry was changing its environment and tasks, until women
not only could tolerate them but were sometimes better suited to
them than men. Large-scale business and industry required the
development of extensive systems of communication and control
whose letters and records were best typed by women. The increased
economic productivity of the nation led to a corresponding rise in the

standard of living, creating an opportunity for the American people to move beyond the mere necessities of life to cultural and recreational luxuries which made new demands on feminine talent. The same high standard of living made possible the purchase of labor-saving devices, ready-made clothes, and ready-to-eat foods, which freed the housewife from bondage to stove, sink, and needle. The productivity of the American economy required the development of advertising to create markets for consumer goods. This advertising succeeded so well that women with increased appetites for goods wanted to go to work so that they could raise the family level of living still further and faster. All these factors, accentuated by another world war and another period of prosperity, combined to create an intensified demand for women workers, and by women to work.

The result has been a dramatic rise in the proportion of married women employed outside the home. For single women, self-support has long since been taken for granted. The innovation is that it is no longer the wedding but the first pregnancy which brings this working span to a halt. Even then the halt is often temporary as an increasing number of middle-aged mothers go back to work to put their children through college or to fill the gap left by the departure of those children.

The productivity of the American economy has also made possible the luxury of the education of women (as in turn it has created a demand for educated women employees). Today more girls than boys graduate from high school, since the latter often drop out to go to work. Even at the college level there are now nearly half as many women as men enrolled.

The employment and education of women have given them resources which their grandmothers didn't have. The pay check of the working wife is a contribution to the family which would be expected to give her a greater interest in financial decisions—and greater respect from her husband. The participation of the wife in the outside world through her job gives her contacts with fellow workers which lessen her dependence on her husband for emotional support and increase the knowledge and skill she brings to decision-making.

Such factors have produced a new generation of American wives who are more resourceful and competent than their grandmothers.

They are no longer content to sit quietly by while their husbands make the decisions. This is not to say that there is necessarily exact equality between husbands and wives in contemporary America but that the predominance of the male has been so thoroughly undermined that we no longer live in a patriarchal system.

THE CONTEMPORARY PATTERN OF POWER

In order to measure the precise balance of power between husbands and wives one would have to assess their influence in all the family decisions which had ever been made—or at least all those which had been made over a considerable period of time. Such an exhaustive undertaking would exceed the capacities of husbands' and wives' memories.

Since a complete record of decisions is unobtainable, any study of marriage must rely on a sample of decisions to represent the larger whole. In this study, eight decisions were selected to provide an estimate of the relative balance of power between husband and wife.

The eight decisions are:

1) What job the husband should take.
2) What car to get.
3) Whether or not to buy life insurance.
4) Where to go on a vacation.
5) What house or apartment to take.
6) Whether or not the wife should go to work or quit work.
7) What doctor to have when someone is sick.
8) How much money the family can afford to spend per week on food.

These eight were selected because they are all relatively important (compared to deciding whether to go to a movie tonight). They are also questions which nearly all couples have to face. (This is why no questions were asked relating to children.) Only three per cent of the couples at most answered any question in hypothetical terms (the three per cent who had never bought a car and the similar number who hadn't yet taken a vacation). The remaining criterion for these questions was that they should range from typically masculine to typically feminine decisions—but should always affect the family as a whole.

It was assumed in advance that contemporary husbands and wives would often talk things over in the process of arriving at a decision. Even a patriarchal husband may consult his wife as one source of opinion and one factor to be taken into consideration while he makes up his mind. The crucial question is not who takes part in the discussion but who makes the final decision. To get this information the lead-in statement to the battery of questions was as follows:

"In every family somebody has to decide such things as where the family will live and so on. Many couples talk such things over first, but the *final* decision often has to be made by the husband or the wife. For instance, who usually makes the final decision about. . . ?"

In order to provide comparable answers, the respondents were given a choice of "husband always," "husband more than wife," "husband and wife exactly the same," "wife more than husband," and "wife always" as response categories.

Who Decides?

The wives' answers to the eight questions are shown in Table 1 with the items arranged in order of decreasing male participation.

Two decisions are primarily the husband's province (his job and the car), two the wife's (her work and the food), while all the others are joint decisions in the sense of having more "same" responses than anything else. Even the wife's working turns out to be a quite middling decision from the standpoint of the mean score, leaving only the food expenditures preponderantly in the wife's hands. Only the two male decisions are made more than half the time by a particular partner.

Sex Roles. The distribution of decisions by sex is not surprising. The husband's work is his chief role in life. From it he derives his greatest sense of well-being or malaise, and there he invests the greatest part of his energies. His work is so one-sidedly important to him that almost all the wives leave him alone for his final decision.

Automobiles are associated with the mechanical aptitude of males

Table 1

Allocation of Power in Decision-making Areas

(731 Detroit Families)

WHO DECIDES?				DECISION				
	Husband's job	Car	Insur-ance	Vaca-tion	House	Wife's work	Doctor	Food
(5) Husband always	90%	56%	31%	12%	12%	26%	7%	10%
(4) Husband more than wife	4	12	11	6	6	5	3	2
(3) Husband and wife exactly the same	3	25	41	68	58	18	45	32
(2) Wife more than husband	0	2	4	4	10	9	11	11
(1) Wife always	1	3	10	7	13	39	31	41
N.A.	2	1	2	3	1	3	3	3
Total	100	99	99	100	100	100	100	99
Husband's mean power*	4.86	4.18	3.50	3.12	2.94	2.69	2.53	2.26

* The mean for each column is computed on the basis of the weights shown, e.g., "husband always" = 5.

(Scheinfeld, 1943). Moreover, a large proportion of the driving in the United States is done by males, giving them added interest in the choice of car.

At the other extreme, meal-planning is part of the wife's role in the division of labor (as will be documented in the next chapter), giving to the wife the major responsibility for food expenditures.

The choice of doctor falls to the wife especially often where there are dependent children in the home, so that it is associated with her role as mother. However, it also reflects the general tendency of women to play a nurturant role for the sick and helpless.

The family vacation and the choice of house are most frequently joint decisions. Is this because they most clearly affect both partners equally?

The fact that insurance decisions are made somewhat more often by the husband may reflect the technical financial questions involved. If so, the financial training involved in his money-earning role gives him extra competence.

That the husband should be more involved in his wife's job decisions than she with his is understandable. For one thing, her work is seldom her major preoccupation in life the way it is for a man. Even if she works just as many hours a week, she does not usually make the same life-long commitment to the world of work. Nor is her pay check as indispensable to the family finances (if only because it is usually smaller). In such ways the choice whether to work or not is less vital to a woman than to a man.

In addition, the wife's decisions about working have repercussions on the husband. If his wife goes to work, he will have to help out more around the house. If he is a business executive, he may prefer to have her concentrate her energy on entertaining prospective clients at home. As a small businessman or independent professional, he may need her services in his own enterprise. On the other hand, regardless of his own occupation, he may want her to work in order to help him buy a house or a business or pay for the children's education.

It may be, then, that the work role is so much the responsibility of the husband in marriage that even the wife's work is but an adjunct of his instrumental leadership, leaving this decision frequently in his hands.

The Balance of Power

Whether families are patriarchal in general is far more important than whether they sometimes conform to patriarchal norms in a single area of decision-making. With eight questions so widely distributed between masculine and feminine roles, the Detroit families as a whole could not look very patriarchal when their answers to the whole battery of questions are totalled up. Even so, there might still be considerable variation between families, if in some the husbands consistently make the decisions while in others wives consistently do.

In actual practice, such consistency is rare. Less than one half of one per cent of the Detroit husbands make all eight decisions and a similarly small proportion of wives are all-powerful. Nevertheless such extremes do exist and exemplify the fact that it is possible to find all kinds of power-balances from the most patriarchal to the most matriarchal.

Given these eight particular questions, the aggregate balance of power falls slightly in the husband's direction. When the total scores for the eight questions, weighted as shown in Table 1, are converted into a ten-point scale reflecting the amount of influence exerted by the husband, the average score for all families is 5.09 (whereas a score of 4.00 is the equivalent of "husband and wife exactly the same").

Although families can be found varying all the way from one extreme to the other, most families bunch together around this mean score. Forty-six per cent of all the Detroit families have scores of four to six. Though slightly skewed to the husband's side in absolute terms, it seems preferable to label these as relatively equalitarian couples. This leaves twenty-two per cent with scores of seven or more who can be called relatively male-dominant and another twenty-two per cent with scores of three or less who are relatively female-dominant.[1] Even these extreme groups cluster close to the central group. This means that Detroit families, on the whole, are extraordinarily alike when it comes to the balance of decision-making.

The middle group of equalitarian marriages can be differentiated further according to whether they make most of their decisions jointly or whether they assign equal numbers of separate decisions to both partners. The former type is called "syncratic" and the latter "autonomic" (Herbst in Oeser and Hammond, 1954). Despite the fact that these four types (husband-dominant, syncratic, autonomic, and wife-dominant) are concentrated in the middle range of power, they still differ enough from each other to provide important distinctions between families in many respects.

The impression that the average Detroit marriage is properly labelled equalitarian is supported by answers to the question: "When you and your husband differ about something, do you usually give in and do it your husband's way, or does he usually come around to your point of view?" Thirty-four per cent say that they usually or always give in under these circumstances, twenty-four per cent say the husband does, but the remaining forty per cent (two per cent, no answer) give equalitarian responses. This forty per cent undoubtedly underestimates the proportion of equalitarian marriages because many wives made it entirely clear that they and their husbands agree

---

1. The remaining 10 per cent are unknown because they failed to answer one or more of the eight decision questions.

on most things most of the time, leaving this question to apply only to marginal disagreements. When viewed against the relatively small margin of husband-winning over wife-winning cases, Detroit marriages have clearly moved a long way from nineteenth century patriarchalism.

THE SOURCES OF POWER IN MARRIAGE

Having designated some marriages as relatively husband-dominant, let us search for the segments of the population in which the patriarchal tradition apparently still survives. Presumably it should be found intact among those families which have been less exposed to urban, industrial, and educational influences.

Where is the Patriarchal Family?

The groups which would be expected to be patriarchal are families now or formerly living on farms, immigrant families, old couples, uneducated couples, and Catholic marriages (because of the Catholic advocacy of the patriarchal ideal). However, none of these expectations is confirmed.

Farm Families? The typical number of decisions made by Michigan farm husbands is exactly the same as the score for city husbands. This does not necessarily mean that living on a farm no longer contributes to the husband's power. But it certainly means that its influence may be entirely nullified by other factors, at least on farms that are within the sphere of influence of a giant metropolis.

With no difference between the families living on farms and those living in the city, patriarchal survivals cannot be expected among people within the city who grew up on farms. The differences between migrants and Detroit-born families actually lie in the opposite direction from what was expected (with migrant wives making more rather than less of the decisions). This is probably due to their low social status rather than a reflection of any matriarchal cultural pattern.

Immigrant Families? A second place where patriarchal culture might survive is among immigrants from the old country. Families brought up under patriarchal norms would be expected to live by the ideals that they learned in their youth even after moving to a new country.

These expectations are refuted, again. Immigrants turn out to be less patriarchal than native Americans (see Table 2). Again the dif-

Table 2

Husband's Power in Native-born and Foreign-born Families

	WIFE'S PLACE OF BIRTH	
	Native-born	Foreign-born
Husband's mean power*	5.24	4.94
Number of families	494	60

* Those interested in the statistical significance of differences between means of subsamples on this power index (assuming that the variance of the subsamples is the same as that of the total sample) may keep in mind that the probability is less than .05 of finding as great as .34, when the subsamples are around 200 cases each, or .69 when the subsamples are around 50 cases each, in size. (See Table A4 in Appendix A.) In all cross-tabulations, cases not ascertained on either variable have been omitted for the sake of simplicity.

ferences which exist in this table are probably not a reflection of different ideas but of the relatively low-status position which immigrants hold in our society.

Catholic Families? A third place where patriarchal ideas might hold sway is among Catholics. This is because the Catholic Church has always made a special point of New Testament prescriptions that wives should obey their husbands. Both Catholic literature and Catholic sermons expound this ideal whereas Protestant sources much more often speak of equality in marriage.

At first glance, Catholic marriages are more patriarchal (with a mean power score for active Catholics of 5.10 compared to 4.89 for active non-Catholics).[2] However, Table 3 shows that this difference is entirely a reflection of the large number of Negro Protestants, since husbands of active white Protestants have just as much power as husbands of active Catholics (all of whom are white).

One further check is possible into the effects of religious ideas on power patterns. If Catholic preaching is influential, active Catholic marriages should conform more closely to the patriarchal norm than less active families. Table 3 shows the reverse to be true—husbands

---

2. "Active" is defined as attending church at least once a week.

Table 3

Husband's Power in Catholic and Non-Catholic Families, by Wife's Church Attendance and by Race

HUSBAND'S MEAN POWER BY RACE	WIFE'S CHURCH PREFERENCE AND ATTENDANCE			
	CATHOLIC		NON-CATHOLIC	
	Active	Inactive	Active	Inactive
White	5.10	5.20	5.09	5.36
	(171)*	(55)	(116)	(210)
Negro	——	3.00	4.44	4.46
		(4)	(45)	(54)
Total	5.10	5.06	4.89	5.17
	(171)	(59)	(161)	(264)

* The numbers in parentheses are the number of families on which the average (mean) power scores are computed.

actually have slightly less say in active Catholic families than in inactive ones. (A similar and slightly larger difference exists between active and inactive non-Catholics). The fact that active Catholic families are less patriarchal than inactive ones certainly does not mean that Detroit priests have been preaching equalitarianism, nor does it probably mean that Catholic wives have been rebelling against what they hear in church. Rather, the organizational participation of the wife in going to church may account for the husband's lessened dominance. (This will be discussed soon.) In any case, these data clearly indicate that active Catholics as a whole are not a patriarchal enclave in American society.[3]

Old Couples? A fourth locale for surviving patriarchalism should be among the older generation. It is difficult to say what the dividing line is between the older generation and the younger generation. However, World War I is often said to have marked the end of one era

3. A controlled analysis, holding occupation of husband constant, shows that the correlation of husband's power with lesser religious activity is a stable one which persists within both major religious groups and three of the four occupational strata. There is some tendency of white-collar Catholics to be more patriarchal than white-collar Protestants (5.83 vs. 5.34). However, since this comparison barely achieves statistical significance (with samples of 81 and 127), is reversed at the blue-collar level, and since inactive Catholic couples are the most patriarchal, this limited tendency hardly confirms a generalized Catholic patriarchalism.

and the beginning of a new one. Presumably, the trend since then has been for shared decision-making to spread increasingly through American society.

Unfortunately, it is impossible to go back into the early 1900's and measure how families operated then in comparison to now. The best that can be done is to take couples who first got married in those days and see whether their patriarchal pattern has survived to the present time.

Table 4

Husband's Power, by Age of Wife

Age of Wife	Husband's Mean power	Estimated Year of Marriage*	Number of Families
Under 21	6.23	1952–55	13
21–29	5.62	1947–55	124
30–34	5.54	1942–46	102
35–39	5.13	1937–41	93
40–44	4.85	1933–36	48
45–49	4.70	1928–32	56
50–54	4.75	1923–27	44
55–59	4.31	1918–22	29
60–64	5.05	1913–17	22
65+	5.43	before 1913	21

* These estimates show the approximate range in date of marriage for typical couples, based on census figures showing median age at marriage as 20 years, in 1950, and 22 years, in 1890 (Glick, 1955).

Table 4 shows that the very oldest couples are indeed somewhat more patriarchal than those married in the 1920's and 1930's. However, the highest power scores belong not to the older generation but to the young post-World War II crop of marriages.

Even the most conservative interpretation would have to be that patriarchy was already weakened by 1912 and died a sudden death in World War I. If this is true, the generation which is still influenced by the old norm is already in the high mortality ages and will soon exist no more. From the standpoint of the changing times, therefore, patriarchy as a cultural norm is either already gone or rapidly disappearing. In view of the contemporary popularity of equalitarian ideas, it is doubtful that the high-power scores of the younger generation represent the emergence of a new belief in patriarchy. Even among the elders, the differences may be life-cycle ones rather than cultural prescriptions.[4]

Uneducated Couples? The final place where a lingering patriarchy might be found is among couples who haven't been exposed to the unsettling influences of modern education, especially higher education. Supposedly, equalitarianism is the new enlightened norm which grade school graduates are unfamiliar with, but to which college students especially subscribe. This is the theme of many textbooks on marriage, under such meaningful titles as *Marriage for Moderns* (Bowman 1960).

Table 5

Husband's Power, by Husband's and Wife's Education

HUSBAND'S MEAN POWER	YEARS OF EDUCATION					
	Under 6	7–8	9–11	12	13–15	16 +
By husband's	4.87	4.73	5.17	5.41	5.70	5.46
education	(53)	(98)	(121)	(173)	(54)	(50)
By wife's	4.83	5.07	5.10	5.43	5.25	4.87
education	(46)	(82)	(136)	(229)	(36)	(23)

Table 5 shows that there is indeed a relationship between exposure to education and the amount of power the husband has—but that it is in the opposite direction from the theory of eroding patriarchalism. As usual, the opposite conclusion does not follow—that high schools and colleges are teaching their graduates (especially their male graduates) to be patriarchal. The contribution of education to the power structure seems likely to be non-ideological in nature (see below). For both husbands and wives, education seems to be a source of personal power vis-à-vis the partner. This will become clearer later when the relationship of the comparative education of husband and wife to power is explored.

We have looked in five directions for evidence that patriarchal subcultures still linger in contemporary American society—and without success. Neither the farm families, nor immigrants from other

---

4. Such an interpretation of these age differences is made later in this chapter. Interpretation of differences between age groups is always difficult because they may be due to aging of the individuals, to length of marriage, or to historical changes. Nevertheless, the attempt must be made. Usually in this study a life-cycle type of interpretation seems more plausible than an historical one.

countries, nor Catholic families, nor the older generation, nor poorly educated families adhere to a patriarchal way of life. In some cases, they are no different from the families which were expected to be more "modern" in their decision-making. In other cases, they are significantly less patriarchal than those which were supposed to be most "emancipated" from the bonds of tradition.

Under these circumstances, the weight of evidence suggests that the patriarchal family is dead. This does not mean there is no such thing as an American family in which the husband makes most of the decisions. Nor does it mean that no *groups* of American families can be found in which the husbands have a great deal of power. What it does mean is that wherever husbands exercise power today, it is not because they and their wives subscribe to a patriarchal belief system which says that it is only right and proper to have this kind of marriage.

Pragmatic Sources of Power

Having exhausted the fruitfulness of the ideological theory of power, it is desirable to turn to the pragmatic theory. To restate it simply, this proposes that the balance of power in particular families and in whole categories of families is determined by the comparative resourcefulness of the two partners and by the life circumstances within which they live.

Some husbands today are just as powerful as their grandfathers were—but they can no longer take for granted the *authority* held by older generations of men. No longer is the husband able to exercise power just because he is "the man of the house." Rather, he must prove his right to power, or win power by virtue of his own skills and accomplishments in competition with his wife.

This reflects a new unpredictability in family life. Under former historical circumstances, the husband's economic and social role almost automatically gave him pre-eminence. Under modern conditions, the roles of men and women have changed so much that husbands and wives are potential equals—with the balance of power tipped sometimes one way, sometimes the other. It is no longer possible to assume that just because a man is a man, he is the boss. Once upon a time, the function of culture was to rationalize the predominance of the male sex. Today the function of culture is to develop a philosophy of

equal rights under which the saying goes, "May the best man win!"—
and the best man is sometimes a woman. The role of culture has
shifted from sanctioning a competent sex over an incompetent sex to
sanctioning the competent marriage partner over the incompetent
one, regardless of sex.

Under these circumstances, it seems wise to abandon the use of
the term "patriarchal" because of its implication of prescribed authority. Preferable instead is the term "husband-dominant" which is
the modern equivalent of the old patriarchate, minus the supporting
sanctions.

The Husband's Position in the Community

Although society no longer insists upon a particular balance of
power in marriage, the larger community still affects husband-wife relationships. Today, the more successful the husband is in the eyes of
the community, the more dominant his part in marital decision-making.

Earlier it was suggested that the low social status of Southern
farm migrants, foreign immigrants, and poorly educated husbands
might account for their low power. Now it is desirable to look directly
at indices of success in the community.

Occupation. Table 6 shows that, generally speaking, the higher
the husband's occupational prestige, the greater his voice in marital
decisions.[5] The major break comes between white-collar occupations
and blue-collar occupations.

Why should the average white-collar husband have more say at
home than blue-collar ones? Perhaps the prestige of white-collar
work provides self-confidence in his own eyes and respect in the eyes
of his wife. In addition, white-collar work involves reliance on the
interpersonal skills of discussion and argument which are involved in
decision-making. Moreover, husbands accustomed to responsible roles
on the job would understandably be inclined to take responsibility in

---

5. The generalization that husband's power is correlated with occupational
status also holds within the Negro race (4.31, 4.60, no cases, and 5.00 respectively).

When controls for the wife's employment are instituted, there is one reversal at the blue-collar level among housewife families: 5.31, 5.16, 5.50, 5.68,
while working-wife families show no difference at the blue-collar level: 4.22,
4.22, 4.77, 4.85.

Table 6

Husband's Power, by Occupational Status

HUSBAND'S OCCUPATION

	BLUE COLLAR		WHITE COLLAR	
	Low*	High	Low	High
Husband's mean power	5.07	4.98	5.36	5.52
Number of families	162	161	78	151

* Low-blue-collar jobs are semi-skilled, unskilled, and service. High-blue-collar: skilled workers and foremen. Low-white-collar: sales and clerical. High-white-collar: business and professional.

the home. As a result of such factors, white-collar husbands are extra-equipped with the knowledge and skills required for decision-making, and their wives correspondingly inclined to recognize their husband's competence along these lines.

Income. Because his work is his chief role in life, occupational success is the crucial index of a man's competence. But the kind of job a man has is not the only measure of occupational achievement. After all, many men simply follow in their fathers' footsteps. The son of a professional man will usually be a white-collar worker too, and though this gives him prestige in the eyes of the community, it may not reflect an unusually competent personality.

A better measure of success on the job is how much money the husband earns. In part, this is simply a reflection of occupation. But extreme income differences go beyond this to sort out the most successful from the least successful workers.

Table 7

Husband's Power, by Income

HUSBAND'S INCOME

	Under $3,000	$3,000 –4,999	$5,000 –6,999	$7,000 –9,999	$10,000+
Husband's mean power	4.58	5.00	5.25	5.38	5.83
Number of families	57	165	185	84	48

Table 7 shows that the husband's earnings are an even more sensitive indicator of his power than his occupation. Partly this is because the families are now split into five groups instead of four. Mostly this is because smaller groups are separated out at both extremes. Husbands with less than $3,000 income are the least successful of the low-blue-collar workers, and those earning more than $10,000 the most successful of the high-white-collar workers (such as doctors and big businessmen).

Bringing home the bacon is a prime example of contributing a resource to marriage. That top-income-bracket husbands should be most influential in marriage reflects the magnitude of their contribution to the family exchequer. By contrast, where the total income of the family (rather than the husband's alone) is taken into consideration, the balance of power is altered in the wife's direction. As a result of the supplementary contribution of other family members (principally the wives themselves), the number of families in the $7–10,000 income bracket jumps from 84 to 131 while the husband's power falls drastically from 5.38 to 4.85. Above the $10,000 mark there are 78 multiple-income families compared to 48 one-income units, and the husband's power is reduced from 5.83 to 5.41. This comparison shows how the balance of power reflects the husband's resources alone only as long as other things are equal. So, high-income husbands are most powerful if their wives contribute no income.

Social Status. Income and occupation are interrelated variables. The husband's education is also related to the amount of power that he has. These are the sorts of variables that sociologists often group together to summarize the social position or status of a family in the community. The Social Status Index used here is an aggregate of these three factors (occupation, income, and education) plus the prestige-ranking of the husband's ethnic or nationality background. The combined index gives a rough picture of a family's over-all prestige in the eyes of the community from the standpoint of these four characteristics.[6]

For the community as a whole, the husband's power is directly related to his social status: 4.39, 4.79, 5.00, 5.33, 5.56. However, the

---

6. Income and education scores were assigned on the basis of the percentiles of the Detroit population falling at the various rank levels. Occupation scores used the percentile prestige ratings developed by the National Opinion Research Center. The ethnic scale was developed from ratings by 195 University of Michigan students from the Detroit area. The over-all score is a simple average of these four individual scores. Examples of scores are: $5,000 income, 61 points; factory worker, 26 points; 11 years of schooling, 42 points; Polish ancestry, 34 points. Such a family would have a Social Status Index of 40.75. (Further details are given in Lenski, 1954.)

Table 8

Husband's Power, by Social Status

	PERCENTILE RANKING ON SOCIAL STATUS INDEX				
	0–19	20–39	40–59	60–79	80–99
Husband's mean power	5.33	5.02	4.97	5.37	5.57
Number of families	12	87	194	174	84

few white husbands in the lowest social status group differ sharply from their powerless Negro counterparts. Presumably these are old men comparable to the pre-World War I marriages in Table 4. If this small group is dismissed as likely to be affected by factors other than status alone, the general conclusion from Table 8 is that the higher the husband's social status, the greater his power.

Do high-status husbands exercise control equally over all eight decision areas? Examination of the relationship between social status and the eight separate decisions shows that high-status husbands make more decisions in only three areas: whether to buy life insurance, what house or apartment to get, and especially whether the wife should go to work or quit work. Actually what happens is not that more high-status husbands make these decisions unilaterally, but that fewer wives do. In other words, high-status husbands take a more active part rather than the wife making the decision by herself.

Are there any reasons why high-status husbands would want to control these particular areas? Chapter 3 will show that high-status husbands are more apt to handle the money and bills. The reason for this appears to be that there is a larger increment of money involved beyond the level of daily necessities. At high-status levels, insurance correspondingly becomes more than burial insurance. As a major expenditure, it necessarily interests the husband. Such husbands are also making a major investment when it comes to choice of a house, whereas for low-status families one flat is about as good as another. Finally, the low-status wife more often feels she has a right to decide for herself whether she will go to work or not, whereas the high-status husband again takes more of an interest in these matters. This does not necessarily mean that high-status husbands are worried about a threat to their prestige if their wives go to work, but that they are concerned about the problems involved in the reorganization of their family life around a working wife. If such reasoning is sound, insurance, housing, and the wife's employment are all matters of special interest to the high-status husband.

In general then, social-status differences in decision-making lie in the more active sharing of responsibility by high-status husbands, whereas low-status men more often fail to take part in the decision-making process. This is the first of many signs which will appear of patterns of sharing in the middle class and of *apartheid* in the working class. The latter pattern often orients the husband outside the family, leaving the wife saddled with the burden of making family decisions unaided. In terms of the four kinds of decision-making, this means that middle-class families are more often syncratic (shared-equal), whereas working-class families tend to be more wife-dominant in their power structure.

Race. The perceptive reader will already have noted that Negro husbands have unusually low power. Table 3 showed that Negro husbands in all major religious categories make fewer decisions than the corresponding whites. Footnote 2 showed that Negro husbands make fewer decisions in the three major occupational strata where comparison is possible (low-blue, high-blue, and high-white collar). This last point is especially important because it shows that the lower power of Negro husbands as a whole (4.40 compared to 5.20 for whites) is not due to status differences alone. To be sure, the label "black" is almost a synonym for low status in our society—and Detroit Negroes are no exception in having less education, lower incomes, inferior jobs, and lower prestige generally than whites. Since low-status white husbands make relatively few decisions, we would expect Negro husbands to exercise little power, too.

Negro families differ among themselves at least as much as white families—and sometimes more. By and large, they are affected by the same sources of power as white families.[7] But in looking at any one resource, white husbands are always more powerful than their Negro status equals. This is true within each occupational stratum, each income bracket, and each social-status level.

---

7. The chief exception to this generalization is that 35 high-income Negro husbands (over $4,000) have lower mean power (4.09) than their 68 less affluent colleagues (4.56). Such peculiar reversals of white trends occur often enough within the Negro community to lead us to treat Negro families separately throughout this book.

Hence there appears to be a specific racial difference between white and Negro families. This need not mean a biological factor. Rather this is the cumulative result of the discrimination in jobs ("last hired—first fired"), the segregated housing, and the poor schooling of Negro men. Such factors undermine the morale of the Negro male, weakening his position in the eyes of his family to the place where it is easy for him to desert altogether. Faced with an undependable husband, the Negro wife has become accustomed to having to hold the family together by hard work and responsible decision-making (Frazier, 1939).

Table 9
Balance of Power in White and Negro Families

BALANCE OF POWER*		RACE		
		White	Negro	Total
Husband dominant		26%	19%	25%
Equal		54	38	51
Wife dominant		20	44	24
	Total	100	101	100
Number of families		554	103	657

*Husband-dominant couples have scores above 6.00 on the scale used for computing husband's mean power in this chapter. Equalitarian scores are 4.00–6.00. Wife-dominant scores are below 4.00.

The over-all picture of wife-dominance in Negro families is apparent in Table 9. Whereas the majority of white families are equalitarian, the largest percentage of Negro families are dominated by the wife.

The biggest difference between Negro and white families comes in the area of insurance, which 24 per cent of the Negro wives decide unilaterally. Presumably much of this is the burial insurance for which Detroit Negro wives customarily make small weekly payments to a collector who comes to the door. Although the other differences are not as great, more Negro wives also make every single one of the other decisions. Curiously enough, there are also slightly more Negro men who make unilateral decisions on five of the eight issues—but not enough more to catch up with the wives. Mostly this reflects the substantial difference between Negro and white sharing of decisions, with only 2.34 decisions shared equally by the average Negro family, compared to 3.07 for the average white family. Table 9 tells the same story since the increased number of Negro wife-dominated families is more at the expense of equalitarianism than of husband-dominance.

Suburban Residence. The final index of the husband's position in the community which we will examine is suburbanization. Families living in Detroit suburbs are more husband-dominant (mean power, 5.44) than those which live in the city of Detroit (4.79). At first glance, this might be due to the concentration of the Negro population in the central city, but control on race shows that it is not. Again, it might be due to the high status of suburban families, but segregating the white families by social status shows that suburban families are more husband-dominant at every status level than their urban peers. Indeed, the most dominant suburban husbands are the ten low-status ones who live in comparatively high-status suburbs.

This last little group provides a possible clue to why suburban husbands have more power. Perhaps suburban wives feel indebted to their husbands for providing them with a place to live which is more attractive than the industrial city of Detroit. If so, this fits the theory that power accrues to those husbands who are able to provide for their wives especially well. In any case, the fact that these suburban husbands participate more actively in family decision-making confirms Jaco and Belknap (1953) in their suggestion that the suburban father plays a more prominent role in the family than his urban counterpart. It also casts serious doubt on the notion that the absence of the father from the suburb during the day leads to a "matricentric" form of marriage, at least as far as husband-wife relationships are concerned (Burgess and Locke, 1953).

This discussion of the ways in which the husband's position in the community contributes to his power in the family may be concluded with a reminder that high-status husbands do not appear to be coercing their wives into submission. Such husbands have more to offer to their marriages because of their unusual competence and resourcefulness; it is this contributing to marriage which brings with it greater freedom for the husband to participate in decision-making and greater willingness by the wife for him to do so.

The Comparative Resources of Husband and Wife

The social status of a family is largely determined by the husband as the representative of the family in the community. His occupation, his income, his education help to establish the family's prestige in the eyes of the community to a great extent, regardless of the wife's characteristics.

However, the balance of power is, after all, an interpersonal affair, and the wife's own characteristics cannot long be disregarded if we are to understand who makes the decisions. Wherever possible, it is desirable to compare the wife and the husband on the same characteristic, for then the comparative resourcefulness and competence of the two partners can be discovered. Once we know which partner has more education, more organizational experience, a higher status background, etc. we will know who tends to make most of the decisions.

Education. Table 5 showed that the more education the husband had, the greater his power. However, for wives the relationship seems to be curvilinear. By putting the education of the husband and the wife together, it is possible to resolve this apparent contradiction.

The Detroit data shows that where the wife has at least five more years of schooling than the husband his power is only 4.29, but when the tables are reversed, his power is 5.68. The conclusion is clear that the more one partner's education exceeds that of the other, the larger his share in marital decision-making will be.

Such a relationship might be due simply to the fact that only comparatively high-status (and therefore powerful) husbands exceed their wives in education by five or more years, while it takes a comparatively low-status husband to be that much inferior to his wife. However, controlling by the husband's occupation does not wipe out the relationship (see Table 10). Instead, high-white-collar husbands continue to gain power if they exceed the wife's education, and to lose it if they fall short of the wife. And the same trends hold within the low-white-collar and the high-blue-collar groups, leaving only one low-blue-collar reversal.

Since comparative education influences marital decision-making at all occupational levels, it proves to be a highly consistent resource for marital power.

Schooling trains people in verbal skills and knowledge which facilitate decision-making quite directly. In addition, schooling contributes to the effective participation of the individual in the community (through paid or voluntary participation) which in turn strengthens the power position of the individual. So whether directly

Table 10

Husband's Power, by Comparative Education of Husband and Wife within Occupational Strata

HUSBAND'S MEAN POWER BY HUSBAND'S OCCUPATION	COMPARATIVE EDUCATION		
	Wife more	Equal	Husband more
High-white-collar	5.32	5.45	5.65
	(31)	(42)	(78)
Low-white-collar	4.92	5.20	5.59
	(12)	(30)	(37)
High-blue-collar	4.80	5.08	5.28
	(117)	(84)	(82)
Low-blue-collar	4.79	5.44	4.88
	(14)	(16)	(8)

or indirectly, the better-educated partner brings greater resources to the decision arena.

Organizational Participation. Activity in a formal organization provides the wife with a resource analogous to the husband's success on the job. Getting outside the home brings knowledge pertinent to settling household issues. Moreover, a person who has enough initiative to be active in the community seems also more likely to participate actively in family decision-making. By contrast, stay-at-home spouses may lack the personal and community-derived resources to play as active a role in making decisions.

Unfortunately, the questionnaire used in this study did not include information on the frequency with which husbands attend organizational meetings. However, it does yield the number of types of organizations both partners belong to.[8] Table 11 shows that the partner who belongs to more types of organizations—aside from a church —takes a more active part in family decisions. At the extremes, wives who belong to at least two more organizations depress the husband's power to 4.45 whereas the converse husbands raise it to 5.45. Pre-

---

8. Most Detroiters belong to very few organizations aside from a church. Forty-two per cent of the wives and 19 per cent of the husbands belong to no non-church organizations at all, while 28 per cent and 40 per cent respectively belong to only one type (e.g., labor unions or lodges). Even this membership is often nominal, for almost a fourth of those women who belong to one or more organizations hadn't attended a single meeting in the three months prior to being interviewed.

Table 11

Husband's Power, by Comparative Organizational Membership of Husband and Wife

	COMPARATIVE ORGANIZATIONAL MEMBERSHIP		
	Wife more	Equal	Husband more
Husband's mean power	5.05	5.14	5.36
Number of families	85	216	250

sumably knowledge of the partners' comparative degree of activity in their organizations would yield an even better picture of the skills and resources they bring to the marriage.

Church membership was excluded from Table 11 because sociologists have traditionally viewed church membership as a conventional matter unlikely to signify much about the persons involved. The separate analysis of comparative church attendance in Table 12 suggests that separation is unnecessary—churches should be looked upon as another example of a formal organization. (Indeed labor unions with their much lower percentage of attendance at meetings are correspondingly less meaningful organizations to the rank and file.)[9]

Table 12

Husband's Power, by Comparative Church Attendance of Husband and Wife

(same church only)

	COMPARATIVE FREQUENCY OF CHURCH ATTENDANCE		
	Wife more	Equal	Husband more
Husband's mean power	4.72	5.21	5.70
Number of families	99	370	20

Table 12 shows that the more often the husband attends church, the more power he has. Churches are not unique in this respect. This is another example of the kind of influence attached to participation in any organization outside the home. Perhaps in a society where church-going is so much the norm, we should put it the other way around and say that individuals who attend *less* often than their part-

---

9. The median Detroit wife attends church every week, the typical husband about every two weeks.

ners tend to put themselves at a disadvantage and weaken their basis for participating in family decisions.

Work. Participation in organizations is in many ways the equivalent of holding a job. Both involve coming to the family from a point of independent leverage. Both involve outside contacts which bolster the resources in knowledge and interpersonal skill which the participating partner brings to the marriage. Working, of course, involves the additional contribution of money—the most tangible of all resources. For both reasons, we would expect the comparative work participation of the two partners to affect the balance of power.

Table 13

Husband's Power, by Comparative Work Participation of Husband and Wife

COMPARATIVE WORK PARTICIPATION

	WIFE NOT EMPLOYED			WIFE EMPLOYED		
	Husband overtime	Husband full-time	Husband none	Husband overtime	Husband full-time	Husband none
Husband's mean power	5.62	5.28	4.88	4.50	4.46	2.67
Number of families	195	218	25	44	57	3

Table 13 shows that whichever partner works more gains power thereby. This is true not only for working wives versus non-working wives but even reflects the number of hours the husband works, with overtime husbands edging out husbands who work only a forty-hour week.

It is difficult to know where to place in this series the families in which neither partner is employed. In some respects, they might seem equivalent to couples where both partners work full time. However their equality in not working is tempered by the fact that many of these wives never worked. This may be why the husband's power is greater than that of two-income families.

Marital power reflects not only the current working relationship of the partners but the length of time the wife works after marriage. The more years the wife has worked since marriage, the more power she has (see Table 14). Only one-third of the wives who have ever worked since marriage are currently employed. Nevertheless, the number of years worked correlate with the wife's power regardless of whether she is still working.[10]

Table 14

Husband's Power, by Length of Wife's Work Participation since Marriage

	WIFE'S WORK PARTICIPATION IN YEARS				
	0	Under 1	1–4	5–9	10+
Husband's mean power	5.80	5.65	4.97	4.66	4.29
Number of families	154	85	183	70	55

The relationship between the wife's employment and her power is complicated by the fact that more wives are employed in the wife-dominant, low-status segment of the community. Indeed this is one reason why low-status husbands on the whole have less power. However, controlling on social status and race shows that working wives have substantially more power on the average than non-working wives at all status levels. Indeed the comparative work participation of husband and wife is related far more closely to the balance of power in marriage than is the social status of the husband in the community taken by itself. This is not, however, to reject the importance of considering the husband's social position, for both his own community role and his wife's comparative resources contribute to the over-all balance of power in marriage.

Life-cycle Changes. The final index of individual resources is the couple's stage in the family-life cycle. This can best be gauged by noting the age of the oldest child in the family.

At first glance, the stage in life cycle does not look much different from what Table 4 showed about the husband's power in relation to the age of the wife. The similarity in total mean scores between the four child-rearing stages and the age spans in Table 4 from twenty to forty-five reflect the fact that most wives bear their first child in their twenties and "launch" him into the outside world in their forties.

---

10. This generalization applies primarily to wives who work apart from their husbands. Gold and Slater (1958) find that young independent business-men and professionals are more often patriarchal than junior corporation executives, despite the fact that the formers' wives often assist them in their work, whereas the latter do not. Apparently helping one's husband involves submission to his leadership and therefore should not be considered an independent resource for the wife in the same sense that working for someone else is.

Table 15

Husband's Power, by Stage in Family-life Cycle

HUSBAND'S MEAN POWER	STAGE IN FAMILY-LIFE CYCLE*					
Childrearing stages:	Preschool	Preadolescent	Adolescent	Unlaunched		
	5.71	5.41	5.06	4.68		
	(127)	(130)	(96)	(53)		
Childless stages:	Honeymoon				Postparental	Retired
	5.35				4.79	4.44
	(17)				(77)	(9)
Childless couples:	5.30	4.72	4.20			
	(10)	(25)	(10)			

* The honeymoon stage consists of childless couples married less than four years. The childrearing stages are defined by age of oldest child: under 6, 6–12, 13–18, 19 or over. Those couples who fail to bear or adopt children are listed below the corresponding childrearing stages by the equivalent length of marriage: 4–7, 8–15, and 16–22 years respectively. Postparental couples are listed below unlaunched ones because of the overlapping length of marriage of these two groups. Retired couples involve non-employed husbands age 60 or more.

The normal sequence of stages is honeymoon, preschool, preadolescent, adolescent, postparental, and retired. Deviant sequences include permanent childlessness (which after 22 years of marriage we have merged with the postparental and retired groups) or retaining unlaunched adult children at home.

However, growing older and having children affect power separately. Having a young child creates needs for the wife which lead her to depend more on her husband for help, financial support, and making decisions. As children grow up, they shift from being burdens to being resources whom the wife draws upon in marital decision-making. They also become resources in other ways, providing companionship and emotional support which make the wife less dependent on her husband.

However, the resources which growing children provide are meager in comparison to the extra-familial resources on which childless women can draw. Childlessness allows a continuation of the honeymoon state of mutual emotional and financial interdependence with the husband. Moreover, the continued participation of the wife in the occupational world accelerates her own maturity toward decision-making resourcefulness. So the childless wife's need for one-sided dependence is less and her skill in independent decision-making greater. Hence, the wife's greater power throughout the deviant childless sequence.

For the wife, it appears that marriage is not as great a role transition as becoming a mother. As a working wife, she continues to participate in community life on a par with her husband. But as the mother of a new baby, she gives up her job and is confined to her home by the heavy demands of child-care.[11] Not only is she cut off from contact with her fellow workers but even the opportunity to participate in recreational activities and organizational meetings is impaired by her baby-sitting responsibilities. Under these circumstances, parenthood brings a sudden loss of resources to the wife combined with increased need for husbandly support. It is no wonder, therefore, that the wife's dependence increases.

Table 4 fails to disclose this "crisis" which parenthood brings. (Le Masters, 1957). Looking at the age of the wife alone masks this transition—the small number of childless young wives being overshadowed by the young wives with children. Hence, looking at both age of wife and stage in family-life cycle gives a clearer picture of what is happening than either would alone (refining Lansing and Kish, 1957).

Such analysis suggests that parenthood may be especially critical for the woman whose first child is born later than usual, for she has achieved greater power by working a larger number of years (cf. Table 14). By contrast, the typical young bride in her twenties marries so fast and bears children so fast that she never has time to work out a very equalitarian relationship.[12] Apparently, then, parenthood is a differential crisis, of minimum proportions for the young marriage-oriented bride but requiring a drastic alteration of life patterns for the woman whose first child has been delayed beyond the usual child-bearing age.

At the other end of the family-life cycle, the phenomena are more

---

11. One study quoted by Folsom (1943) found that the wife's housework jumps from 50 to 94 hours a week at this point, then gradually tapers off as the child grows older.

12. This is especially true for the 13 brides under the age of 21. Table 4 showed these couples with by far the most husband dominance (6.23) of any age group. The origin of this dependence on the husband is the unusually large number of young children whom these young brides have already accumulated. Five have one child, five more have two, and three already have three children. This extraordinary fertility at so young an age creates an acute need for dependence on the husband's resources.

difficult to interpret. The reduced power of retired husbands in Table 15 presumably reflects their withdrawal from resource-giving participation in the occupational world. Short of retirement, however, Table 4 suggests that the husband's power tends to rise late in life. Do wives past age sixty depend more on their husbands because of growing emotional needs in old age? This seems doubtful since men age faster than women, creating even greater male dependency needs. Perhaps the very mortality of older men leads wives to increased deference to those men who survive. If so, the husband's hand is strengthened by his scarcity value, and the wife's need to depend on him arises in comparison with her widowed friends. We have also suggested previously that these may be the few remaining survivors of a patriarchal era. Which hypothesis is correct only time and further research can tell.[13]

In any case, middle age appears to be a time of peak wife-dominance in Detroit (as in Kansas City according to Neugarten, 1956). Women in their forties and fifties appear to achieve a strength and self-confidence which younger women seldom know.

THE POWER TO MAKE DECISIONS

In summary, the power to make decisions stems primarily from the resources which the individual can provide to meet the needs of his marriage partner and to upgrade his decision-making skill. Because it is based on such tangible and relevant criteria, the balance of power may be said to be adapted to the interpersonal relationship of the two partners involved.

Contemporary married couples are freed from the "dead hand" of patriarchal tradition to work out their own destiny in the way best suited to them. This does not mean that they can work out their decision-making pattern in any fashion whatever, but that they are not bound by any "cake of custom" which arbitrarily installs one sex in

---

13. The increased husband-dominance in old age is not a reflection of differential longevity among high-status people but occurs at all social levels when social status is held constant. The stability of this phenomenon is seen in the fact that wives over 60 make fewer decisions in every single one of the eight decison areas.

power. Whereas in the past, custom often dictated that all families should be patriarchal, today the rise of women produces considerable variation between families (and even within families with the passage of time). With less sex-linked cultural norms, such variation incurs less penalty than it once would have. Indeed, the emerging norm may not be a particular pattern of male-dominance or equalitarianism but, rather, the idea of appropriateness. If a wife is working today, it is appropriate that she should have more voice in decisions, rather than be subjugated to an arbitrary standard.

Only at the wife-dominant extreme is there evidence of deviance from the norm today. It may be appropriate for the wife who is the sole support of her family to make most of the decisions, but it certainly is not normal for the marital roles to be reversed in this way. We will find throughout this study dissatisfaction associated with wife-dominance. This is not, however, simply a reflection of breaking social rules. Rather, the circumstances which lead to the wife's dominance involve corresponding inadequacies and incompetencies on the husband's part. An inadequate husband is by definition unable to make a satisfactory marriage partner. So the dominant wife is not exultant over her "victory," but exercises power regretfully by default of her "no good" or incapacitated husband.

Within the range from husband-dominance to extreme equalitarianism, appropriateness appears to be linked with satisfaction. A wife who doesn't get to make many decisions does get to have her needs met by a resourceful husband, and the husband who "has to" share his power with his wife has the compensation of her greater contributions to the marriage.

Under these circumstances, power in American marriages is not a matter of brute coercion and unwilling defeat so much as a mutual recognition of individual skills in particular areas of competence and of the partners' dual stake in areas of joint concern. Given such a natural working out of particular decisions under varying circumstances, it is no wonder that most wives cannot say *why* they make decisions at home the way they do.[14] All they are aware of is that somehow their balance of power "just growed" and that it is right.

Only when American marriages are looked at *en masse* is it clear

14. This question proved completely unworkable in early pretests of the questionnaire.

why power is patterned the way it is—and why it seems right to the couples involved. The answer lies in the tangible resources and skills which the two partners pool in marriage. Today's marriages have a variable balance of power which is not determined by the assignment of authority to one sex, but by the interplay of dynamic forces which affect the marriage from within and without.

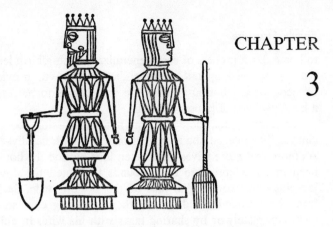

THE DIVISION OF LABOR

IN ORDER TO carry on a marriage, decisions must be not only made but carried out. This chapter is concerned with the everyday tasks that have to be performed in every family in order to keep the home going. How do the husband and wife divide up or share the work around the house? Chapter Four will examine the work which husband and/or wife do outside the home to provide the family's economic support.

The American family has changed its authority pattern from one of patriarchal male dominance to one of equalitarian sharing. Has the division of labor changed, too?

THE TRADITIONAL PATTERN

Traditionally, husbands did "men's work" and wives did "women's work." Men's work was strenuous and dangerous, the difficult tasks in field and woods which women were not considered strong enough to undertake. Women's work centered in the home, not only because women were incapable of the heaviest outside work but because women are the childbearers. Pregnancy, child birth, and breast feeding make it necessary and convenient for the woman to stay close to home. By a process of easy generalization, childbirth leads to child-rearing, to feeding and clothing the children, to providing similar services for the husband. Thus the wife comes to be responsible for a large package of household tasks.

In recent years, there has been much discussion about the American family's alleged abandonment of this traditional division of labor. As more and more wives have taken jobs outside the home, there has been increased pressure on husbands to lighten the double load of job-plus-housework which falls on the working wife. Such assistance from the husband could come either by taking over some feminine tasks completely or by sharing tasks with his wife. In either case the new conception is one of sharing.

To a considerable extent, the idea of shared work is incompatible with the most efficient division of labor. Much of the progress of our modern economy rests upon the increasing specialization of its division of labor. A specialist is able to develop his particular skills in a way a jack-of-all-trades never can.

Family life has always required a multitude of skills of its practitioners, so that a husband or wife must necessarily perform many different tasks. Nevertheless, as long as the wife stuck to her cooking and the husband to his hunting, some of the advantages of specialization accrued. Such advantages would be lost if husband and wife were to merge their work completely.

The very threat of such a loss is one brake on the trend to undivided work. Individual preferences for particular tasks are another. The greatest preventive, however, is the continuing biological differences between men and women which even in the Israeli Kibbutz—with its ideological dedication to the abolition of sex roles within a communal framework—continue to influence the division of labor (Spiro, 1956).

It seems unlikely, therefore, that traditional sex roles in the home will be abandoned within the foreseeable future. At least they are still very much in evidence.

THE CONTEMPORARY PATTERN

To keep track of all the work done by a husband and wife has sometimes been attempted through the co-operation of small numbers of research-minded volunteer families. For a large-scale study of a cross section of a whole community, such comprehensive information is impossible to secure.

As in the case of decisions, one must be satisfied with a small group of family tasks as an index of the over-all division of labor. The eight tasks used in this research are:

1) Who repairs things around the house?
2) Who mows the lawn?
3) Who shovels the sidewalk?
4) Who keeps track of the money and the bills?
5) Who does the grocery-shopping?
6) Who gets the husband's breakfast on work days?
7) Who straightens up the living room when company is coming?
8) Who does the evening dishes?

The questions were chosen because they concern tasks which most families perform.[1] (Since one third of the respondents have no children, childcare tasks could not be included.) They also are tasks which theoretically either partner could perform (hence the emphasis on *dinner* dishes since both partners are usually home in the evening).

Facets of the Division of Labor

The division of labor actually covers a variety of concepts. First is the amount of work done at home by each partner. This will be referred to as the *relative task participation* of the couple and is equivalent to the balance of power in decision-making. Scores are computed in terms of the wife's mean task participation, with five points where she always does a task, four points for husband-more-than-wife, and so on (see Table 16 below).

In addition to knowing how *much* work is done by each partner, we must also know which tasks each does. Some of the eight tasks have been traditionally done by men and others by women. The degree of *adherence to male roles* refers to the extent to which the hus-

---

1. Those couples whose tasks are performed by children or servants were asked which partner they thought would do the task if no one else were available. Apartment dwellers similarly gave hypothetical answers about lawn and sidewalk. Since the hypothetical answers were few in number and were distributed in similar fashion to the "actual" answers, they were grouped together for purposes of analysis.

band does the repairs, mowing, and shovelling. The degree of *adherence to female roles* is the extent to which the wife is responsible for the groceries, breakfast, living room, and dishes.[2] Combined, these two indices provide a measure of the degree of *adherence to traditional sex roles* in the marriage.

Whereas the previous measures vary in degree, it is sometimes valuable to know how many tasks are done exclusively by the traditional partner. This gives a measure of the degree of *role stereotypy* in marriage; it may vary from none to a maximum of seven tasks performed exclusively according to the stereotyped pattern.

Table 16
Division of Labor, by Household Tasks

(731 Detroit Families)

WHO DOES IT?	TASK							
	Repairs	Lawn	Walk	Bills	Groceries	Break-fast	Living room	Dishes
(1) Husband always	73%	66%	61%	19%	7%	16%	1%	1%
(2) Husband more than wife	11	9	13	6	7	5	1	2
(3) Husband and wife exactly the same	6	6	8	34	29	4	17	13
(4) Wife more than husband	3	6	7	11	20	7	15	12
(5) Wife always	3	7	7	30	36	66	65	70
N.A.	4	6	4	—	1	2	1	2
Total	100	100	100	100	100	100	100	100
Wife's mean task performance	1.46	1.71	1.81	3.27	3.72	4.04	4.44	4.52

Closely related to stereotypy is the degree of *role specialization*. This is the number of tasks performed exclusively by one partner but not necessarily by the traditional partner. This refers to the degree of differentiation of roles between the two partners, rather than to their conformity to conventional patterns. In a completely specialized marriage, all eight of the battery of tasks are performed unilaterally. The

---

2. Keeping track of the money and bills has been omitted from these computations because we are not sure whether this should be considered traditionally a masculine function. However, this item is included in all computations of the relative amount of work done by the husband and wife.

reciprocal of role specialization is the extent of *role-sharing*. This is restricted to the number of tasks out of the eight which are done by the husband and wife "exactly the same." These two measures of specialization and sharing deal with the extreme cases, ignoring those tasks which are partially shared, done by one partner more than the other.

Relative task performance, traditional role adherence and stereotypy, specialization and sharing provide a comprehensive series of perspectives on the division of labor in marriage. What is the American pattern today?

Who Does What?

Masculine Tasks. Table 16 shows that most husbands do the lawn-mowing, snow-shovelling, and repairing, while the wives do the dishes, straightening up, and cooking. The remaining two items are neither the husband's nor the wife's in a majority of families though they tend to be done more by wives.

The predominant picture reveals specialized task performance along traditional sex lines. The extent of this conformity to conventional patterns is greatest for the three male tasks, since the median Detroit husband performs over 90 per cent of them. Since grocery-shopping is less exclusively a feminine task, the median adherence to traditional feminine tasks is a bit less, but still substantial (76 per cent). Combined, the performance of these seven tasks follows traditional lines most of the time in the typical Detroit family.

If we pose the more rigorous question, "How many families adhere completely to traditional sex lines?" the answer is only 6 per cent. However, the median family has a completely stereotyped allocation of five of the seven tasks, leaving only two for even marginal variation.

The reasons for this sharp division of labor along traditional sex lines are presumably those discussed already. Lawn-mowing and snow-shovelling exemplify tasks capitalizing on male musculature. Doing household repairs similarly utilizes the mechanical aptitude which men in our society possess more than women. (Scheinfeld, 1943).

Feminine Tasks. The feminine tasks are less directly determined by biological or mental aptitudes, but are examples of the household "package" usually associated with the role of mother.[3] Probably the number of husbands participating in grocery-shopping has increased since the neighborhood store gave way to supermarkets which can be reached only by car—husbands being the usual custodian of the American car.

Administrative Tasks. Keeping track of the money and bills lacks a generally accepted pattern of allocation. Handling the money is a sensitive operation, allied with such other household tasks as shopping but tied up, too, with the relative power of the husband and wife. Those wives who do more housework also tend to keep track of the money and bills. On the other hand, there is a high correlation between money-handling and decision-making. (Where the wife always keeps track of the money and bills the mean power score is only 4.29, whereas husbands who always handle the money have a mean power of 6.13.)

Apparently keeping track of the money and bills is a crucial administrative function in the home, standing midway between the making of financial decisions and carrying them out through actual purchases. For all four of the financial decisions in this study, the partner who makes the decision is the one who is most apt to keep track of the money and bills. The relationship is especially marked in the case of decisions about how much money to spend on food and whether to buy life insurance, since these questions were phrased quite directly in financial terms. Clearly, the person who makes major financial decisions in marriage tends to be the one who follows through in seeing where the money goes and doling it out to the billing agencies. Apparently making decisions about money and keeping track of money are two functions which tend to reinforce each other. They are not easily separable between one partner as boss and the other as bookkeeper.

To summarize, the pattern of task performance is one of marked specialization. Taken task by task, six of the eight are usually performed in a completely specialized manner. Taken family by family,

---

3. The husband's breakfast would be an even more exclusively feminine task had the "husband always" category not been misleadingly inflated by so classifying the appreciable minority of cases where the husband eats no breakfast or eats out. What should have been done was to ask these respondents to give a hypothetical answer.

the median couple split up the same six tasks in the same specialized way. At the same time, the median couple share only one task fifty-fifty, leaving only one of the eight to be done primarily but not exclusively by one partner.

Doing and Deciding: The Structure of American Marriages

How does this division of labor compare with the pattern of decision-making in American marriage? Both are equalitarian in the sense that both husbands and wives participate. But whereas the division of labor is highly specialized, the process of decision-making is considerably less unilateral. The typical pattern in Detroit is to make only half the decisions unilaterally (compared to three-fourths of the tasks). Conversely, three decisions are typically shared equally by the two partners, compared to only one task. As a result of these differences, decision-making is also less stereotyped than task performance, there being substantially more variation from family to family in who decides than in who does things at home.

These differences are great enough to produce a general impression of flexible sharing in decision-making in contrast with stereotyped specialization in the division of labor.[4] The typical family is therefore like a corporation which makes its decisions in staff conferences but executes them through technical experts.

Miller and Swanson (1958) have a name for this type of family. They call it the "colleague" family because it resembles co-workers "with equal, interdependent, but distinct and mutually recognized competencies." They speculate that the traditional American patriarchal family changed first into Burgess and Locke's "companionship family" which shared both decisions and tasks in an entrepreneurial competitive society. The companionship family then evolved into the colleague type as American husbands were increasingly employed in bureaucratic organizations.

However, Gold and Slater (1958) were unable to find any evidence at the present time of the predicted relationship between

---

4. The omission from our data of information about childrearing tasks neglects the chief area which American husbands have begun to enter. Miller and Swanson (1958) found that 38 per cent of husbands get up at night with children at least occasionally. Even so, however, the wife's greater time at home means that there is only part-time sharing of childrearing tasks.

entrepreneurial occupations and companionship families or between bureaucratic occupations and colleague families. Perhaps a few ardent feminists did establish companionship-type families in the days of their "flaming youth" (the 1920's), but the major shift in American family patterns seems to be directly from the patriarchate to the colleague form.

However, even to say that the contemporary pattern is "colleague-ish" is only to describe the median family. Relatively few families fit any of the three "types" (traditional, companionship, or colleague), if rigorous criteria are used. Gold and Slater were able to "type" less than half of the families in the Detroit sample since there is no room in the three classical types for any wife-dominant families nor for those husband-dominant ones in which housework is shared.

This is not to say that there is no connection between power and the division of labor. Actually there is a considerable tendency for couples who share more than half their decisions to do more housework together, and at the other extreme for couples who make few joint decisions to do correspondingly little work together. But the two variables are related continuously to each other rather than clustering where the classical typology says they should. As a result, the "companionship family" and the "colleague family" may be looked upon as useful ideas but not as discrete categories into which families can be neatly separated. Power and the division of labor are aspects of marriage which may coexist in almost any combination. As a result, they are best considered separately rather than welded into artificial combinations.

DETERMINANTS OF THE DIVISION OF LABOR

Although the pattern of task allocation is rather inflexible for the community as a whole, it still differs appreciably from family to family. What social factors account for some of these variations between families? Under what circumstances do wives take a larger share of the work? Which families hew closest to the cultural line in task allocation and which are most radical?

Answers to these questions may be sought in three general directions: (1) What segments of the community follow traditional norms in their division of labor—just because they are traditional? (2) What situational factors affect the participation of husband and wife in household tasks? Especially, how important is the relative availability of the two partners? (3) What changes occur within marriages with the passage of time?

This task is complicated because one must look not only at the relative amount of work done by each partner but at the particular tasks each does. The traditional norm isn't so much the amount of work done (as in the case of patriarchal authority) as the degree of adherence to traditional sex roles. Nevertheless, differences in the amount of work done by the two partners are important, too.

Where Is the Traditional Family?

A completely traditional family would be one in which the husband always did the male tasks (repairing, lawn-mowing, and snow-shovelling) and the wife always devoted herself to her traditional role (cooking, dish-washing, house-cleaning, and shopping). Since only six per cent of the families are this traditional, it is necessary to look for groups in the community which are simply more stereotyped than average. The standard of comparison here is the mean stereotypy score for the total sample (4.50). As with power, we expected immigrants, Catholics, and farm families to be the most traditional.

Immigrants? Since most immigrants were raised in traditional societies, they should be especially influenced by conventional norms. At first glance they are—for those couples where both partners were born overseas have a high stereotypy score of 4.97. However, this difference disappears when the age of the immigrants is taken into consideration. Most foreign-born Detroiters came to America a long time ago, and their division of labor is affected more by their age than by their place of birth. By contrast, young immigrants who have spent most of their life to-date overseas and have only recently arrived in America are less stereotyped (4.20) than average in their allocation of tasks. If it is true that immigrants do bring "old-fashioned" ideas with them to America, circumstances must outweigh those ideas in determining their division of labor.

Catholics? The same conclusion emerges from looking at Catholic and Protestant families. Catholics should follow the traditional division of labor more closely because Catholic teaching places special emphasis on prescribed roles for men and women. However Catholic stereotypy, at 4.46, is a shade less than average, and the Protestant average a shade higher (4.53). Moreover, devout Catholics are not more traditional but less so than inactive Catholics (4.39 versus 4.64). This is the opposite of what would be expected in theory. Hence, the Catholic parish is quite clearly not a traditional segment of the Detroit community.

Farmers? Finally, the farm families may be examined. They have the same median number of stereotyped task allocations (five) as the city families. So, again, there is no more adherence to tradition in a segment where it is rumored to exist.

Following the previous more thorough, but equally futile, attempt to locate patriarchal segments of the community, this new search for tradition-bound task-allocation patterns can be ended more quickly. Just as it was impossible to find subcultures which still determine their balance of power by traditional norms, so traditional ideas do not seem to be an effective determinant of the division of labor. Rather than being motivated by ideological concerns, American families seem to be quite pragmatic in settling who does what around the house.

This doesn't mean that families cannot be found which are traditional in form. The question is whether they are traditional *because* of conventional beliefs and value patterns or for other reasons. As with decision-making, the choice lies between culturological and dynamic theories. In both power and the division of labor, the answer seems clear. The culturological approach fails to account for variations between families, but pragmatic factors do provide workable interpretations. In the case of the division of labor, the general contemporary pattern happens to be traditional. While sheer conservatism may account for some of this behavior, the chief causes seem to be those bio-social factors which produced the tradition in the first place. Hence, the most traditionally patterned families in Detroit may not shape their division of labor from ideological considerations any more than the most unusually patterned families. Rather, both extremes reflect concrete, tangible factors at work in the interrelationships of husband, wife, and the community.

Resources for Getting Things Done

Nothing could be more pragmatic and non-ideological than the sheer availability of one partner to do the household tasks. This is precisely what seems to be the prime determinant of the division of labor.

If the dishes need washing and the lawn needs mowing, somebody must do it. As far as the needs of the family are concerned, what matters is not who does it but that someone does it. As long as the option is equally available to either partner, the work is usually done along traditional lines. But if circumstances arise which make it impossible for the customary performer to do his duty, the "show must go on." In this sense, every husband is a "stand in" for his wife, and every wife for her husband. It is true that he may not have learned her lines very well or consciously prepared himself for this emergency. But when the emergency arises, he is under pressure to take over her roles lest the household functioning break down. Not every spouse rises to the occasion, but the moral pressure and the practical urgency are there. If he doesn't, he presumably must face the criticism of the incapacitated partner—and perhaps that of his own conscience as well.

As in the case of decision-making, the moral norm which determines how families ought to differ from one another in their division of labor is appropriateness. Ordinarily, it is appropriate that the husband do the male tasks and the wife the feminine ones, because these tie in efficiently with masculine constitutions and feminine childbearing. But in extraordinary circumstances, it is appropriate for the alternate partner to come to the rescue of his overburdened or unavailable spouse even if it means playing an unfamiliar role.

Time as a Resource. Availability is partly a matter of space, partly of time. To be able to help out at home, an individual must be home. So, factors which keep the husband or wife away from home reduce his or her participation in household tasks. But even if both partners are home, they are not always equally available. The husband may be home in body but not in mind, his thoughts preoccupied with occupational responsibilities. Such a husband is not likely to be much use to his wife. Or the wife may be so heavily burdened with childcare responsibilities that she just plain runs out of time. Then the only way of getting the work done is to tap the husband's time.

Table 17

Unilateral Performance of Specific Household Tasks, by Farm and City Wives

(178 Farm Families, 731 City Families)

FAMILIES WHERE
WIFE ONLY
PERFORMS TASK*   TASK

	Repairs	Lawn	Walk	Bills	Groceries	Breakfast	Living room	Dishes
On farm	6%	13%	6%	25%	45%	86%	86%	88%
In city	3	7	7	30	36	66	65	70

* Reciprocal percentages of the 178 farm husbands and 731 city husbands help with these tasks at least occasionally.

Farm and City Schedules. Differential availability seems to explain why farm wives do so much more housework than city wives. Superficially one might expect farm husbands to do more around the house because they don't have to leave home to go to work. Yet Table 17 shows farm husbands doing less of everything except the farm-relevant account-keeping and shovelling a path to the barn. Not only do farm wives do more feminine tasks but they even do more of the other two masculine tasks. (The small differences shown in this table are compounded at the other end of the scale where only 44 per cent of the farmers do all the lawn mowing compared to 66 per cent of the city husbands, while the city husbands similarly edge out the farmers on exclusive home-repairing, 73 per cent to 55 per cent.)

In the aggregate, these differences add up to a much larger percentage of farm wives who do more than half of the tasks all by themselves. Whereas only 39 per cent of the city wives handle this many tasks, 70 per cent of the farm wives are found at this hard-working end of the continuum.

The fact that farm wives perform more of both female and male tasks explains why there is a rural-urban difference in the amount of work done without a difference in the aggregate conformity to traditional norms. Although farm wives adhere more closely to the traditional pattern on feminine tasks, they more often invade the masculine sphere, producing low masculine stereotypy.

How can this rural diligence be explained? Since farm couples are comparatively unstereotyped on male tasks, the differential output can hardly be attributed to rural conservatism. Perhaps some people would say city wives are spoiled, but does that mean rural husbands are, too? Surely not.

The very confidence with which it can be said that the American farmer is no slouch provides a clue to the mystery. In many ways, farm work is like women's work—it's never done. Not only is there an endless amount of painting, fence-mending, and wood-chopping that could be done on the typical farm, but it's always so near at hand that it provides the husband with counterclaims to any demands that might come from the wife. The typical city worker leaves his job behind when he punches the time clock at 5:00. While this allows him more leisure, it also leaves him morally defenseless when there are tasks to be done at home.

If this interpretation is correct, the farmer's perennial involvement in his work makes him relatively unavailable for household tasks, whereas the city husband's separation from his place of work makes him highly available for part-time "employment" at home.[5]

Urban Occupations. Urban husbands differ among themselves, however, in the extent to which they leave their jobs behind. Generalizations about separation of work-place and residence apply primarily to blue-collar workers since they seldom have reason to be preoccupied with business problems in their spare time. The boss, however, doesn't have it so easy. As an executive, he has problems to solve that plague him over the weekend and keep him awake nights. Even if he doesn't bring his paper work home in the proverbial briefcase, his mind will not easily forget. So, whether working late at the office, figuring in his study, or puzzling over a problem in his easy chair, the responsible executive is unavailable for housework. The more responsible he is, the less available he becomes—for the means to promotion is overtime work, and the consequence of promotion is more overtime work.

In Detroit, the differences between entire occupational groups are minor, although the business and professional group does have the highest task performance by the wife (5.49) and the low-blue-collar group the least (5.20). The big difference between city husbands is not between occupations as such but reflects the amount of involvement of the husband in his occupation.

---

5. For a more extended discussion of this question see Blood (1958).

Occupational Preoccupation. Two measures of the husband's success in his occupation are available. The first is the amount of income he earns. Presumably the more time and energy a man invests in his job, the more he is financially rewarded.

Table 18
Household Task Performance, by Husband's Income

	HUSBAND'S INCOME			
	Under $3,000	*$3,000–6,999*	*$7,000–9,999*	*$10,000+*
Wife's mean task performance	5.11	5.27	5.65	6.21
Number of families	61	357	86	52

The evidence from Table 18 is unmistakable: high-income husbands do less work around the house. It is important to remember that this is not just because wealthy men hire gardners to mow the lawn. Since this is the *relative* division of labor between husband and wife, for everything the successful man does less of, his wife does correspondingly more. She, too, of course, may have more servants and more labor-saving devices to cut down on her own household tasks. But the rise in her index of task performance shows that the housework as a whole becomes increasingly her responsibility because her husband is so absorbed in his career.

Table 19
Household Task Performance, by Husband's Intergenerational
Occupational Mobility

	HUSBAND'S INTERGENERATIONAL MOBILITY		
	Downward	*Stable*	*Upward*
Wife's mean task performance	5.10	5.28	5.67
Number of families	162	176	207

A second measure of occupational success involves comparing the husband's occupation with that of his father before him. Those who now hold a better job have been "upward mobile," in comparison to those who have stayed in the same occupational stratum or moved downward.[6]

---

6. Occupations were rated on the National Opinion Research Center's scale of occupational prestige. "Stable" husbands were those who had not moved more than 5 percentile points from their father's rating.

The differences shown in Table 19 are not great but they sub-
stantiate the generalization that the more successful the husband is in
his occupation, the less the wife can count on his help at home. Not
that successful husbands disdain household tasks—they are just too
busy being successful to have the time.

Table 20
Household Task Performance, by Husband's Social Status

(for families in which the wife is not currently employed)

	PERCENTILE RANKING ON SOCIAL STATUS INDEX				
	0–19	20–39	40–59	60–79	80–99
Wife's mean task performance	6.00	6.03	5.54	5.73	5.54
Number of families	13	65	144	153	79

In talking about successful husbands, it is necessary to stress that
they are not identical with high-status husbands. Social status, as
Table 20 shows, has a somewhat irregular relationship to the division
of labor even when limited to families in which all the wives are
home. Since what little difference there is lies in the opposite direction
from what we have seen, for income and occupation, it means that
there is a countertendency at work among stable high-status people
to the one noted among self-made, occupationally-oriented men.

This tendency for the established high-status man to be more
family oriented is suggested also in the fact that high status suburban
husbands do a good deal around home (wife's task score = 5.19).
Perhaps the "station-wagon set" is represented here with its larger
number of children, its do-it-yourself movement, and other indices of
family-orientedness.

The man who struggles to get ahead does so at the expense of
family participation. But the man who has a secure position in the
community, because of family background and higher education, can
afford to orient himself more toward the enjoyment of life in family
activities. The social-status index is therefore a composite of familistic
and occupationalistic criteria which pull in opposite directions when it
comes to the division of labor. So a distinction must be made between
the high-status husband who is still immersed in his occupational advancement and the equally high-status man who is less occupationally
preoccupied and therefore more available for tasks around the home.

Table 20 shows one other group of husbands who participate just as much in household tasks as the highest status husbands, namely the middle range. Such husbands are well-enough socialized to be sensitive to the wife's needs but not so successful occupationally that their work interferes with their availability for housework. The next to the top group is where mobility strivings appear to interfere more.

In the case of low-status families, it is not jobs that get in the way of male assistance but other factors. Insensitivity? Preoccupation with "the boys"? TV? Whatever the causes, low-status husbands clearly do the least housework.

Job-involved Wives. So far, only the husband's involvement outside the home has been mentioned. But since many wives also work, both partners' employment influences their availability for household tasks.

Table 21

Household Task Performance and Adherence to Male and Female Roles, by Comparative Work Participation of Husband and Wife

| | COMPARATIVE WORK PARTICIPATION | | | | | |
| | WIFE NOT EMPLOYED | | | WIFE EMPLOYED | | |
	Husband overtime	Husband full-time	Husband none	Husband overtime	Husband full-time	Husband none
Wife's mean task performance	5.81	5.57	5.64	4.66	3.40	2.33
Adherence to female roles	6.20	6.12	6.33	4.88	4.32	1.33
Adherence to male roles	6.64	7.00	7.26	7.51	7.90	8.33
Minimum number of families*	198	218	28	50	58	3

* Each cell in the column above a particular number contains at least the number of families indicated, with minor variation upward wherever the number of "Not Ascertained" cases diminishes. For example, in the first column above, the actual numbers on which the means are computed are 198, 206, and 204 (reading from top to bottom). This nomenclature will be used throughout the book whenever compound tables utilize the same independent variable for a series of dependent variables with slightly differing non-response rates.

Table 21 shows a striking difference between wives who are not employed (and therefore fully available for household tasks) and those whose jobs take them out of the home. When the wife is away most of the day (nearly all working wives in Detroit have full-time jobs), she faces the potential burden of two jobs: paid work plus housework. Under these circumstances, the husband feels obliged to help out more at home and takes over an appreciably larger share of the housework. The working wife still has a more strenuous life than the housewife, no doubt, but the husband may come to her rescue sufficiently to cushion the physical strain on her and to minimize resentment against him.

However, his ability to come to her aid depends on the extent to which he works himself. If he is home all the time, the three cases in Table 21 suggest that he can pretty much take over the housework even if he is unable to hold a regular job. But if he has two jobs himself (as many over-time husbands do), there will be less reason and less possibility for him to help out with the wife's second area of responsibility.

The comparative availability of the husband has the same effect when the wife is not working—but it makes less difference then. If the wife is home all the time, she can do her traditional tasks without much help from the husband. Even if he's home full-time (as when neither partner works), he is not likely to invade her sphere as long as she is capable of doing her own traditional work. Most non-working couples involve a husband who has retired but spends his time largely in puttering around rather than in doing half of the housework.

This suggests a limitation on the principle of comparative availability: *under conditions of strain,* tasks will be reallocated in the direction of the more available partner. From this point of view, the full-time housewife whose husband is employed full-time is the normal pattern. She has full-time to devote to the feminine tasks and he has his spare-time in which to get around to the masculine tasks.

When the husband retires, there is no additional strain on the division of labor because the wife still has plenty of time to get her work done. Only if she takes a job does a stay-at-home husband come under pressure to change his role.

On the other hand, if the husband works evenings and weekends, it may be difficult for him to accomplish even the traditional male tasks—so the wife who is home all the time may find herself taking over his tasks.

For the husband to work overtime puts less strain on the traditional division of labor than for the wife to go outside the home to work. This is a simple question of the number of hours in the week. Husbands rarely put in as much as forty hours overtime but this is the usual outside investment of the wife who goes to work. The ability of the husband to respond to this major deficit in his wife's time budget may be seen by comparing the size of the changes in household participation according to the varying amounts of time the husband has available. Overtime husbands, with the least time to spare, still manage to squeeze out a major shift in task performance of 1.15 points in response to the radical alteration of the wife's daily schedule when she works. But husbands with a normal complement of spare time shift even more (2.17 points difference), while men retired from the labor market make the biggest shift of all (3.31 points).

To summarize, (1) the more the conventional division of labor is disrupted, the more tasks must be reallocated; and (2) tasks are reassigned to the other partner in proportion to the amount of time he has available.

Comparison of two-income and one-income families by degree of stereotypy in the allocation of tasks shows that working wife families depart appreciably from traditional roles.[7] However, this overall difference holds primarily for families where the husband's income is less than $5,000. At this low income level, 32 per cent of the two-income families but only 15 per cent of the one-income families have unstereotyped roles (less than half of the tasks done in the traditional manner).

Do higher income families have more resources with which to adapt to the strain of the wife going to work? Perhaps their financial position enables them to employ substitute task-performers under the supervision of the traditional partner and to mechanize the latter's work sufficiently to enable her to do her tasks in what little time is available. Apparently, then, it is especially at low-income levels that the wife's departure leaves no alternative but for the husband to pitch in and help out.

Actually, total role stereotypy is an ambiguous way of looking at changes which reflect the lessened availability of one partner. A decrease in the availability of one partner tends to reduce stereotypy in his role area but to increase it in the partner's area. This occurs in

7. The authors are indebted to Buse (1955) for preliminary analysis of this area.

farm families where the husband's lessened availability results in the wife invading his role but doing her own tasks all the more one-sidedly. The same is true when the wife goes to work—but in the reverse direction.

Table 21 shows that the extra pressure on husbands of working wives causes them to help their wives out more with feminine tasks at the same time that they do more of their own tasks. The result is that two-income families are more stereotyped in the masculine area and less so in the feminine area. This dual shift occurs at both low and high income levels, though not quite symmetrically. Above $5,000, the wife's working prompts the husband to do more of his own tasks, with the net result that high-income marriages move slightly in the traditional direction on total stereotypy. Lower-income husbands, however, not only increase their masculine work, but move even more substantially into the female area, producing a net shift away from general stereotypy.

It is incorrect, therefore, to say that two-income families are more companionable than one-income families in their division of labor. To be sure they share the bread-winning responsibility. They also share the feminine tasks. But they do not share the masculine tasks as much. The net result is greater equality in decision-making between husband and wife, and more participation by the husband in the total task of running the household—but not more collective participation in all task areas. Rather, the wife drops out of the husband's task areas as he moves into hers.[8]

Examination of the various tasks in relation to the wife's employment shows that husbands help out more with the working wife's home-centered tasks (getting the breakfast, doing the dishes, and picking up the living room) but the wife continues to do just as much of the grocery shopping. There her time shortage may be offset by the ease of shopping on the way home from work. On the other hand, the husband gets less of the working wife's help with his outdoor tasks (snow-shovelling, lawn-mowing), but there is no shift in household repairing. Perhaps the latter depends so much on technical skill that

---

8. This modifies Kligler's conclusion that working-wife families are consistently less bound by traditional lines separating husband-wife domains in the performance of traditional roles (1954).

only the competent partner can do it. All the time in the world doesn't help if one lacks the know-how.

In keeping track of the money and bills, the distinction lies not between wives who are currently employed and those who are home but between those who have *ever* worked and those who never have since marriage. Apparently participation in the world of work trains the wife in financial competence which is reflected in keeping the books (and making financial decisions) long after she quits working. Again, skill seems more important than time in this administrative task.

To summarize, husbands of working wives can expect to help out more in the home and get less help themselves outside the home— except where tasks are so technical in nature that the relative competence of the two partners matters more than their availability. The case of the working wife, therefore, requires further modification of the general thesis to say that families differ in their division of labor according to how easy it is for either partner to do it. Ease is a combination of time and skill. Another way of putting it would be to return to the concept of resources. Time is a resource for getting work done. So is skill. Hence, the division of labor is determined by the comparative resourcefulness of the two partners in accomplishing the necessary household tasks.

Unresponsive Husbands. Even for ordinary tasks which require little skill, more than time is needed. With most husbands, a wife's shortage of time is enough to get him to respond with help. But some husbands fail to respond despite clear evidence of need. These are the deviant cases where the husband has no excuse but laziness or irresponsibility—and where the wife resents his inertia correspondingly.

Where in the community are these inadequate husbands clustered?

One place is the working-class Negro family. Whereas low-blue-collar white husbands help out more around the house, Negroes at this occupational level do not, despite the fact that their wives are most apt to be working out of the home. Rather than respond to the needs of their wives, the husbands cling to traditional male roles (mean of 4.85 compared to 4.27 for whites). Could this be because their sense of masculinity is threatened by frequent unemployment? In any case, their wives have to keep up their own tasks relatively unaided.

But inadequacy is not confined to one race. Although there is generally little relationship between power and the division of labor in the family, wife-dominant families present a surprising picture. Instead of Caspar Milquetoast submissively doing his wife's bidding as the cartoons suggest, his wife does far more household tasks than any other type of wife (mean task performance is 5.81 for dominant Negro wives, 5.92 for dominant white wives). This counters the common assumption that powerful spouses compel their partners to carry out their bidding, and is further evidence of the non-coercive nature of marital power.

One possible reason why powerful wives do so much work is the same reason they are powerful—namely, the inadequacy of their husbands. Where men are indecisive, women must make the decisions. And if men are unable or unwilling to do their share of the housework, their wives must do it themselves.

It is pertinent to recall not only the paradox of powerful wives powerless to motivate their husbands to work, but the added paradox that these hard-working wives are also more apt to be working outside the home and therefore more urgently need their husbands' assistance. Perhaps this notion of inadequate husbands explains another paradox. One would expect that the more hours the wife works outside the home, the fewer tasks would be done by her at home. Actually the reverse is true. Those wives who work outside the home more than 40 hours a week get the least help from their husbands of any group of working wives. (Average task performance by overtime wives is 4.58 compared to 4.05 for other working wives controlled on amount of work to be done at home by excluding working mothers with preschool children.) This group is also highly specialized in task allocation, reflecting anew the husband's failure to share the wife's burden.

Such unresponsiveness contrasts with the incapacitated husbands shown in Table 21 who take over so many tasks at home to make up for their inability to work outside. This contrast heightens the impression that some wives whom one would most expect to be assisted at home are not, simply because of the unwillingness of their husbands. Understandably, such wives are most dissatisfied with their marriages.

Skill as a Resource. Skill is more important than time in determining whether the husband or the wife will repair things and keep track of the finances. No other information on mechanical skill is available but bookkeeping ability can be gauged in various ways. For instance, whichever partner has more education keeps track of the money and bills (even when controlled on the husband's occupational level).

Table 22
Wife's Financial Task Performance, by Husband's Income

	HUSBAND'S INCOME			
	Under $3,000	$3,000 –4,999	$5,000 –6,999	$7,000 –9,999	$10,000+
Wife's mean financial task performance *	3.20	3.32	3.30	3.11	2.88
Number of families	70	181	198	88	57

* Keeping track of the money and bills.

Of even greater significance, however, is the husband's income. Once he gets above $7,000 a year and especially when he gets over $10,000, he assumes the financial responsibility more often. Below $7,000, most of the money goes for groceries and other subsistence items anyway. But when income exceeds this level, problems of investment and savings arise which swing insurance decisions to the husband. When money gets to be this plentiful and decisions about it correspondingly complicated, the successful husband's extra experience with money becomes doubly valuable.

Changes in the Division of Labor

The resources which the husband and wife bring to the family are partly skills acquired before the couple get married. Partly they are resources of time which the partners are able to contribute to marriage by default of external involvements or by intentional interest in the family.

Role Differentiation. Still other differences between families stem from the internal dynamics of family living. One of these is a type of change which is likely to affect any group over the course of time—gradually the members become specialists along differentiated but complementary lines.

When any new group of people first come together, there is a period of tentative trial-and-error searching out of the pattern of who will do what. At first, no one knows how his own skills compare with those of other group members. If the tasks are strange, there is all the more necessity for various members of the group to try them out before it is eventually discovered who is best at each. As such discoveries are made, each person comes to perform those tasks for which he has the greatest skill and other resources. This process of eventual specialization results from what economists call "the principle of least effort"—whoever can get results with the least effort tends to perform that task. He himself finds greatest satisfaction in doing so, and the others more and more defer to his competence. As a result, he plays an increasingly specialized role as time goes on.

In the case of the family, role differentiation has a head start— even for newlyweds. From early childhood, the bride and groom have observed the standardized model of their own parents and of parents generally—the model of traditional role differentiation along sex lines. In the process of being brought up, there has usually been explicit training—especially for the girl—for the tasks that she will perform when she becomes a wife and mother in her own right. So by both informal and formal socialization, the husband and wife have been prepared to enter marriage with similar expectations about how they will divide up their duties.

Despite this preliminary preparation, there is still something in marriage of that initial tentativeness which characterizes all new groups. For one thing, the role expectations the partners bring to marriage are not likely to coincide in every respect. Some tasks crop up which both partners expected to be their own—the money and bills, for example. Other tasks may be mutually wished upon the partner—such as taking out the garbage. Discrepancies in role expectations produce a period of Alphonse-and-Gaston tugging and hauling before a settled pattern emerges.

Moreover, few modern young people come to marriage completely rehearsed in the tasks of keeping house. The less well-trained the partners, the more they must engage in mutual experimentation. The proverbial hard-as-a-rock first buns may well lead to husbandly advice, collaboration in reading the recipe, or even a temporary change of cooks if he has been "baching" it before marriage. Likewise, husbands who have never repaired a broken lamp cord before are apt to find someone looking over their shoulder, proffering assistance.

The collaboration of young husbands and wives in household tasks stems not only from their need for assistance but their enjoyment of doing new things together. One of the charms of courtship is the experience of doing things together for the first time. This novelty continues through the honeymoon into setting up housekeeping. Eventually, the novelty wears off as the seasons roll around for the second time. Even so there may still be a continuing stress on togetherness for its own sake which keeps the couple working at tasks jointly for a while longer. By the time that has worn off, children usually arrive to impose new tasks on the couple, repeating the cycle of tentative exploration and charming firsts with the added factor of pressure on the husband to collaborate in meeting the peremptory needs of the baby.

Eventually, however, the crisis of invasion by helpless children passes. Then nothing remains to prevent the principle of least effort from asserting itself fully. Novelty has gone. Competences have been tested. The stress of household tasks wanes as children become chore-performers instead of simply chores themselves. As for companionship, it may not have disappeared so much as changed its form. Where young couples find companionship in doing the dishes together, middle-aged couples come to take each other for granted sufficiently so that they can appreciate each other's work at separate tasks. No longer is it necessary to work together to prove their love. Love has been tested and accepted. Now they can express their love through each one's separate contribution to a complementary whole. Marriage can now be symbiotic without having to be synchronous all the time.

Table 23

Role Specialization, by Stage in Family-life Cycle

MEAN ROLE SPECIALIZATION		STAGE IN FAMILY-LIFE CYCLE				
Childrearing stages:		Preschool	Preadolescent	Adolescent	Unlaunched	
		5.13	5.22	5.47	6.01	
		(122)	(134)	(95)	(58)	
Childless stages:	Honeymoon				Postparental	Retired
	4.77				5.82	6.00
	(18)				(83)	(9)
Childless couples:		6.22	4.71	5.13		
		(9)	(28)	(8)		

Table 23 shows that the honeymoon period of role experimentation involves more sharing of tasks than any later stage. For most couples, the honeymoon period is followed quickly by the retirement of the wife from work to housewifery, enabling her to begin specializing despite the newness of her tasks. As the children become less of a burden and more of a resource, role differentiation between husband and wife increases at an accelerated pace, reaching its peak when the wife has fully trained children at her disposal, or the retired husband unlimited time to perform his own tasks.

Relative Participation in Tasks. Similar trends occur with respect to the amount of work done by each partner, although specialization and task performance are not identical phenomena.

Table 24

Relative Task Performance, by Stage in Family-life Cycle

WIFE'S MEAN TASK PERFORMANCE	STAGE IN FAMILY-LIFE CYCLE						
	Honeymoon	Preschool	Preadolescent	Adolescent	Unlaunched	Postparental	Retired
Childrearing stages:		5.14 (122)	5.58 (134)	5.53 (95)	5.56 (58)		
Childless stages:	4.55 (18)					5.47 (83)	5.50 (10)
Childless couples:		5.00 (9)	5.11 (28)	5.25 (8)			

Whereas age of wife alone gives a somewhat irregular picture of the changing amount of work, stage in the family-life cycle reflects age, the wife's employment, and the burden of pre-school children sufficiently to provide a clearer trend line. Table 24 shows that the young wife without children does the least work at home. However, the coming of the first child does not deprive her completely of her husband's assistance since she needs his help in adjusting to the increased demands of her new role as mother. By the time her oldest child gets into grade school, she settles into a *hausfrau* pattern, carrying the main responsibility for tasks about the home. Even when the last child leaves, the ending of the mother role hardly affects the wife's share in the performance of household tasks.

The increasing role differentiation with the passage of time is largely a consequence of continued interaction as such. But the wife's increasing share of household tasks reflects other factors. Partly the decreased burden of children out of diapers and in school takes the pressure off the husband to help out. So the need for his sharing diminishes. At the same time, the children themselves begin to acquire competence for doing chores, which makes them a resource for getting the housework done. Since the wife is the chief childrearing agent, the responsibility for organizing and supervising these junior partners falls to the wife. This results in shifting still more of the responsibility of the household to the wife and away from the husband.

The primary determinant of the shifting division of labor is the wife's sex-linked childrearing role. What happens to the husband under these circumstances is not clear. As he participates less and less in household tasks, he also makes fewer family decisions. During the child-rearing span of years he seems to become increasingly alienated from his family, leaving the family responsibility more and more in the hands of his wife.

Little is known, unfortunately, about what the middle-aged husband does with the time he no longer invests in his marriage. At the middle-class level, these are years when promotion often brings heavy work responsibility. Kinsey (1948) finds that middle-class involvement in extra-marital affairs increases in these same middle years. Perhaps the increasingly estranged husband turns to other women in search of the companionship and understanding he loses at home, as his wife becomes preoccupied with the children. With working class men, one substitute may be TV.

Whatever the fate of the husband, the wife's absorption in her children results in serious discontinuity when they grow up and leave home. Child-launching for the wife becomes a role crisis as drastic as retirement for the husband. Here is impetus for three trends which are at work in Detroit to cushion the blow: (1) the continuation of mothering into the grandmother role; (2) the resumption of work by the middle-aged housewife (Chapter Four); and (3) the partially successful restoration of the husband-wife relationship once that is all the wife has left (Chapters Six through Eight).

THE DIVISION OF LABOR IN AMERICAN MARRIAGE

Feeding the family, cleaning the house, mowing the lawn, repairing broken things—these are the maintenance functions which must be performed by the family in order to keep things going. Who does them—whether father, mother, or children—is largely a matter of convenience or economy of effort. A few tasks, such as repairing and bookkeeping, require skills which may not be distributed equally in the family nor easily learned. Hence they are best performed by whoever has the technical know-how. Some tasks, such as lawn-mowing and snow-shovelling require muscular strength in which fathers usually surpass their wives.

But most household tasks are humdrum and menial in nature; the chief resource required is time. Usually the person with the most time is the wife—provided she isn't working outside the home. If she does work, the husband incurs a moral obligation to help her out in what would otherwise be her exclusive task areas. And help her he does unless he is unusually involved in his own work or just plain insensitive to his wife's needs. He is also pressed into extra duty when the wife has her hands full with the new and strenuous tasks of caring for young children.

The rest of the time, though, husbands and wives tend to be specialists who complement rather than duplicate each other's work. The husband specializes in heavy and technical tasks, the wife in functions correlated with her role in life as childbearer and childrearer. Thus, each partner does different things which contribute to the needs of the family as a whole. Each contributes from his own resources to the welfare of the total group—except where the wife gets so involved in her childrearing role that her role as wife atrophies. In the later stages of childrearing, the husband often becomes a marginal member of the family whose resources are turned elsewhere or lie unused.

In general, the division of labor in the modern family coincides with the division of labor in the traditional family. The reason is not so much that contemporary Americans are conservative in principle—for they have altered their pattern of decision-making to fit the times. Rather the same bio-social reasons which shaped the traditional family still supply differential resources which men and women bring to marriage. But where resources differ from man to man or woman to woman, the modern family adjusts its division of labor accordingly. If it clings to traditional patterns under altered circumstances, the condemnation of spouse and observers alike is incurred. For the criterion which governs the contemporary division of labor is not custom but equity, and an equitable division of labor depends on the resources of time, energy, and skill which each family member can contribute to the common task.

Part Two

FAMILY FUNCTIONS

A FAMILY FUNCTION is a service that families perform. Family functions may serve the society at large (by producing and educating new members), the self-maintenance of the family as an on-going unit, or the needs of individual family members. This book is focused on family functions from the standpoint of the individual participants—especially the adult participants (the husband and wife).

Family living is not the only source of need-satisfactions in life but it is an important source. The family is an economic unit through which the husband and often the wife support themselves and their children (Chapter Four). The family is the only unit in our society through which men and women can have the experience of bearing and rearing children (Chapter Five). Companionship is provided elsewhere by cliques and friendships but the marriage vow involves a life-long commitment to togetherness (Chapter Six). New in the world's consciousness is the awareness that marriage is also important to mental health—for better or for worse (Chapter Seven). Finally, marriage provides the old, old function of love and affection to its members (Chapter Eight).

Families differ tremendously in the extent to which they perform these functions. Yet almost all young couples begin marriage optimistically, hoping that they will achieve high performance levels. However, the goals of marriage are not identical for all couples. From parents, a particular example of marriage has been observed and particular values learned. Goals are also influenced by the reference group to which a couple belongs—that segment of the community which provides the standards they seek to achieve. For instance, farm couples usually derive their expectations from other farm families, not from the city.

Marriage goals include such specifics as a certain kind of home, children, and an ideal pattern of love and companionship. To achieve these goals requires tangible efforts. For instance, the husband's success on the job is the chief means to his family's achievement of its desired standard of living. Mental hygiene requires communication between husband and wife. Such activities are instrumental to the achievement of family goals.

The extent to which a family achieves its goals profoundly affects the degree of satisfaction the members feel. Satisfaction depends partly on the objective level of performance, e.g., the higher the family income, the greater the satisfaction with the standard of living, other things being equal. But satisfaction is affected also by differences between the life one has and what one feels one ought to have. Those who achieve their goals feel more satisfied than those who don't—even though the outside observer might see no objective difference between families.

Goals and satisfactions do not remain static throughout life any more than actual behavior patterns do. Levels of aspiration rise as previous goals are achieved—or fall as they appear more and more hopeless. Young couples can be satisfied on very little income as long as the future looks bright. Changing circumstances bring new goals, new behaviors, and correspondingly greater satisfaction or dissatisfaction.

Family functions, therefore, have three facets—the goals the couple hope to achieve, the steps taken to reach them, and the kinds of feelings which come with success or failure.

THE ECONOMIC FUNCTION

AMERICANS ARE uncomfortable about the relationship between money and marriage. We believe that people should marry for love, not money. We frown on alien cultures which require a large dowry or a bride price in cattle. We are disgusted about foreign parents who stress wealth and family background in choosing a bride for their son. We relish stories about rich girls marrying chauffeurs—not because we envy his success in getting rich quick, but because we admire her idealism in abandoning all for true love. For a "nation of capitalists" we are terribly romantic.

Yet there are other sayings, too, that remind us that people can't live on love alone. So, half apologetically we encourage our daughters to marry medical students and be wary of dates who flunk their exams, quit school, or have no ambition.

Squeamishness ends, however, when the wedding vows have been said. From that point on it is obvious to newlyweds and relatives alike that money, job, and success are hard facts of life. From then on, money matters. Promotions are big news. Bonuses are something to get excited about and bills something to worry about.

How many of the other goals of marriage depend on money? It costs money to buy privacy for love, recreation for companionship, shoes for the children. Fundamentally, it costs money to stay alive, and the family has the basic responsibility for providing food, clothing, and shelter, for all save the few unattached or institutionalized people in the world. Few Americans, however, are willing to settle for sheer survival. The American standard of living sets higher goals than keeping the wolf away from the door. In the "Advertising Age," more and more, costlier and costlier products make up the wished-for package. Americans are interested in living well, in enjoying life. They want to do "the right thing" for their children. They aren't greatly interested in saving money because "you can't take it with you," but they are greatly interested in the things that money will buy.

Until they get married, most couples have no TV, no furniture, maybe no car, certainly no house. Every wedding sets in motion another purchasing spree—so much so that the pages of the *Wall Street Journal* gloat over predictions of the flood of new marriages in the coming years. Every couple goes into marriage hoping to have a good life—which means in part hoping to have a good living.

The main task of the economic function in marriage is to provide this living—to provide money which makes it possible to commandeer the goods and services consumed in family living.

For the husband, the economic function is his main job in life. He spends most of his time at work, puts most of his energy into it, derives most of his satisfaction from it. High among those satisfactions for the average working man is the pay check which he brings home to be translated into purchases for the family.

To women, the economic function is less important. Their lives tend to be centered in the home, in bearing and rearing children, entertaining and visiting. If the pay check is adequate, they can take it for granted and concentrate on family relationships. Especially in times of stable prosperity, attention can shift from money matters to the "finer things of life," to the use of leisure time in more enjoyable ways.

THE ECONOMIC GOALS OF MARRIAGE

Michigan families in 1955 took it for granted that a good income would come their way. After more than a dozen years of wartime and postwar prosperity, they listed "the standard of living—the kind of house, clothes, car, and so forth" as the *least* valuable part of marriage when given a chance to choose among five aspects.[1] Only 3 per cent of the Detroit wives felt the standard of living was the most valuable aspect of marriage-in-general; 10 per cent chose it second; 15 per cent third; leaving 71 per cent who did not see it as one of the three major values in being married. The farm wives gave an equally low place to this aspect of marriage.

Wives who mention the standard of living first are largely those who can't take it for granted. For them, the economic function is still a goal to be achieved rather than a present reality.

For instance, 89 per cent of all wives who rank the economic function first are married to men earning less than $5,000 a year (the median income in Detroit). Similarly, wives of downward mobile men (who have failed to achieve the occupational level of their fathers) are doubly likely to be concerned about economic matters in marriage.

How adequate a pay check is depends partly on its size in dollars and its size in comparison to the father-in-law's standard. Important also, however, is how far it must be stretched. Not a single one of the childless young brides ranks money first in marriage—most of them are doubling the husband's income anyway so that capital goods are rapidly accumulating. Mothers of grade school age children stress finances more often than any other group. At this point, most families have reached their maximum size, the children are growing rapidly (consuming more food and clothing) but aren't old enough to bring in supplemental income. Sixty per cent of all wives who choose money first are concentrated at this one stage in the family life cycle (compared to only 23 per cent of the total families). This suggests that the standard of living is a prominent goal for families whose pay checks least adequately cover family needs. For them, the economic function is under par and therefore important. They can't afford to think about such luxuries as companionship. As for having children, they often have more than they want already.

---

1. Most often ranked first was "companionship in doing things together with the husband"; next came "the chance to have children"; third, "the husband's understanding of the wife's problems and feelings"; and fourth, "the husband's expression of love and affection for the wife."

Money is rarely the chief goal in marriage for American wives. Nevertheless, the need for money is always there, ready to assume prominence whenever it is not adequately met.

MEETING THE ECONOMIC NEEDS OF THE FAMILY

In the preindustrial era, families didn't depend on money income but produced their own goods and services. Families were the original business enterprise. By comparison, the corporation is Johnny-come-lately. Even today, the economy of many countries rests on a broad base of family-style production, with a sprinkling of industries on top.

Americans tend to think first of the family farm when they think of family production. But the world has seen many other types of family enterprise. Fishing, weaving, pottery-making, and most other crafts were family centered from the beginning. The underdeveloped countries of the world are still primarily dependent on family production. Even as industrialized a country as Japan produces many cloth and paper products in home industries.

In the West, cottage industry was a passing phase in the industrial revolution. The steam engine was so bulky that it could not be decentralized into small producing units—so the factory came into existence, pulling family members out of the home to work. Although mechanization of agriculture has not destroyed the family farm in

Table 25

Subsistence Production in City and Farm Families

FAMILIES PRODUCING "MOST" OR "ALL" OF EACH ITEM*	PLACE OF RESIDENCE	
	City	Farm
Baked goods	55%	79%
Summer vegetables	9	87
Canned, frozen foods	7	74
Dresses	7	15
Number of families	731	178

* Reciprocal percentages of families produce half or less of the same item. E.g., the remaining 45 per cent of city families bake half or less of their cakes, cookies, and pies.

America, it has increased productivity so fast that fewer and fewer farm families are needed.

As a result of these changes, the economic function of the family rarely involves home production any more. Today, only farm families produce much for sale, and even in the country production for subsistence purposes is beginning to follow the urban decline.

Subsistence Production

Table 25 shows the sharp contrast between city and farm families at the present time. Hardly any wives sew any more, although twice as many farm women as city women make most of their dresses. Food-growing and preserving is the big area of difference between city and country. Partly this is due to the lack of land in the city. Families living in the heart of Detroit garden least of all, as would be expected. While few people in the whole metropolitan area raise very many vegetables, the average family in low-income suburbs manage to raise "some" of their vegetables. Presumably, they combine reasonable opportunity in the form of garden space with considerable need to economize.

City families have an excuse not to grow vegetables (and if they don't grow them, it's less economical to can or freeze them). But what about baking and sewing? Aren't these just as possible for city families as on the farm? Undoubtedly. But not as necessary.

Farm-family income in Michigan (as in the United States as a whole) is low. The median income for the farm sample is about $3,000, hardly more than half the city median.

Subsistence production helps to soften the economic blow for farm families. They don't need as much cash if they can grow their own food. Conversely, if they can't afford to buy food, home production becomes more urgent.

Saving Money vs. Making Money. Many city women would rather bring in income than reduce the need for it. By going to work, they have more purchasing power for store goods, and less time for home production, especially when working more than a forty-hour week (see Table 26).

It is understandable that working wives would have less time to make things at home, since they do less housework in general. The

Table 26

Subsistence Production, by Wife's Employment Status

| | EXTENT OF WIFE'S EMPLOYMENT | | | |
	None	Part-time	Full-time	Over-time
Mean subsistence production*	4.16	3.73	3.72	2.66
Number of families	486	26	75	21

* This is a seven-point scale, in which 4.00 is the equivalent of "some" home production and 4.04 is the mean for the total white sample. A high score means more production.

difference between wives who work full time and those who don't work at all is not so great as might be expected, however. The degree of similarity reflects the marginal place which home production occupies in the work of the average city housewife. Only when the wife works overtime is she so hard pressed that she can't do somewhere near the normal amount of baking. As for other types of production, most city wives do none of them at all.

The consistently low volume of subsistence production in the city helps to explain why it isn't closely related to the economic need of the household.

Table 27

Subsistence Production, by Husband's Income, for Non-working Wives Only

| | HUSBAND'S INCOME | | | | | |
	Under $3,000	$3,000 –4,999	$5,000 –5,999	$6,000 –6,999	$7,000 –9,999	$10,000+
Mean subsistence production	4.27	4.12	4.64	3.83	4.51	3.64
Number of families	30	121	94	69	84	76

Table 27 shows a zigzag pattern of ups and downs in subsistence production from one income group to another. This suggests that producing things at home is no longer an important way of improving the family's economic position under urban conditions.

So uneconomic has it become to try to produce food at home that even farm families and foreign families who move to the city engage in very little subsistence production there. Not that these are lost arts; migrant and immigrant wives probably learned the necessary skills from their mothers. Rather, food growing and processing pay off in the country but are either impossible or not worth the effort in the city. The proverbial rural hoe has been superseded by the urban can-opener.

Today home production for the city wife is an optional aspect of her role rather than a necessary one. If it is valuable, the value is not primarily money saved, but a feeling of personal creativity for herself and perhaps of superior quality for the family consumers. If this is true, then home production has largely ceased being an economic function in the city and almost deserves to be classified as recreation —a hobby to be pursued when the wife feels like it and has time.

Table 28

Subsistence Production, by Stage in Family-life Cycle

MEAN SUBSISTENCE PRODUCTION		STAGE IN FAMILY-LIFE CYCLE					
Childrearing stages:		Preschool	Preadolescent	Adolescent	Unlaunched		
		3.96	4.02	4.15	4.48		
		(130)	(140)	(101)	(66)		
Childless stages:	Honeymoon				Postparental	Retired	
	3.74				3.91	4.82	
	(19)				(89)	(11)	
Childless couples:		3.18	3.72	3.70			
		(11)	(29)	(10)			

The stages in the family-life cycle reflect the factors affecting the minor variations in urban home production (see Table 28). The young wife without children is too busy working outside the home to do very much at home. The mother of young children is home but preoccupied with more urgent tasks and still does less than average. Only the family with older children produces much at home and some of this is probably done by the children themselves. The questionnaire asked how much is produced "at home" and not simply "by the wife." Perhaps mothers of teen agers give their daughters a few baking lessons in preparation for marriage. Perhaps, too, mothers of adult children turn to home production as a substitute for the emotional satisfaction they don't get from their husbands.

On the whole, the data from Detroit reflect the striking decline in home production in modern America—so great that it has largely lost its economic character except for families who still live on the land where ease of production helps meet financial pressures.

In the city, the way to achieve a high level of living is not to produce your own, but to participate in a larger division of labor than the family itself provides. The result of the abandonment of subsistence production is not economic loss but a higher standard of living than would otherwise be possible. The industrial worker participates in a complex organization which is able to produce types of goods which home production could never even approximate.

The Mobility Aspirations of the Husband

The main person expected to take an outside job is the husband. Just as in primitive societies the wife stayed home to tend the fire and care for the children, so today the wife is still involved during much of her life in household responsibilities.

A man's job is not a static thing. Most men go through significant changes in their rates of pay—if nothing else—during their careers. Men who start "on the ground floor" when they are young acquire seniority which enables them to be upgraded into better-paying jobs. The stockroom boy sometimes becomes a buyer, the man on the line a foreman.

At the beginning of their work histories, most men hope to get ahead in one way or another. To do so is to be able to serve the needs of the family more fully, to meet the economic goals of the family more quickly. Hence, the mobility aspirations of the male American symbolize both his own and his dependents' economic goals.

Mobility serves a dual role in the life of the man. It is partly a means to a higher standard of living. But it is also evidence of personal success—a rewarding self-validation.

Upward mobility is the great American dream. Whereas in many parts of the world, the ideal son follows in his father's footsteps, the American ideal is to move beyond the father's achievements. To a remarkable extent, upward mobility is actually achieved. Primarily, this results from the steady expansion of the American economy. Between 1910 and 1950, mechanization dropped the percentage of unskilled workers in the American labor force from 21 per cent to 17.5 per cent and farmers from 32 per cent to 12 per cent. At the same time, the growth of large corporations increased managerial positions from 6 to 10 per cent, while specialization and technical development increased the proportion of professionals in the labor force from 4 to 7 per cent (Freedman, 1956). The opening up of better jobs creates opportunities for upward mobility which many Americans achieve and to which even more aspire.

In Detroit, very few men have followed in their fathers' footsteps. When the present husbands' occupations are compared in prestige with their fathers' jobs a generation ago, only 31 per cent have remained even approximately stable.[2] However, not all of the remainder have succeeded in moving upward. Indeed, the 33 per cent who have moved down is almost as large as the 37 per cent moving up. Therefore, the major fact about Detroit is not that so great a preponderance of men have moved upward but rather that enough have done so to provide a model for the rest.

Table 29

Mobility Aspirations and Expectations, by Age of Wife

	AGE OF WIFE				
	Under 30	30–39	40–49	50–59	60+
Husband has aspirations	66%	48%	36%	22%	8%
	(140)	(202)	(114)	(85)	(40)
Wife's mean expectation of husband's mobility chances*	3.43	3.45	3.17	2.25	1.67
	(92)	(94)	(36)	(16)	(3)

* If the wife believes her husband's chances of succeeding in his mobility aspirations are "certain" he is scored 5.00; "good" = 4.00; "50/50" = 3.00; "poor" = 2.00; "none" = 1.00. Numbers in parentheses show the number of families on which percentages and means are based.

People sometimes think that the days of widespread occupational mobility have passed in the United States. In Detroit, at least, this isn't so. The younger generation (those under forty) have already achieved as much upward mobility as their elders, and by the end of their careers may even surpass them. At least they hope to.

---

2. The comparison is with the father's "usual occupation while your husband was growing up." Occupations which varied within five points up or down on the prestige scale of the National Opinion Research Center were classified as stable for all practical purposes.

The pervasiveness of mobility aspirations in young Americans is visible in Table 29. At the beginning of marriage, almost everyone is not only ambitious but optimistic. As time passes, however, goals are either achieved or seem increasingly inaccessible. Life does not begin at forty for Detroiters as far as mobility is concerned. If success has not been achieved by that time, it's almost too late. After forty, most couples give up hoping for new occupational fields to conquer and even those who still hope become gloomier and gloomier.

Since forty is the age at which expectations fall to fifty-fifty and aspirations become relatively rare, the analysis of mobility needs to be focused on couples under that age.

Table 30

Type of Mobility Desired, by Husband's Occupation

(for Wives Under 40 Years Old)

TYPE OF MOBILITY DESIRED	HUSBAND'S OCCUPATION			
	BLUE COLLAR		WHITE COLLAR	
	Low	High	Low	High
Promotion	16%	14%	32%	32%
Same work but independent	2	7	14	11
New work	15	17	9	1
New work and independent	16	9	7	5
Unknown by wife	8	14	4	4
None	43	39	35	47
Total	100	100	101	100
Number of families	109	80	57	96

Types of Aspirations. What is involved in mobility aspirations is revealed more concretely in Table 30. The most common desire in corporation-dominated Detroit is to be promoted. The remaining three types of mobility are less popular than promotions, interesting less than 10 per cent of the population apiece.

White- and blue-collar workers have significantly different ambitions. Promotions as a line of advancement are desired most often by office and junior management personnel. Even after age forty, sales and clerical workers continue hoping that the company will move them ahead. Low-white-collar workers also are least likely to have no mobility aspirations than other workers.

Since they already have valuable skills, white-collar workers secondarily consider going into business for themselves. Semi-skilled and unskilled workers with little to offer the general public rarely have this ambition.

For blue-collar workers, going into business on their own is more apt to require getting into a new line of work. Because such mobility often requires both training and capital, it is especially difficult to achieve. Many times it is a fanciful daydream, unlikely ever to be realized. Blue-collar workers similarly, but less ambitiously, often want to get a new type of job with an employer—one which can't be classified simply as a promotion because of the shift in duties. Shifting to new work for someone else is especially distasteful to the high-white-collar man. If he is to go into a new line of work, at least he'd like it to be on his own. The big split in career aspirations between white-collar and blue-collar men is between men who are satisfied with their skills but not with their opportunities, and those whose great need is to acquire more skills.[3]

Pressures for Mobility. Mobility aspirations are inspired by a man's reference group. Differential reference groups can be seen where the husband has already moved from his father's occupational level or has married someone from such a different level. Young husbands who have already outstripped their fathers tend to establish themselves in white-collar occupations where they can rely on promotions for further advancement. By contrast, men who have slipped downward are more interested in changing to completely new lines of work, perhaps to regain the success their fathers had.

The same kind of contrast exists between men who marry up and those who marry down. Where the wife's family background is higher or where a farm boy marries a city girl, there are frequent aspirations to get into new lines of work. Is this because ambitious young men seek high-status wives or because such wives put pressure on their husbands to measure up to their fathers' achievements? In either case,

---

3. A majority of the latter are aiming for the very top. Fifty-nine per cent of those interested in changing occupational levels are classified as aiming for high-white-collar occupations. (Partly this is inherent in the classification of most self-employed persons as "entrepreneurs.")

the wife's occupational background seems to set the standard for the husband. Lack of aspiration is rare among this group after forty as well as before, suggesting a continuing orientation to the father-in-law's example.

Farm women who marry city men find it especially difficult to explain what kind of improvement the husband would like to make. Perhaps for them the whole world of urban occupations is too strange to be comprehensible.

In Detroit, as elsewhere in the United States, white-collar jobs are unmistakably more desirable than blue-collar jobs. As a result, men who achieve white-collar jobs tend to be satisfied with them or to rely on the career lines they offer to achieve advancement. Young blue-collar workers, however, begin their marriages with the hope that they too may climb the ladder of success. Sometimes their hope is realized, but often the paths to advancement are already closed by the time a man gets married—for few married men pull up stakes and go to college or even to night school to train themselves. The hopelessness of mobility aspirations dawns rapidly as the years go by. This is one aspect of settling down to marriage—in disillusionment or pride, as the case may be. Disillusionment is likely to result in dissatisfaction with the standard of living. But if the husband is doing a better job than ever before of bringing home the bacon, the result is apt to be satisfaction and high self-esteem.

The Wife's Role in the Husband's Mobility

Most of the occupational success or failure of the husband depends on him alone. Nevertheless, the kind of wife he has is not always irrelevant. William H. Whyte, Jr. (1951), claims that more and more corporations are scrutinizing the wives of potential executives in order to screen out those who would be liabilities. In addition to being innocuous, are there positive things a wife can do to help her husband get ahead? Is there any truth to the old saying that "behind every successful man there stands a woman"? If so, is her function to inspire her husband by her glamor? Or her words? Or to assist in some more tangible way?

Some wives are completely at a loss to answer a question like this, but most wives conceive of themselves as somehow relevant to the husband's potential success (see Table 31).

Table 31

Wife's Role in Husband's Mobility, by Urban and Rural Occupations

WIFE'S MOBILITY ROLE	HUSBAND'S OCCUPATION				
	BLUE COLLAR		WHITE COLLAR		FARMER
	Low	High	Low	High	
1. Collaborative	2%	2%	13%	21%	70%
2. Employment	2	2	3	1	3
3. Supportive					
a. Encouragement	30	22	26	28	4
b. Considerateness	7	8	8	6	4
c. Advice	2	4	1	4	1
d. Entertainment	0	3	6	10	0
4. Peripheral					
a. Housework	20	18	13	11	10
b. Thrift	2	2	2	3	4
c. Nothing	35	38	28	16	4
Total	100	99	100	100	100
Number of families	168	167	87	160	178

The answer for farm wives is clear-cut: they are direct participants in the farm operation—doing chores, running errands, driving the tractor, etc. Most farm wives give not simply one but two ways they help their husbands (but only first answers are tabulated in Table 31).

The urban group most clearly comparable to farm wives are the wives of small businessmen and independent professionals, nearly half of whom report similar collaboration in the family enterprise (see Gold and Slater, 1958). Most urban wives, however, are much farther removed from their husbands' careers. In fact, low-status wives often feel completely irrelevant to the husband's mobility.

For those city wives who do make some sort of contribution, two forms stand out. Simply being a good housekeeper (cooking the husband's meals, caring for his clothes, etc.) is emphasized by low-status women, especially Negro women. On the other hand, Gold and Slater find that wives of white-collar bureaucrats concentrate on encouraging the husband's efforts to get ahead. Such praise-and-push is common with young wives who still hope the husband will succeed. Encouragement is highest of all (40 per cent) among wives of men who want to get out on their own and into a new type of work. Young wives also concentrate on saving money, perhaps for the husband's use in launching his own business.

Comparison of different age groups suggests that an historical trend may be at work. Whereas young wives are apt to play an encouraging role, women in their forties often collaborate with their husband (15 per cent) while those over sixty stress housework (29 per cent). The latter group exemplifies a "traditional" role for women. Those in their forties may be interpreted as "feminists." The young ones under thirty who provide so much encouragement to their husbands (32 per cent) may be thought of as "neo-traditional," i.e., as reoriented to the home but with less stress on housework as such and more on emotional support for the husband.[4]

Negro wives stress earning and saving money. Entertaining business associates and potential clients, on the other hand, is clearly a high-status role which not a single Negro wife mentions.

That advice and "considerate" noninterference are in some respects polar opposites is suggested by the relationship to the husband's power. The more powerful the husband, the more often the wife explicitly avoids worrying him or making demands on him. The more powerful the wife, however, the more apt she is to advise him about his job and how he can get ahead. When asked about their mobility role, powerful wives often refer to such sources of their own power as the fact that they work outside the home. On the other hand, they often feel they can do nothing to help the husband and give him conspicuously little emotional support. In their opinion, his mobility chances are rather slight, perhaps because the aggressiveness he lacks at home is also missing at work.

Parallel Careers. Working wives exhibit three different patterns in relation to the husband's mobility (see Table 32). Negro maids and factory workers are working wives *par excellence* in the sense that they stress the value of their work to the husband more often than other working wives (29 per cent vs. 5.4 per cent).[5] Working women never mention thrift as a contribution except at low-status (blue-collar) levels where money is generally so short that it must be care-

---

4. The terminology here is Morris Janowitz's. Only research in future decades will be able to distinguish how much of these age differences is due to historical trends and how much to life cycle changes.

5. The 2 per cent of non-working wives who mention working are referring to previous employment.

Table 32

Wife's Role in Husband's Mobility, by Wife's Occupation

WIFE'S MOBILITY ROLE	WIFE'S OCCUPATION			
	BLUE COLLAR	WHITE COLLAR		NONE
		Low	High	
1. Collaborative	10%	10%	22%	8%
2. Employment	4	3	6	2
3. Supportive				
a. Encouragement	33	24	17	26
b. Considerateness	2	10	—	7
c. Advice	4	—	6	4
d. Entertainment	2	5	17	4
4. Peripheral				
a. Housework	8	21	—	17
b. Thrift	4	—	—	3
c. Nothing	33	26	33	29
Total	100	99	101	100
Number of families	51	58	18	455

fully guarded by the wife if the husband is to accumulate a business nest-egg.

At the other extreme from blue-collar women are business and professional women. They should probably be labelled "career women," because they have usually had special training for their work and may even be interested in it enough to continue working through the childbearing years. They often collaborate with their husbands in managing a retail business or as nurse-and-doctor-type teams. Although they deprecate housework as such (and probably employ considerable domestic help), they do a lot of entertaining demanded by the husband's own career. They relatively seldom encourage the husband to get ahead and correspondingly often help in no way, perhaps because the husband is already so successful, but also because this is an equalitarian relationship of two matched careers.

Sales and clerical work is the most popular form of employment for American women. It avoids the unpleasant working conditions of factory jobs but doesn't require the arduous preparation of professional work. Hence, it is the sort of work to which middle-class women turn most easily until the children come or after they leave. These low-white-collar wives are quite different from other working women and more like non-working wives. They may be "temporary" working wives whose orientation is toward the housewife role. Table 32 shows that both wives with low-white-collar jobs and those currently without jobs stress their housewifely contributions of housework, encouragement and noninterference, and play down employment itself. Presumably, the role transitions of such women into and out of the labor market are relatively smooth.

Patterns of Assistance. The various ways the wife helps her husband get ahead cluster in certain social strata. (1) The *collaborative* pattern applies only to families which have their own business—whether farm, store, or office. These wives work directly with their husbands to increase the collective profits. Because their contribution is so tangible, they have less need to provide more subtle emotional support and encouragement for their husbands. (2) Also tangible but noncollaborative is the *working wife* pattern of wives of Negro blue-collar workers who go to work in order to supplement the husband's income, perhaps helping him accumulate enough money to get started in a little business of his own. (3) The *supportive* pattern of young, high-status housewives provides emotional support and encouragement for the husband and uses the home as a place of entertainment for his associates and prospects. (4) Finally, the *peripheral* pattern, characteristic of old and low-status couples, sees relatively little that the wife can do to help except keep house for him. Since his work is functionally remote from the home and his chances for mobility slight anyway, she feels little if any connection with his career pattern.

Assistance or Reinforcement? Evaluating the wife's role is difficult. How much does her activity really help the husband's chances? Does his promotion depend so much on his own performance that the kind of wife he has makes very little difference anyway?

An independent report from the husband on the value of his wife's assistance is needed. Unfortunately, we didn't even ask the wife to estimate her own effectiveness. Nevertheless, some assumptions can be made. If the wife feels that her life is completely irrelevant to her husband's mobility, this indicates less vitality in this aspect of marriage than if she feels that she makes some kind of contribution. On the other hand, since some men are too old to advance further, even this interpretation must be made carefully.

Table 31 suggests that working-class marriages function least in this respect (since a majority of wives feel they can either do nothing, or nothing but housework). High-white-collar families are strongest in the city from this point of view—and farm families even stronger.

Table 33

Mobility Expectations, by Wife's Mobility Role

(Aspirant Families Only)

	WIFE'S MOBILITY ROLE			
	Collaborative	Employment*	Supportive	Peripheral
Wife's mean expectation of husband's mobility chances	3.10	4.50	3.41	2.86
Number of families	20	4	126	93

* The number of cases of wives specifying employment as their chief mobility role is too small to be discussed.

Table 33 makes possible a finer differentiation between families based on the husband's probable mobility. Does this show which wifely activities are most effective in boosting him along? Probably not. Rather, it seems to reflect the mobility chances of the husband's career line.

The husband's chances of mobility are less than even where wives play the peripheral roles which characterize low status or old couples. Because the opportunity for mobility is poor, the wife's assistance is largely irrelevant.

Midway in optimism are women who contribute by working with their husbands. These independent entrepreneurs are often small ones whose chances for further advancement are limited by competition from chain stores and large industries. Twice as many collaborative wives are first generation Americans as are found among either immigrants or older Americans, a symptom of the small business pattern of neighborhood grocery stores, restaurants, etc.

The type of wife who has her wagon hitched to a fast rising star is the one whose contribution is supportive. Her husband is typically a professional man or the executive of a large corporation whose career line is clear and promising. The wife may entertain his clients and offer occasional advice, but to a large extent she is sympathetic and undemanding, playing not the role of housewife but of *wife*. She is not economically productive, either in the sense of working outside the home or producing at home. Her role is sharply differentiated from the husband's but symbiotic with it. He carries the exclusive responsibility for the family's standard of living and is his own pace-setter in upward mobility. But in everything he does he has the active interest, the moral support, and the confident appreciation of his wife.

This attitude of confidence is visible in the mobility optimism of wives whose husbands have appreciably more education than they do (mean 3.30) and wives who married up occupationally (3.54). It also appears in optimism about men who have already outstripped their fathers (3.44). As far as such wives are concerned, "nothing succeeds like success."

Some of this faith in "superman" husbands is naive. There is no reason to believe that men who marry down educationally or occupationally gain extra chances of success thereby. Indeed, the earlier discussion of reference groups suggested that such men might even be *less* ambitious. Extra confidence therefore reflects the wife's relationship to her husband.

If the husband has already proven his ability to move ahead, a supportive role by the wife is appropriate. If the wife's confidence in her husband's ability stems only from her own sense of dependence on him, it nevertheless has certain consequences for the way in which she treats him—with respect, deference, loyalty, and support—i.e., encouragement and consideration.

On the other hand, if the wife is superior to the husband in education or background she tends to put achievement pressure on him but deprecates his ability to arrive at the goals she sets for him. Such a wife is unhappily domineering in contrast to the serene confidence and enthusiasm of the dependent wife of the successful man.

In between wife-dominance and husband-dominance are equalitarian marriages created by dual-income and collaborative situations. The equalitarian wife is modest in her expectations of her husband, neither exaggerating nor deprecating his chances.

In general, answers to the question, "What have you tried to do to help your husband along in his work?" disclose more about the wife's relationship to the husband than they do of tangible assistance in the husband's mobility. The reason a woman stands behind a successful man is not so much in order to make him succeed as because that's the kind of man a woman likes to stand behind! This is not to dismiss the wife's role as meaningless but to describe it as negligible in comparison to the personal achievement motive and occupational skills of

the husband. All other things being equal, the wife's support or in-
difference could make a difference in a man's morale and mobility.
But all other things are not equal, so that who the man is becomes
more important than who his wife is—from the standpoint of the economic system. And it is the economic system that determines occupational mobility.

To the marriage, however, what the wife does to help her husband
in his work role is a sensitive indicator of how they feel about each
other, what they mean to each other, what they do for each other.
The nagging wife who undermines her husband's morale differs importantly from the appreciative wife who enhances his self-esteem.
The wife's attitude and behavior in relation to the husband's chief role
in life do much to shape his conception of himself, his ego-feelings.
She is the mirror in which he sees himself—a mirror whose enhancing
or detracting distortions become his image of himself. She is what
Nelson Foote (1956) calls his "audience" whom he tells of the events
of his work life and who listens or turns a deaf ear.

Table 34

Wife's Mobility Role, by Informative Companionship

(extreme categories only)

WIFE'S MOBILITY ROLE	FREQUENCY HUSBAND TELLS WORK EVENTS	
	Daily	Never
Collaborative	12%	8%
Employment	3	3
Supportive	43	21
Peripheral	42	69
Total	100	101
Number of families	245	39

Table 34 supports the conception of the wife as audience to her
husband's work narrative. Supportive wives hear about the husband's
work experiences relatively often. By contrast, peripheral wives seldom do. The coincidence between Tables 33 and 34 reflects the theme
of this discussion: the mobility of the husband is echoed in affirmative
support by the wife. The wife in turn provides an ego-building audience for the husband. But in economically unsuccessful families, the
husband's failure is reflected in mutual estrangement of the husband's
work role from the wife. He ceases to communicate with her about

work events, and she ceases to find relevant ways of responding to his work role. When this happens in relation to the husband's most important role in life, it signifies a profound estrangement indeed.

Working Wives

Only a small proportion of working wives take a job in order to help their husband's occupational prospects. Most do so to supplement his income. This is the chief urban equivalent of the farm wife's subsistence production of vegetables and chickens.

In recent years the number of married women playing this economic role has been rapidly increasing. In 1940 only 15 per cent of American wives were working, compared to 24 per cent in 1950 and 28 per cent in 1955 at the time of this study (Taeuber, 1958). Although city wives usually work more often than the national average, only 24 per cent of the Detroit wives were employed in 1955. The lower rate may be due to the relatively high income of Detroit husbands. Michigan farm wives also work less than the national farm average, only 9 per cent being employed. Though the income of Michigan farmers is low compared to Detroit, it is high compared to typical American farm income. Hence, there is less economic pressure on both the city respondents and the farm respondents to go to work than there would be in many parts of the United States.

Why do farm wives work less often than city wives when they are so short of money? Lack of job opportunities in the country and transportation problems for getting into town are two obstacles. Whether as cause or effect, farm wives turn instead to greater home production, carrying a larger share of household tasks and collaborating with the husband in his farm operations.

Table 35
Wife's Employment Status, by Husband's Income

WIFE'S EMPLOYMENT	HUSBAND'S INCOME				
	Under $3,000	$3,000 –4,999	$5,000 –6,999	$7,000 –9,999	$10,000+
Part or full time	24%	19%	16%	13%	5%
Over-time	8	5	1	2	0
Not employed	68	76	83	85	95
Total	100	100	100	100	100
Number of families	71	184	199	88	57

Economic Pressures. Within the city, the evidence for economic pressure as the primary motive in the employment of married women is clear. Table 35 shows that six times as many wives work in the bottom income bracket as in the top, with regular steps in between. Moreover, working long hours (over forty hours a week) is especially concentrated where the economic need is greatest.

This evidence of economic pressure is reinforced by comparing Negro and white families. Thirty-one per cent of Detroit Negro wives are employed, compared to only 22 per cent of the white wives.[6] Since all the wives interviewed are living with their husbands, the difference in employment is not due to desertion (at least at the moment) but to the low pay and irregularity of Negro employment. The extra pressure on Negro wives is also visible in the fact that 25 per cent of all Negro working wives put in more than forty hours a week compared to 17 per cent of white working wives.

Thus Negro wives are more apt to have to work in the first place —and when they do work, they put in more hours in order to make ends meet. In addition to resulting from the husband's inadequacies, the Negro working wife's comparatively long hours reflect the low status of the jobs she gets. Whereas 60 per cent of the white working wives have white-collar jobs (mostly sales and clerical), only 19 per cent of the Negroes do. More than half of the latter have bottom status low-blue-collar jobs with correspondingly low hourly wages.

Standards of Comparison. At rock-bottom levels, poverty as such forces the wife to go to work. As the husband's income rises, its adequacy depends increasingly on what the wife uses as her standard of comparison. If her standard is different from the husband's, her evaluation of the need for more money differs correspondingly. One index of differential standards is the comparative education of the husband and wife. If the wife has less education than the husband, the chances are she will be unusually satisfied with his income and less apt to go to work herself. On the other hand, if she has more education than he, she has probably acquired more expensive tastes than he can satisfy. She will tend to take a job herself to supplement what she feels is an inadequate income. Again economic pressure is motivating employment, pressure for keeping up with one's classmates (see Table 36).

---

6. The national percentage of Negro working wives was 30.2 per cent in 1950 (Glick, 1957).

Table 36

Wife's Employment Status, by Comparative Education of Husband and Wife and by Husband's Income

(Exclusive of Retired Couples)

PERCENTAGE OF WIVES CURRENTLY EMPLOYED, BY HUSBAND'S INCOME*	COMPARATIVE EDUCATION		
	Husband More	Equal	Wife More
Under $5,000	23%	25%	31%
	(81)	(77)	(91)
$5,000 and over	9	16	20
	(133)	(108)	(90)

* Numbers in parentheses refer to the number of families on which each percentage is based. The reciprocal percentages are not currently employed.

Another clue to the economic motivation for working is the impact of the husband's occupational mobility. Table 37 shows that the more successful the husband is in his occupation, the less often the wife works. This distinction does not apply to blue-collar families but is accentuated in high-white-collar households. Wives who go to work when the husband slips downward are either attempting to hold the line on their declining standard of living or else hoping to aid the husband in attaining the occupational success his father had. In either case, the father's occupation represents a standard against which these couples measure their own achievement—and the discrepancy puts pressure on the wife to go to work.

Table 37

Wife's Employment Status, by Husband's Intergenerational Occupational Mobility

(White-collar Husbands Only)

WIFE'S EMPLOYMENT STATUS	HUSBAND'S PRESENT JOB AND INTERGENERATIONAL MOBILITY					
	BUSINESS, PROFESSIONAL			SALES, CLERICAL		
	Down	Stable	Up	Down	Stable	Up
Working	30%	14%	9%	27%	24%	19%
Not working	70	86	91	73	76	81
Total	100	100	100	100	100	100
Number of families	23	57	79	26	29	26

The pressure of the husband's failure relative to his father is visible also in the amount of time which working wives put in outside the home. In downward mobile families, only seven wives work part-time whereas ten work overtime. Conversely, in upward mobile families, nine wives work part-time but only three work overtime. The number of cases is small but the direction of the relationship is consistent. The accentuation of the need factor by the mobility standard of comparison produces the biggest trend to part-time work among upward-mobile high-white-collar families, whereas the biggest trend to overtime work is among downward mobile low-blue-collar families. This suggests that although the husband's mobility does not affect *whether* the blue-collar wife will be employed, it does affect the number of hours she will work.

Employment and Marital Satisfaction. From the traditional point of view, housekeeping is the expected role for the married woman, and employment outside the home a source of strain upon the marriage. Yet previous research by Locke (1951) showed no difference in the proportion of happily married and divorcing wives who were employed. In the present study, the average marital satisfaction scores of working and non-working wives are likewise similar (4.68 and 4.72).

Yet the preceding analyses of factors impelling wives to go to work suggests that marital relationships are likely to be somehow affected despite this over-all similarity. What is needed is a more complex analysis which will take the motivating factor of economic pressure into consideration. Table 38 shows that when economic necessity is related to the wife's employment status, a pattern of differential marital satisfaction emerges.

Two contrasting categories of wives turn out to be equally satisfied with their marriages: working wives of low-income husbands and non-working wives of high-income husbands. The remaining wives on the average are somewhat less satisfied.

Why should this be true? The difference lies in the gains and losses from working at these two income levels. When the husband's income is below average, the wife's earnings make a big difference in the family's ability to gain its desired standard of living. Working seems urgently desirable both to the wife and to her husband who rewards her with understanding and appreciation. Thus her work strengthens the marriage bonds. If she were to stay home under these

Table 38

Wife's Marital Satisfaction, by Employment Status of Wife and by Husband's Income

WIFE'S MARITAL SATISFACTION BY HUSBAND'S INCOME*	WIFE'S EMPLOYMENT STATUS	
	Working	Not Working
Under $5,000	4.78	4.60
	(60)	(159)
$5,000 or more	4.54	4.78
	(43)	(257)

* Wife's marital satisfaction is computed by weighting her reported satisfaction with standard of living, companionship, understanding, and love and affection (plus the congruity of her expected and desired number of children), by the comparative importance she attaches to each of these five aspects of marriage. Numbers in parentheses refer to the number of families on which each mean is based.

circumstances, the total family income would be cut to the quick, and the economic strain on the family would increase dissatisfaction with the husband, impairing the marriage relationship.

As the husband's income rises, however, the wife's income becomes steadily less useful. Eventually a point of diminishing returns is reached, where what she adds to the standard of living is more than offset by the loss of her services in the home. The husband presumably resents the pressure her "unnecessary" work puts on him to help out around home and the lost time and attention she is too busy to give him. If she doesn't have economic necessity as a legitimate excuse, the wife may be working *because* she is dissatisfied with her husband. Feeling her marriage has let her down, she turns to the world of work in search of the satisfactions everybody needs in life.

An interesting parallel is available from the question of who makes the decision whether the wife goes to work or quits work. In low-status families, it is the wife who overwhelmingly makes this decision by herself. Since she is the one who decides what contribution she will make to the family exchequer, the husband is especially indebted to her when she volunteers to help out. In high-status families, however, the husband takes a much more active part in this decision. At the highest levels, he decides unilaterally even more often than she does. It is impossible to know for sure whether dissatisfied high-status working wives have been ordered to work against their will or have gone to work contrary to orders. Perhaps neither. But outside work for wives in high-status families clearly tends to be associated with disgruntled husbands and disappointed wives.

The disgruntlement of husbands may not result very much from abstract ideas about the rightness and wrongness of wives working (though ideological rationalizations could probably be found to justify husbandly approval or disapproval of their wives' conduct). One reason for thinking ideological statements about the propriety of wives working are after-thoughts rather than forethoughts is that there is so little variation in feminine employment between segments of the population with different cultural backgrounds. For instance, first and second generation Americans have practically identical rates of working wives. Wives born overseas work less, but this difference applies only to the relatively aged, total immigrant group and not to young new immigrants who have only been in America a short time. Similarly, recent migrants from Northern farms have fewer working wives but Southern farm couples have more. In view of these contradictions, attitudes toward the working wife seem to be determined more by the net profit or loss it will bring to the family's total life than by abstract patriarchal or equalitarian ideas.

Working vs. Mothering. How does the wife's working relate to the family-life cycle? The answer is complicated by the current trend toward increased work. If there were no change under way, one would expect older women to have an accumulatingly larger percentage who had ever worked. Table 39 shows that the reverse is actually the case. Fewer women in the older age brackets have ever worked. Obviously

Table 39

Wife's Employment after Marriage, by Age of Wife

	AGE OF WIFE						
	Under 30	30–39	40–49	50–54	55–59	60–64	65+
Percentage who ever worked since marriage	78%*	75%	72%	69%	58%	55%	39%
Estimated year of marriage	1947–55	1937–46	1928–36	1923–27	1918–22	1913–17	Before 1913
Number of families	143	208	117	45	36	31	23

* Reciprocal percentages of wives have never worked after marriage.

this is not *caused* by living longer. It reflects the fact that in former decades most women quit work when they got married.

Table 39 shows that an exceedingly large proportion of young wives have worked at some time since marriage. The saturation point may not have been reached even yet. The general American trend is for girls to get married younger but to postpone the birth of their first child until a couple of years after marriage (Glick, 1955). During this new period of childlessness in early marriage almost all young couples now take joint working for granted. Some of the remainder will go to work after their children are grown. We are rapidly approaching an era in American history when almost all women will work at some time after marriage. Often this will be both before and after the child-rearing phase of their life. The chief exceptions will be wives whose early work phase is cut off by early pregnancy (like the teen-age brides in Detroit) and those whose husbands are so well-to-do that voluntary activities are more attractive than paid employment.[7]

Table 39 shows that there was a time when most American women didn't work after marriage. But one must go all the way back to those married before World War I to find such a pattern. The big change seems to have occurred among women who married between that war and the Depression. Perhaps youthful feminism had something to do with the trend. More likely, the employment boom of World War II and after involved these women after their children were out of diapers.

In any case, diapered children urgently require their mothers' attention. Table 40 shows that hardly any mothers of pre-school children work when the husband's income is adequate. This is true not only when the *oldest* child is under 6 but also for 112 additional mothers whose *youngest* child is under 6. Indeed, the employment of the mother is geared much more closely to the age of the youngest child than it is to the age of the oldest. This explains why the proportion working dips among low-income mothers whose oldest child is over eighteen. When all mothers at this stage are subdivided by the age of their youngest child, the proportion working is zero where the youngest is under six, and 8 per cent for ages six through eighteen, but

---

7. Only 49 per cent of the wives of men earning more than $10,000 have ever worked since marriage.

Table 40

Wife's Employment Status, by Stage in Family-life Cycle and Husband's Income

WIVES CURRENTLY EMPLOYED, BY HUSBAND'S INCOME		STAGE IN FAMILY-LIFE CYCLE					
Childrearing stages:		Preschool	Preadolescent	Adolescent	Unlaunched		
Under $5,000		16%	23%	27%	18%		
		(55)	(48)	(33)	(28)		
$5,000+		3	10	19	23		
		(70)	(92)	(64)	(35)		
Childless stages:	Honeymoon					Postparental	Retired
Under $5,000	62%*					19%	0%
	(13)					(32)	(11)
$5,000+	43					16	—
	(7)					(50)	—
Childless couples:							
Under $5,000		— — — — — 60% — — — — —					
		(30)					
$5,000+		— — — — — 38 — — — — — —					
		(16)					

* Numbers in parentheses show the number of families on which each percentage is based. Reciprocal percentages of wives are not currently employed.

climbs all the way to 36 per cent where the only children living at home have reached adulthood and can look out for themselves.

Remembering that the national trend is toward increased employment in the middle years, it is possible to predict what the pattern of employment throughout the family-life cycle may look like in the future: (1) Nearly all wives are likely to work after marriage until their first pregnancy. (2) Very few mothers of preschool children (mostly hardship cases of severe economic necessity) will work even part-time away from their children. (3) When the last child enters first grade, employment will rise sharply and continue to increase until the last child leaves home or reaches adulthood when employment will reach a second peak. This figure may not equal the pre-childbearing starting point, since by this time most families have purchased a house and accumulated the major capital goods, diminishing their economic need. However, the increasing proportion of American children seeking increasingly expensive college educations provide a new financial incentive for mothers to work in the early postparental years.

As children grow up, the decision whether the wife should go back to work is increasingly left in her hands. When the wife is under thirty, the husband is usually deeply involved in the work decision, but by the time she gets into her forties and fifties, the issue is typically decided by the wife herself. This reflects the fact that in the early phases of marriage, the couple urgently need to accumulate funds for furniture, car, and the down payment on a house. At the same time, the relationship between the wife's employment and the coming of the first child is also a matter of great concern. By contrast, a forty- or fifty-year-old woman has raised her children to the place where they can look out for themselves, if they're not already completely on their own. This gives her freedom to leave home for work if she wishes to. But the diminished economic pressure on the family makes her work even more optional. So the decision is often left up to her.

With the exception of hardship cases (and a few career-oriented wives), the employment of women is geared closely to the family-life cycle. This is true not only with respect to the ages of the children but also to the number of children. Table 41 shows how greatly children cut down the length of time she works outside the home.

Table 41

Length of Wife's Employment after Marriage, by Number of Children Ever Born

LENGTH OF WIFE'S EMPLOYMENT AFTER MARRIAGE	NUMBER OF CHILDREN EVER BORN				
	0	1	2	3	4+
Two years or more	62%	52%	42%	41%	32%
Under two years	22	26	30	26	21
None	16	22	28	33	47
Total	100	100	100	100	100
Number of families	83	136	181	108	99

The large number of mothers of four or more children who have never worked resembles the current teen-age brides. Women who have large families tend to begin their childbearing so early in marriage that they have little opportunity to work. Subsequently, their childcaring responsibilities are so heavy for so long that working later is often impossible. Although economic need increases with the size of the family, the task of meeting it falls primarily on the husband's or older children's shoulders, rather than the wife's. Perhaps the husband can take a second job evenings or work overtime. Only when the number of children is limited does economic need lead directly to the wife's employment.

The wife's role in American marriage therefore goes through two main phases before ending up in a more indeterminate one. Her first role after marriage is to work along with her husband to help the household get off to a good start financially. Once the children start coming, the role shifts dramatically to full-time housewife and mother. Then gradually as the children mature and depart, she acquires not one but several options. She may, if she wishes, return to work. On the other hand, she may concentrate instead on such alternatives as church work, club work, civic leadership, visiting her grand-children, and enjoying her new leisure time (Havighurst, 1956).

As more American women find themselves in middle age with the time, the energy, and the opportunity to work, they are choosing that option. Hence, the American wife's life is increasingly being determined by two main factors—the desire for a high standard of living and the desire for children. Since she can't produce both at once, she is learning to undertake them one at a time: first money, then children, then money again. As she does so, she is making an increasingly substantial contribution to the economic function in the American family.

SATISFACTION WITH THE STANDARD OF LIVING

How well do most couples achieve the economic goals they set for themselves? Measured by the wife's satisfaction with her standard of living, most couples do pretty well.

Table 42 shows that enthusiasm is rare (but this may be due to the impossibility of conceiving that "it couldn't be better"). At the other extreme, strong complaints are even more rare. A clear majority of wives express genuine satisfaction with the husband's accomplishments in this field.

The 38 per cent of all city wives who are less than "quite satisfied" (and can be thought of as at least mildly dissatisfied) are relatively many, however, compared to feelings about other aspects of marriage.

Table 42

Satisfaction with Standard of Living in City and Farm Families, by Race

WIFE'S FEELING ABOUT OWN STANDARD OF LIVING	RESIDENCE AND RACE		
	CITY		FARM
	Negro	White	
(1)* Pretty disappointed—I'm really missing out on that	10%	1%	1%
(2) It would be nice to have more.	30	17	15
(3) It's all right, I guess—I can't complain.	32	16	23
(4) Quite satisfied—I'm lucky the way it is.	27	60	54
(5) Enthusiastic—it couldn't be better.	1	6	7
Total	100	100	100
Mean satisfaction	2.79	3.53	3.51
Number of families	114	595	176

* Numbers in parentheses are used in computing mean satisfaction in subsequent tables.

Only 31 per cent are similarly dissatisfied about companionship and even fewer (25 per cent) about love and affection.

Standards of Comparison

The similarity between city and farm wives in Table 42 is striking. In view of their low incomes, farm wives might be expected to be less satisfied. The fact that they are not presumably reflects the relativity of satisfactions—which depend on the standard of comparison used. If farm wives compared themselves with city wives, they would have to acknowledge that they are not as well supplied with housing, clothes, cars, etc. But they don't. Their husbands aren't city workers. As farmers they tend to be measured against other farmers. By definition, the average farmer compares as favorably with other farmers as city husbands do with *their* reference group. Cash income underestimates the standard of living a farm provides. Subsistence production helps fill the money gap. Besides, there are intangible satisfactions in country living which some women prize. Those who do not are most likely to have moved to the city in the great stream of rural-urban migration, leaving behind a relatively satisfied group of farm women.

Money. Within the city, by contrast, incomes do get measured against each other. Table 43 shows a marked relationship between the amount of money the husband earns and the degree of satisfaction the wife feels with her standard of living.

Table 43

Satisfaction with Standard of Living, by Husband's Income for All White Families, Jewish Families, and Negro Families

WIFE'S MEAN SATISFACTION WITH STANDARD OF LIVING	HUSBAND'S INCOME				
	Under $3,000	$3,000 –4,999	$5,000 –6,999	$7,000 –9,999	$10,000+
For all white families	3.21 (67)*	3.34 (178)	3.64 (193)	3.58 (88)	3.99 (56)
In Jewish families	2.00 (7)		3.20 (5)		3.67 (6)
In Negro families	2.68 (41)	2.78 (54)	3.00 (12)		

* Numbers in parentheses refer to the number of families on which each mean is based.

Satisfaction is almost unanimous among high income families. The three women at this level who "can't complain" and the four who wish they had more must have an especially well-to-do reference group!

At the two extremes, a sizable 18 per cent of the wives are "enthusiastic," about $10,000 incomes, but only 47 per cent are either enthusiastic or satisfied with less than $3,000 (vs. 66 per cent for all whites). To find this many still satisfied on less than $3,000 may seem surprising until it is realized that they are mostly elderly couples in retirement. Relatively few Detroiters can be satisfied with $3,000 as a peak income in life. But retired couples have fewer economic pressures and a different set of income expectations than younger ones. Hence it is possible for wives over sixty to be just as satisfied on less than $3,000 as most families are on $3,000–$5,000.

Any family in the community which comes up to the city-wide average feels minimally satisfied no matter what the reference group.

All the Detroit wives who feel they have "really missed out" on the standard of living are struggling along on less than $5,000.

Ethnic Standards. Perhaps because they have the highest average income of any religious group and also because they are concentrated in business and professional occupations, Jewish families have an unusually high standard of comparison. As long as their income reaches this standard, they are just as satisfied as anyone else, but those who fall below it are acutely dissatisfied. Mean satisfaction for Jewish families with incomes between $5,000 and $7,000 is as low as that for other white families earning less than $3,000. For Jewish families earning less than the Detroit average income of $5,000, the mean is much lower than any other group.

If many Jewish wives are lukewarm about their standard of living because of an especially high reference group, the dissatisfaction of Negro respondents has a quite different source. Low income, segregated housing, and similar tangible obstacles combine to leave only 1 Negro wife in 114 enthusiastic and hardly more than a fourth even satisfied. Even when income levels are held constant, Negro wives find their standard of living less adequate than white wives but not as hard to take as low-income Jewish wives.

Differential Standards. If the husband is doing the best he can, the wife tends to withhold criticism. Greater enthusiasm is expressed by wives of men who are working overtime, especially when the wife is working herself. If she works just as hard as he, and especially if she *had* to go to work because his income was low, she may complain. But if he works longer hours than she does, it becomes appropriate to be satisfied and say "it couldn't be better." After all, there are only so many hours in a week!

Satisfaction for the wife depends partly on the current efforts of the husband and wife, partly on their comparative backgrounds. Farm girls who marry city men tend to be extra satisfied with their new standard of living. Similarly, satisfaction is even higher (3.79) for city girls who marry men from a much higher socio-economic background. Such husbands can usually offer the wife a better standard of living no matter how successful or unsuccessful they may be as individuals. However, women married to men from only slightly higher backgrounds, similar backgrounds, or even substantially lower backgrounds are all about equally satisfied. Perhaps the latter case involves men ambitious enough to be able to satisfy their wives' desires.

Age Differences. The ability of a husband to satisfy his wife is also tested when the ages of the two partners differ (see Table 44).

Table 44

Satisfaction with Standard of Living, by Comparative Age of Husband and Wife

| | COMPARATIVE AGE | | | | |
| | WIFE OLDER | | EQUAL | HUSBAND OLDER | |
	4+ years	1–3 years		1–3 years	4+ years
Wife's mean satisfaction with standard of living	2.75	3.52	3.75	3.59	3.48
Number of families	16	61	65	206	247

Homogamous couples are the most satisfied. Satisfaction declines as the age gap increases in either direction. It drops faster where the husband is younger than the wife, presumably because of occupational inadequacies among these men. Many of them marry older women as mother substitutes, on whom they can depend for emotional security. While wives may find emotional gratification in being able to nurture such dependent husbands, the aggressiveness necessary for occupational success is usually lacking. Although the number of such marriages in this sample is too small to test this interpretation conclusively, their economic dissatisfiaction is conspicuous.

Why older husbands also provide a less satisfactory standard of living is more difficult to interpret. Perhaps the greater satisfaction of homogamous wives stems from a feeling of joint responsibility for what is achieved. Relevant here is the fact that syncratic couples (who decide things together) are more satisfied with their standard of living than autonomic (separate-but-equal) or husband-dominant ones. As would be expected from Table 44, wife-dominant couples are least satisfied of all.

Changing Needs and Resources

Satisfaction with the standard of living depends not only on what one has at the moment but on what one expects to acquire in the future. As a result, newly-weds are most optimistic. However, disillusionment sets in rapidly. After a few years of marriage, enthusiasm settles down into satisfaction. In the middle years of childrearing, there is a growing wish for more to live on. By the later years of marriage, even this wish often gives way to uncomplaining resignation or to bitter disappointment.

Table 45

Satisfaction with Standard of Living, by Stage in Family-life Cycle and Husband's Income

WIFE'S MEAN SATISFACTION WITH STANDARD OF LIVING, BY HUSBAND'S INCOME		STAGE IN FAMILY-LIFE CYCLE			
Childrearing stages:		Preschool	Preadolescent	Adolescent	Unlaunched
Under $5,000		3.37 (54)	3.21 (48)	3.23 (31)	3.37 (27)
$5,000+		3.89 (72)	3.66 (91)	3.44 (63)	3.53 (36)
Childless stages:	Honeymoon			Postparental	Retired
Under $5,000	3.54 (13)*			3.16 (31)	3.50 (10)
$5,000+	4.00 (7)			3.75 (52)	—
Childless couples:					
Under $5,000		— — — — — 3.45 — — — — — (29)			
$5,000+		— — — — — 3.76 — — — — — (17)			

* Numbers in small type give the number of families for which each mean is computed.

Table 45 shows that satisfaction with the standard of living declines with the onslaught of children, ebbing still further as they acquire school-age appetites and wardrobes. In low-income families, economic recovery begins when the oldest child acquires the ability to earn money at adolescence. By contrast, teen agers in wealthier families remain a growing expense rather than a financial asset. Only with the departure of the last child do high-income families achieve a level of satisfaction equal to that which childless couples enjoy all along. Whether launched or unlaunched, however, children normally become financially independent when they reach maturity, easing the strain on parental incomes.

The life-cycle trends shown in Table 45 hold up when controlled by age of wife and by number of children in the family. However, the standard of living is greatly depressed in families with four or more children, even at high-income levels.

Except where handicapped by race, by large numbers of children, or by unusual personal inadequacy, most husbands manage to provide their wives with a standard of living close to their economic goals. Consequently, most wives feel satisfied enough in this area to be able to rate it a relatively unimportant aspect of marriage.

THE ECONOMIC FUNCTION

The economic function in today's urban marriages differs sharply from what it still does on contemporary farms and what it once did in the average American family. Moving off the land has separated the work place from the family residence. As a result, the city family cannot function as an economic team except in those few families which operate a family business. By and large, the economic system has been divorced from the family system with remarkable thoroughness.

As a result, the economic function of the family depends primarily on the efforts of the husband who goes out of the family to participate in the economic system. His occupational success determines the economic resources available to the family. Whether the wife is satisfied with these resources depends, however, on how they compare with her frame of reference. Despite the "leveling-up" influence of the mass media and modern advertising, special family origins or ethnic communities can provide higher than average norms resulting in dissatisfaction with even substantial economic resources.

A dissatisfied wife has two main alternatives. She can put pressure on her husband to do better—but if he hasn't got what it takes, that won't do much good. Or she can go to work herself. If family finances had been strained to a great extent, her work may increase the family income so much that everybody feels better. If not, her work may only irritate the husband and strain the marriage. At the beginning of marriage, however, work is taken for granted by most wives—so great is the need for getting off to a good financial start, and so unnecessary the wife's remaining at home when there are no children. Later in life, after the children grow up, re-employment is more optional for the wife, an option which more and more women are taking up.

Quite unimportant, today, is the production of goods at home like grandmother used to make—so unimportant that home production has hardly any economic meaning today and is largely an art instead. It, too, is optional.

More significant, however, for the wife who stays home is her attitude toward her husband's work. Few men start out at the peak of their careers and almost every young bride hopes her man will progress beyond his starting job or pay. As time goes on and those hopes are fulfilled or proven empty, her feeling for him changes correspondingly. Either he comes to be appreciated all the more for his achievements in life, or he is resented a bit for disappointing her. In any case, the relationship between the husband and the wife is affected by the way he plays his economic role. If he plays it well, the economic function is a source of strength to the marriage, with the wife an applauding audience to her husband's performance. If he plays it badly, he retires in disgrace behind a curtain of silence and she turns her attention to her own role in life.

The economic function of the family is therefore primarily the husband's function. Even when the wife works, the reasons why she works and the relative permanence of her work reflects his career. He is the one whose main job and permanent job it is to provide for the economic needs of the family. Her job uniquely is to bear the children —which is the subject of the next chapter.

CHAPTER 5

HAVING CHILDREN

IN MANY traditional societies, a woman is not considered really married until she bears her first child. Lesser men as well as Oriental potentates have often returned wives who didn't bear children satisfactorily. Western civilization has been less interested in exchangeable wives but hardly less disappointed by barrenness.

The traditional emphasis on having children is no accident. Indeed, it springs from multiple sources. In agricultural societies deriving their wealth from the land, the family plot acquires almost sacred value from the family's dependence upon it. One reason for having children is to pass this treasure on from generation to generation, unsullied by strangers who may not appreciate it.

If such a society is illiterate, immortality tends to be centered in the family line. Where neither books nor diaries nor birth certificates record one's existence, oblivion ensues unless there are progeny to keep one's memory alive. If ancestor worship is the obligation of the living, children provide spiritual social security.

The combined urgency of inheritance and ancestor worship sadden childless couples and stimulate social inventiveness. One means of filling vacancies in the on-coming generation is to legitimize the children of extramarital liaisons. Moreover, adoption may be extended beyond orphans and illegitimate children to adults who may be available for this purpose.

In many societies, it is not enough to have children if there are only daughters and no sons. If women may not inherit property and may not provide the proper reverence for ancestors, a man with only daughters is to be pitied as much as a childless one. If maiden names change at marriage, sons are necessary to carry on the family name. Hence, societies have devised means of supplying sons where they are missing. In Japan, poor young men often filled this gap by abandoning their own "maiden" name to be enrolled in the family "tree" of a household without sons, marrying one of the brother-less daughters.

Fortunate the man who has a son to follow in his footsteps. But life in such societies is often hard. Life expectancy may be short, infant mortality high. In order to assure the survival of one son to maturity, it is well to have two sons. The large number of children born in traditional societies is often impressive—but so is the number of child-sized tombstones in old New England cemeteries.

Another reason why farmers may want children is financial. In a primitive society, it is hard for a man to raise crops or handle flocks all by himself. Many tasks require the co-operative effort of several persons. Children provide a captive labor supply which is a tangible family asset. With little or no schooling to pre-empt their time, children take on chores almost from the time they can walk. At an early age they become economic assets instead of liabilities. Happy the man who has many children to work with him. Happy the family which can share the produce of a large work force.

In a barter economy, it is impossible to save up for old age. Grain will spoil in time, animals must be cared for to be kept alive. There are no pensions, social security systems, retirement annuities, or homes for the aged. Admittedly, few people in primitive societies live to be seventy. But senility is a relative matter. A tribesman of thirty-five may be as old physiologically as a modern man twice his age. Malnutrition, disease, and crippling injuries leave dependency as much of a problem in a short-lived society as in a septuagenarian one.

If it is impossible to protect oneself against starvation in old age, one must depend on others. And who is more dependable than children? To American ears, such a statement may seem questionable. But in primitive societies, children become the expected, accepted means of support for their feeble elders. Having children is therefore a form of material (as well as spiritual) social security—the more children, the more security.

A subsistence economy may also come to view children as wealth in themselves, symbols of prestige, or proof of virility. Where children have functional values, they tend to acquire symbolic value as well. Stycos tells how large families are an ego-satisfying demonstration of masculinity to the Puerto Rican working man (1955). If an economic system produces only subsistence goods—food, clothing, and shelter —kids may be the equivalent to Cadillacs as badges of affluence.

The Place of Children in Modern Life

Economic assets, social security, ancestor worship, proof of virility —the strangeness of these concepts to American readers is proof of the new world we live in. The coming of the machine revolutionized the family as well as industry. Machines can produce more than children, making large work crews no longer necessary. The removal of production from home to factory has broken up the parent-child work team. Also, machines produce so much that an economy can rise above the subsistence margin and afford the luxuries of schools and the withdrawal of children from the labor market until they are sixteen, eighteen, or twenty. Once children become obsolete as producers, they *ipso facto* are economic liabilities instead of assets.

The mechanization of agriculture and industry, the flowering of prosperity and modern medicine, the urbanization of the population— these are some of the changes which have made children more optional than they once were. They now might be thought of as consumer goods to be purchased on an eighteen-year installment plan, as economic responsibilities not to be assumed lightly.

This does not mean that children have become nuisances to be avoided. The American baby boom proves that children are still wanted. The reasons for wanting children may have changed and the number of children desired may be less than it used to be, but Americans are still interested in having children.

When asked where they see children fitting into marriage, modern wives count them second only to companionship with the husband. Twenty-six per cent of the Detroit wives list the chance to have children as the most valuable part of marriage and 28 per cent more list it second. Paradoxically, however, fewer farm wives (22 per cent) mention children first, so far has the Michigan farm changed from the subsistence economy's emphasis on children.

CHILDREN AS A GOAL OF MARRIAGE

Further evidence of the value placed on children in contemporary marriages is the near universality of wanting children. Marriages which are childless by choice are practically nonexistent (see Table 46).

Table 46

Preferred Number of Children in City and Farm Families

PREFERRED NUMBER OF CHILDREN*	PLACE OF RESIDENCE	
	City	Farm
None	3%	1%
One	2	3
Two	23	18
Three	24	25
Four	36	37
Five	5	6
Six	4	7
More than Six	3	3
Total	100	100
Mean	3.42	3.57
Number of families	724	174

* "If you could choose, or if you could start over again, how many children would you want to have?"

Wanting one child is just as rare as wanting none. The common opinion that only children are spoiled or unhappy is undoubtedly reflected in the unpopularity of this size family.

Table 46 shows that four children is the most popular number. A majority of both the city wives and the farm wives want either three or four and the over-all average falls between these two numbers. Eighty per cent or more of the city and farm wives prefer either two, three, or four children, suggesting that this is the normal range of variation in contemporary family goals.

This "normal range" appears even more strikingly when women are asked, "as things now are, what do you think is the ideal number of children for the average American family?" Ninety-three per cent of the city wives and almost as many farm wives give answers between two and four. Most of those who personally would like to have fewer than two or more than four children do not expect other American families to follow their example.

Under these circumstances, the differences between segments of the community are small. Nevertheless, marginal differences in preferred numbers of children provide insights into family patterns.

Table 46 shows a tendency for contemporary farm families to desire more children than city families. Child labor laws do not apply to chores on father's farm. Even long bus rides to school may not prevent farm children from doing appreciable work before supper and during vacations. Farm children often drive tractors at what city folk consider a remarkably early age. Not only do farm children pay some of their own keep by their work, but the farm vegetable garden makes it easier to feed another mouth. Even so, only one Michigan farm wife in seven proposes to feed an extra mouth.

Table 47

Preferred Number of Children, by Degree of Urbanization

	PLACE LIVED MOST OF LIFE BEFORE DETROIT			
	CITY		FARM	
	Over 50,000*	Under 50,000	Southern	Northern
Mean preferred number of children	3.37	3.48	3.53	3.79
Number of Families	350	178	19	33

* Includes native Detroiters.

Migrants and Immigrants. Table 47 shows that this higher goal of farm families tends to survive migration to the city. Women raised on farms prefer more children than city-bred women while those from smaller towns fall in between. Apparently, large-family ideals are not simply a response to rural economic conditions but are inculcated in the process of being raised in a rural environment, and resist change when people move to the city.

Although the data are not conclusive, old-wave immigrants, who came to Detroit before World War I, appear to have very high family goals whereas more recent immigrants prefer relatively few children.

The larger family ideals of old-wave immigrants reflect many factors beside the culture in which they were raised. Their religious affiliation, their age, and their social status all conspire to reinforce their preference for relatively many children.

Old-wave immigrants are mostly Catholics. Catholics generally prefer larger families than non-Catholics. In Detroit, the average Catholic wife prefers 3.63 children, compared to only 3.19 for white Protestants and 3.21 for Jewish wives. This is one aspect of family life where religious teaching is effective, though we shall see later that it affects the verbalization of family goals more than their fulfillment.

Old-wave immigrants are by definition members of the older generation and share its preference for larger families. Women over forty-five prefer 3.48 children whereas those thirty through forty-four want only 3.39 and those under thirty only 3.26. This steadily dwindling mean does not indicate that the American family is heading toward childlessness. On the contrary, there are fewer young wives than older ones who would like to be completely childless. Nor is a one-child family becoming more popular. Rather, the average shrinks entirely at the expense of big families. The number of wives wanting more than four children drops from 16 per cent to 13 per cent to 10 per cent as one compares the oldest, middle, and youngest age groups. The result is that an increasingly large percentage of American women's personal preferences fall within the limits of what they consider ideal for American families as a whole. This trend includes a steady upswing in the popularity of the three-child family, in particular, which may eventually eclipse four as the most common goal of urban families. In any case, two is at least holding its own as the minimum desirable number, while four is becoming a tighter and tighter ceiling on family aspirations.

What factors have contributed to this homogenization of American attitudes? The closing of the door on mass immigration may be one since it cuts off the influx of immigrants with big-family ideas and allows more time for blending in the melting pot the ideas of those already here. The mechanization of agriculture has similarly whittled away at the quantitative propensities of the rural sources of urban recruiting. Medical advances have narrowed the gap between the number of children born and the number who survive the hazards of childhood. Hence extra children for insurance are less necessary.

Standards for Children. The American emphasis has shifted from quantity to quality with respect to children. Having fewer children may not guarantee a better life but, other things being equal, parental resources don't have to be spread so thin. More education, more recreation, and better medical care cost money. Although the real income of the average family has increased, rising incomes may have intensified rather than satisfied the desire to give each child more.

Historical proof of increasing standards for children is difficult. However, hints are available in the well-known paradox that the people who want the largest number of children are those who can least afford them. Thus, in Detroit, women whose husbands bring home less than $4,000 a year would like to have 3.51 children on the average; whereas moderate income families prefer 3.42; and families above $6,000, only 3.33. Fewer high-income families want no children at all (only one out of 13 wives with this deviant preference has above $6,000 income). But this minor positive correlation with income is more than offset by low-income wives who want big families. High-income wives are like young wives, more convinced than anyone else that two to four children is the right size to aim at. Hence it appears probable that as the American standard of living continues to rise, the concentration of preferences within this span will be accentuated.

Table 48

Preferred Number of Children, by Husband's Intergenerational Occupational Mobility

	HUSBAND'S INTERGENERATIONAL MOBILITY				
	DOWNWARD		STABLE	UPWARD	
	Extreme	Moderate		Moderate	Extreme
Wife's mean preferred number of children	3.31	3.47	3.51	3.48	3.23
Number of Families	87	97	185	101	113

The relativity of economic provision for children is nowhere more apparent than in the relationship between childbearing preferences and the husband's occupational mobility. Table 48 shows that where a major shift in prestige-level of his occupation occurs, the wife is less interested in having children. Where the husband's career moves downward, he cannot provide for his children as well as his father did for him. The child-endowment standards he learned from experience will not allow him to have as many children of his own on a more limited income.

Upwardly mobile men may find children a handicap in the quest for success. Children take time, energy, and money which could otherwise be devoted to the career ladder.

Educated Preferences. Closely correlated with economic trends have been educational ones. Over the decades, the average number of years of school completed has risen for both men and women. With the patriarchal family in eclipse, the views of the wife take on added importance in family size decisions. As women get more education, their family size preferences become more standardized (see Table 49).

Table 49

Preferred Number of Children, by Education of Wife

PREFERRED NUMBER OF CHILDREN	YEARS OF EDUCATION*		
	Grade School	High School	College
None	5%	2%	—
One	1	1	1
Two	19	25	22
Three	18	26	37
Four	39	35	29
Five	5	5	8
Six or more	13	7	2
Total	100	101	99
Mean	3.52	3.34	3.31
Number of families	149	393	65

* Grade school: 8 years or less. High school: 9–12 years. College: 13 years or more.

Better-educated women less often want either no children at all or unusually large families. Although they do not differ appreciably on the average from high schooled women, those who have been to college are more heavily concentrated in the two-to-four child range and foreshadow the wave of the future in their distinctive preference for precisely three children.

The effect of education in narrowing the range of preferences is twofold. In practically eliminating subnormal preferences, education provides women with husbands sufficiently prosperous to release the more or less universal American desire to have one child for the sake of the parents and at least one more for the sake of the first. In reducing preferences for outsize families, education creates in women more interests outside the home, not at the expense of having any children but certainly at the expense of being tied down by a long string of them. Educated women are also familiar with child psychology and its emphasis on giving love and affection to each child. The easiest way a mother can give more attention to each child is to have fewer of them. By and large, most Americans say that they want fewer children because they love them so much, not because they like them so little. Children are not nuisances to be avoided, but individuals who deserve a fair deal within the limits of the parents' ability to provide for them.

The Place of Children in Marriage. Giving children a good life means, above all, raising them in a happy home. Hence, nothing reduces the preferred number of children more severely than marital unhappiness (see Table 50).

Table 50
Preferred Number of Children, by Marital Satisfaction

	MARITAL SATISFACTION				
	Very low	Low	Moderate	High	Very high
Mean preferred number of children	2.50	3.31	3.53	3.53	3.24
Number of families	16	48	165	186	144

Whereas having fewer children is usually designed to improve their lot, the dissatisfied wives in Table 50 often feel that children would be better not born at all than to come into an unhappy home. Four of the sixteen unhappiest wives would rather have no children at all if they had their lives to live over again (compared to only one wife who is more than moderately satisfied). The mean preference of unhappy wives would be even lower, were it not for a countertendency among a few such wives to want a very large family to make up for the husband's inadequacies. In general, marital dissatisfaction tends to discourage the usual preferences for three or four children.

The smaller preference of the very satisfied wives requires other interpretations. This may reflect higher aspirations for children (the modal preference is for three). There may, in addition, be some tendency for such wives to want to hold on to their good relationship to their husbands by not introducing too many distractions. Their near unanimity in wanting at least one child (143 out of 144) indicates that they are not interested in avoiding children altogether in order to preserve their marriage, but wish to keep marriage and parenthood in balance by confining their choices to the two to four range.

The child bearing goals of American marriages may be summarized by the numbers two, three, and four. Within this range, wives with especially high standards for the welfare of their children tend to choose three as the magic number. Wanting more than four is mostly an old-fashioned, rural idea. Wanting less than two usually reflects severe financial or emotional deprivation. Most wives agree remarkably well on what they would like for themselves and for other Americans, too.

THE ACHIEVEMENT OF CHILDBEARING GOALS

One might expect most wives to accommodate the number of children they say they would like to have to the number they actually have (or expect to have in the case of younger women). Yet only 38 per cent of the white wives interviewed expect to reach their goals, and the Negro batting average is even lower. So the record of actual or expected achievement of childbearing goals is conspicuously poor.

Table 51

Extent of Discrepancies between Preferred and Expected Number of Children

Extent of Discrepancy	Per Cent of Families
Surplus (8 per cent)	
3 or more children	3
2 children	2
1 child	3
No Discrepancy	38
Deficiency (54 per cent)	
1 child	18
2 children	20
3 children	8
4 or more children	8
Total	100
Number of families	578

Most wives expect to miss the target, some of them by a good deal. Table 51 shows that nearly all the misses involve falling short of the mark rather than exceeding it. Nearly nine-tenths of those who miss the mark expect a deficiency, leaving only a small number who complain of more children than they would like.

Optimism and Realism. At the beginning of marriage, a wife's hopes are usually her only basis for saying how many children she expects. New brides are as optimistic about having children as they are about the husband's chances of getting ahead in his job. It doesn't take long, however, for the wife to begin to accumulate experience which may throw cold water on her optimism. Difficulties in conceiving, miscarriages, "accidental" conceptions, and financial reverses rapidly lead to pessimism.

Table 52

Childbearing Preferences, Performance, Expectations, and Discrepancies, by Length of Marriage

	LENGTH OF MARRIAGE				
	Under 3 Years (1953–55)*	3–9 Years (1946–52)	10–19 Years (1936–45)	20–29 Years (1926–35)	30+ Years (Before 1926)
A. Preferred number	3.08	3.27	3.51	3.57	3.45
B. Number born to date	.78	1.75	2.17	2.06	2.75
C. Expected number†	2.91	2.84	2.41	2.21	—
	(33)	(191)	(161)	(33)	
D. Discrepancy					
Surplus	3%	12%	4%	7%	21%
No discrepancy	78	47	34	17	32%
Deficiency	19	41	62	76	56
Total	100	100	100	100	100
Minimum number of families	36	191	191	89	99

* Dates in parentheses show when these couples were married.

† For women under 45, the numbers of families are given in parentheses because this is a subsample of the total sample. The "minimum numbers" given at the bottom of the table refer to the computations in sections A, B, and D of the table, which are based on the total sample unrestricted by age.

Table 52 shows widespread optimism in wives married less than three years, followed by sharp cuts in the expected number of children and increases in the number of discrepancies. Much of the initial optimism must be dismissed as naivete. If it is discounted, less than half the urban wives seem likely to achieve their childbearing goals.

With the advent of modern methods of contraception, surplus children have become largely a thing of the past. The identical percentages of surplus children for the 30 plus and 3–9 years of marriage hide a significant difference in extent of surplus: most of the former surplus involves 3 or more excess children, whereas most of the younger group expect to exceed their goal by only one child. Some of the latter's feelings may change as more years elapse, for most of them have several preschool age children on their hands. As their children mature and become less burdensome, they may feel more satisfied. At least, this may explain the rise in the preferred number of children during the early decades of marriage.

Economic Trends

The widespread deficiencies among wives married 20–29 years reflect the economic hardships of the Great Depression.

Table 52 shows the great frustration experienced by women who married between 1926 and 1935. The 1930's were years of economic catastrophe which delayed many marriages and delayed even more childbearing until too late. The tragedy of the depression years is clearly indicated in the low number of children actually born, despite the high number preferred. Indeed, perhaps the high preferences are one manifestation of feelings of frustration.

Since World War II began, America has experienced a baby boom unlike anything known since World War I. Already by 1955, Detroit wives in their early thirties had borne more children than their mothers' generation (those in their fifties). Since this does not reflect an enlarged ideal about the desirable number of children, the younger generation's more prolific childbearing represents the fulfillment of dreams made possible by years of economic prosperity. Many of these same young women expect to have still more children before they are through. As they do, their average number will move toward that of women married before World War I. However, their higher average will result from a concentration of families in the ideal range of two to four children. Already, more young than old wives have at least two children. The latter had many extra-large families but also more subnormal childless and one-child families than the younger generation will have.

One would think from the importance of economic conditions

that well-to-do people would come closest to having the number of children they want, but Table 53 shows that they excel only in avoiding unwanted children.

Table 53

Childbearing Preferences, Performance, Expectations, and Discrepancies, by Husband's Income

	HUSBAND'S INCOME				
	Under $3,000	$3,000 –4,999	$5,000 –6,999	$7,000 –9,999	$10,000+
A. Preferred number	3.69	3.30	3.47	3.18	3.56
B. Number born to date	2.22	2.04	1.99	2.18	1.74
C. Expected Number*	2.24	2.80	2.76	2.45	2.21
	(33)	(130)	(138)	(64)	(34)
D. Discrepancy					
Surplus	13%	10%	8%	7%	2%
No discrepancy	43	42	34	35	33
Deficiency	43	48	58	58	65
Total	99	100	100	100	100
Minimum number of families	69	181	196	88	57

* For women under age 45.

Why do prosperous families so often fail to achieve their goal when national prosperity tends to foster success in this regard? At least the reasons are *not* financial. Only one of the 37 "deficient" wives whose husbands now earn more than $10,000 says they didn't have as many as they wanted because they couldn't afford it. Most of them specify physical obstacles (like roughly half of all women with deficiencies in childbearing). Wives of top-income men are also apt to marry later in life, not past menopause but enough past the usual childbearing years (the early twenties) to depress their childbearing achievements. This, in a sense, is another physical obstacle.

According to Table 53, a husband's income has to be less than $3,000 a year, before economic pressure whittles down the number of children a couple expect to have.

The previous chapter demonstrated what a relative matter money is. Whether one feels he can afford children depends very much on what his standards are. Intergenerational mobility is usually an indicator of such differential standards.

Table 54

Childbearing Preferences, Performance, Expectations, and Discrepancies, by Husband's Intergenerational Occupational Mobility

| | HUSBAND'S INTERGENERATIONAL MOBILITY | | | | |
| | DOWNWARD | | STABLE | UPWARD | |
	Extreme	Moderate		Moderate	Extreme
A. Preferred number	3.31	3.47	3.51	3.48	3.23
B. Number born to date	2.16	2.03	2.03	2.17	1.89
C. Expected number*	2.53	2.83	2.61	2.81	2.56
	(56)	(56)	(128)	(78)	(75)
D. Discrepancy					
Surplus	15%	6%	8%	6%	10%
None	33	41	32	47	44
Deficiency	51	53	60	46	47
Total	99	100	100	99	101
Minimum number of families	87	96	185	101	112

* For wives under 45.

Table 54 shows a tendency for women whose husbands have suffered severe economic reverses to feel that they have too many children. Often these wives feel they have at least two children too many. Economic failure may make children already born seem unwanted—it may also dissuade couples from having children in the first place. At least, wives in downward-mobile families are especially apt to attribute deficiencies to economic hardships (25 per cent of deficient downward-mobile wives give this reason vs. 17 per cent of stable and 20 per cent of upward-mobile wives).

When husbands are economically successful, there is the greatest satisfaction with the number of children born. Husbands who have traveled upward the furthest have the fewest children to date due to economic preoccupation and concern for giving their children extra advantages in life. Apparently, husbands who manage their occupational roles successfully also succeed quite well in achieving their modest childbearing goals.

There is little evidence, however, that satisfaction with one's standard of living leads people to want to have more children. Rather, influences seem to flow in the other direction: large numbers of children tend to lower the family's standard of living (see Table 55).

Very few wives feel severely deprived in their standard of living except those who have unusually large families. Four of the seven

Table 55

Number of Children Born, by Satisfaction with Standard of Living, by Age of Wife

NUMBER OF CHILDREN BORN	SATISFACTION WITH STANDARD OF LIVING				
	Pretty Disappointed	Would Like More	Can't Complain	Quite Satisfied	Enthusiastic
Women under 40	—	2.33	1.92	1.85	1.50
		(61)	(48)	(220)	(20)
Women over 40	4.14	1.97	2.42	2.01	1.69
	(7)	(39)	(48)	(138)	(16)

wives who complain most about their standard of living wish they had at least three fewer children than they now have.

At the opposite extreme, wives who are enthusiastic about their standard of living are unusually apt to have only one child. None of them has more than four.

Even when families are divided into high- and low-income groups, the incompatibility of the economic and childbearing goals of the family tends to persist. Below $5,000, the wife's satisfaction with her standard of living declines appreciably with the addition of each child to the family. Above $5,000, the same pattern holds with only one exception. Families with three children are more satisfied with their standard of living than any others, not excluding childless families. This could not mean that adding a third child improves the standard of living but that well-to-do families are especially apt to prefer this number of children.

A high standard of living and children may be incompatible goals in life but most wives are very clear which is more important. Children rank second only to companionship as a valuable aspect of marriage whereas the standard of living ranks last of all. This means that few wives would ever intentionally go childless no matter how deprived they felt economically. Most wives want their minimum two, no matter what. But beyond this point, economic questions become increasingly important—not money as such but personal standards about the kind of life another child deserves and the kind parents prize for themselves.

The pervasiveness of economic reasoning is seen in the fact that 75 per cent of all wives who give other than physical reasons for not having more children specify economic ones. By contrast only 15 per cent of them say they couldn't give more children adequate personal care and the remaining 10 per cent say that they couldn't take the additional anxiety and trouble.

A family cannot have both many children and many material things unless the husband is unusually prosperous. Each goal must be limited if the other is not to suffer unduly. Childbearing usually takes precedence up to a point—but if physical factors do not intervene, that limiting point will be determined largely on economic grounds.

Social Status and Children

As far as economic factors are concerned, high status appears to be correlated with fewer children. However, educational factors appear to operate somewhat differently (see Table 56).

Table 56

Childbearing Preferences, Performance, Expectations, and Discrepancies, by Wife's Education

	YEARS OF EDUCATION		
	Grade School	High School	College
A. Preferred number	3.52	3.34	3.31
	(149)	(393)	(65)
B. Number born to date*	2.74	1.76	1.88
	(100)	(74)	(25)
C. Expected number†	2.51	2.64	2.86
	(50)	(318)	(40)
D. Discrepancy			
Surplus	15%	6%	5%
No discrepancy	24	42	46
Deficiency	60	52	49
Total	99	100	100
	(149)	(392)	(65)

* Wives over age 45.
† Wives under age 45.

Poorly educated women (like low-income women) tend more than others to have more children than they want (Table 56). The pattern of discrepancies, however, reverses the tendency of high income to be associated with deficiencies. College-educated wives appear to achieve their goals more often or to be more satisfied with their achievements than wives with less education. Does a college education give a woman more competence in planning her own destiny, or are women graduates so young on the average that this figure simply reflects youthful optimism? The record of accomplishment to date by educational groups is similar to the pattern by income groups (Table 56-B). Women who never went beyond grade school have had many more children than better-educated ones. Thirty-eight per cent of those with less than eight years of education have had at least four children, many of them seven or more, whereas only 7 per cent of college-educated women have had as many as four to date.

When age differences are cancelled out by limiting the analysis to women under forty-five, a quite different picture presents itself (see Table 56-C). When younger women are asked how many children they expect to have, it is the better-educated wives who expect the most children. This rarely means more than four, since big families are largely the province of poorly educated women. But so many young wives with only a grade school education expect to have no children at all and so few expect three or four that their predicted average is low. Both grade school and high school graduates modally expect to have two children. By contrast, those who have been to college within the past twenty-five years expect most often to wind up with three or four.

If these expectations are fulfilled it would mean a dramatic change in the accustomed way of behaving for higher status people.[1] Is this evidence of the "station-wagon set" of young wives whose children overcrowd ordinary sedans? The most tangible way of testing this question is to compare the number of children young wives already have with the completed family size of their elders. Table 57-B shows a striking contrast between the older and younger generations in this respect. In the older generation, the higher the status, the smaller the family. In the younger generation, exactly the opposite is true.[2] It re-

---

1. Demographer David Goldberg (1957) is convinced from an intensive analysis of the expectation predictions in this sample that "the expectations should come fairly close to the final product."

2. When analyzed by husband's occupation, wives over and under 40 have almost identical numbers of surviving children in every occupational category except among low-blue-collar workers. Young wives in that occupational category have the fewest children to date (1.73) whereas older wives in the same job group have the highest average (2.52).

mains to be seen whether the *completed* families of high-status wives are larger than those of low-status wives. Their predictions are quite irregular. Up to the time interviewed, however, the younger generation seems to be establishing a new pattern.

Table 57

Childbearing Preferences, Performance, Expectations, and Discrepancies, by Social Status

	PERCENTILE RANKING ON SOCIAL STATUS INDEX				
	0–19	20–39	40–59	60–79	80–99
A. Preferred number	2.82	3.41	3.39	3.54	3.28
	(17)	(97)	(210)	(190)	(93)
B. Number born to date					
Wives under 40	1.22	1.81	1.91	1.97	2.13
	(9)	(47)	(136)	(109)	(53)
Wives over 40	4.25	2.54	2.15	2.07	1.55
	(8)	(50)	(74)	(81)	(40)
Total wives	2.65	2.26	2.00	2.02	1.88
	(17)	(97)	(210)	(190)	(93)
C. Expected number of children*	2.78	2.42	2.66	2.70	2.62
	(9)	(50)	(158)	(127)	(63)
D. Discrepancy					
Surplus	29%	13%	10%	6%	5%
No discrepancy	59	34	40	35	38
Deficiency	12	52	50	60	57
Total	100	99	100	101	100
	(17)	(97)	(210)	(190)	(93)

* Wives under age 45.

The new pattern may be described as follows: children in threes have become popular with college graduates and with high-status people generally. The end of the Depression has enabled couples combining superior education and adequate income to achieve their childbearing goals more easily than their elders. Conservatism in childbearing goals, on the other hand, has begun to characterize two groups: those whose income is severely limited and those who are oriented toward the achievement of higher social status. Such occupationally preoccupied persons seldom avoid childbearing altogether, but are more apt to limit the number they desire to two and also more often actually wind up with none at all.

Marriage Patterns and Childbearing

Comparative success in reaching their childbearing goals characterizes equalitarian marriages (see Table 58).

Table 58

Childbearing Preferences, Performance, Expectations, and Discrepancies, by Balance of Power

	BALANCE OF POWER		
	Husband-dominant	Equal	Wife-dominant
A. Preferred number	3.54	3.36	3.34
B. Number born	2.00	2.08	1.91
C. Expected number*	2.80	2.66	2.51
	(104)	(217)	(61)
D. Discrepancy			
Surplus	10%	7%	11%
None	35	43	30
Deficiency	55	50	59
Total	100	100	100
Minimum number of families	144	297	111

* Wives under 45.

Equalitarian wives report fewer discrepancies in either direction than wives who dominate or are dominated by their husbands. Presumably, mutuality in decision-making produces plans which more effectively implement the wishes of both partners.

Husband-dominant and wife-dominant marriages resemble each other in their discrepancy rates but are polar opposites in terms of the expected number of children. At first glance, this might appear to indicate that dominant husbands are brutes who force their wives to bear unwanted children, whereas wives who manage to get power into their own hands have as few children as possible. However, such an interpretation would require fewer discrepancies among powerful wives (rather than the greater number who actually appear). Hence, some other interpretation is necessary.

Some of the differences between husband-dominant and wife-dominant marriages which emerged in Chapter Two provide such an alternative. Dominant wives, generally speaking, are unhappy wives whose husbands are unable to meet their needs satisfactorily. A few such wives throw themselves into childbearing as a substitute for marital satisfaction, but far more (15 per cent of the total) either cannot or choose not to have any children at all. This works both ways because childless women tend to take jobs outside the home which bolsters their power in the process. For more of the dominant wives, however, their smaller number of children is a matter of regret rather than of satisfaction.

Powerful husbands, on the other hand, tend to be successful in the community and their success enables them to have more children, insofar as it doesn't involve excessive mobility striving.

These differences help to explain several contrasts between husband-dominant and wife-dominant marriages which were found by Goldberg (1957). Thus, husband-dominant families expect to have more children if the husband is highly educated and the husband and wife belong to many organizations. By contrast, in wife-dominant families, these factors are reversed. Better-educated wives married to inadequate husbands expect to have *fewer* children and participate in organizations as a substitute for having children. Less educated ones throw themselves into home-centered patterns of leisure-time activities, subsistence production, and visiting with relatives. Within this context, preoccupation with children may anaesthetize dissatisfaction with the spouse.

Children and the Husband-Wife Relationship. Husband-dominant marriages, therefore, present a consistent pattern in which high social status provides a secure place for children. Dominant wives, however, may react from their unhappiness in either of two ways—by shifting their attention from the role of wife to mothering a large brood in traditional style, or by escaping from family roles altogether into satisfaction outside the home. Perhaps in the old days the mothering alternative was popular, but among young wives nowadays the unhappy wife more often takes refuge in outside activities.

This interpretation fits the pattern revealed in Table 59. Dissatisfied wives tend to expect either very few children (none or one) or an excessively large number. Two children predominate for the intermediate families while having three or four is associated with high marital satisfaction.

The most dissatisfied wives often exceed their preferences and complain of surplus children. The most satisfied wives, on the other hand, expect to have more children than anyone else despite the fact

Table 59

Expected Number of Children, by Marital Satisfaction for Wives under 45

EXPECTED NUMBER OF CHILDREN	MARITAL SATISFACTION			
	Low*	Moderate	High	Very high
None	18%	15%	5%	3%
One	29	15	12	6
Two	16	32	36	24
Three	13	17	21	32
Four	5	13	18	25
Five or more	19	8	8	10
Total	100	100	100	100
Mean	2.29	2.27	2.61	3.01
Number of families	28	86	134	134

* Because comparatively few wives under age 45 are dissatisfied, the two lowest categories have been combined in this table.

that they do not prefer the largest number. This does not mean that they expect to have surplus children, too, but that in reaching their more modest goal they will exceed those who aim higher but fall farther short.[3]

Religious Ideologies

Differences between the major American religious groups lie in the expected directions. Catholics have the highest preferred number of children, the highest number born to date, and the highest expectations of young wives for completed size of family. Due perhaps to their religious philosophy, relatively few express a desire for a different number of children than they expect to have. On the other hand, this low discrepancy rate may involve optimism resulting from the known youthfulness of Detroit Catholics.

Protestants, as a whole, lie intermediate on all childbearing measures, though some denominations present unusual patterns. Episcopalians bear especially many children while Fundamentalists tend toward considerable deficiencies in childbearing. No other groups can compare in deficiencies, however, with the small groups of Greek

---

3. This analysis is complicated by the reciprocity of the relationships. Marital satisfaction and childbearing preferences and expectations tend to interact upon each other in both directions.

Table 60

Childbearing Preferences, Performance, Expectations, and Discrepancies, by Wife's Church Preference

	RELIGIOUS AFFILIATION			
	Catholic	Protestant	Jewish	Greek Orthodox
A. Preferred number of children	3.63	3.18	3.15	3.31
B. Number born to date	2.17	2.01	1.65	1.44
C. Expected number*	2.79	2.66	1.27	1.40
	(183)	(211)	(11)	(10)
D. Discrepancy				
Surplus	7%	10%	5%	12%
No discrepancy	44	36	20	19
Deficiency	49	55	75	69
Total	100	101	100	100
Minimum number of families	251	311	20	16

* Wives under age 45.

Orthodox and Jewish wives. Not a single young Jewish wife expects to have more than two children, and only one Greek Orthodox wife expects a large family. These are both small groups, but the differences are extremely great. Some of the Jewish experience may be due to unusually high standards for their children—yet they express a preference for as many children as Protestants. Perhaps factors beyond their control such as marrying at a comparatively late age (perhaps postponed by many years of education) produce their low fertility.[4] The Greek Orthodox resemble other young immigrants, hard pressed and anxious to get ahead economically, their wives often too busy collaborating in the family enterprise to take time out for having children.

In summary, the 909 American wives remarkably often report failure in achieving their childbearing goals. Rarely nowadays is having too many children a problem, but the Great Depression left a whole generation of wives feeling deprived of the number of children they wanted. If the future is prosperous, the number of wives who forego

---

4. How many children a wife can have depends greatly on how old she is when she gets married. Surplus children are heavily concentrated among women who married before they were 18 years old (23 per cent of whom have surpluses) and deficiencies correspondingly among those who didn't get married until after they were 30 (83 per cent of whom fall short of their goal).

children for economic reasons may decrease. As for biological obstacles, modern medicine may whittle these, too. As of the present
time, however, American marriages have a long way to go to achieve
anywhere near general success in reaching childbearing goals.

THE CONSEQUENCES OF NOT HAVING CHILDREN

Since practically every couple would like to have children, it is not
surprising that childless wives (11 per cent of the sample) tend to feel
frustrated unless they have married so recently that they are justi-
fiably optimistic. When asked what have been some of the good things
about not having children, 36 per cent of the childless wives can think
of nothing good at all, reflecting an inability to rationalize their fate.

The most common benefit (mentioned by 27 per cent) is freedom
from responsibility—the same sort of freedom which wives revel in
who have launched their last child (Deutscher, 1959). Eighteen per
cent mentioned the financial advantages in having fewer dependents
and about 9 per cent each appreciate not having to care for children
and being able to enjoy the husband's companionship unencumbered
by children.

Data elsewhere in this book suggest that such advantages in not
having children correspond to genuine disadvantages in having them.
Nevertheless, most childless wives are quite convinced that children
would be well worth any disadvantages they may involve.

What do these wives say they have missed in not having children?
Primarily their companionship—it's lonely being a childless wife, say
45 per cent, especially those who can't have them for biological reasons. Twenty-seven per cent more feel that life without children lacks
purpose, their home its completion, or their role as women its fulfillment. Such losses reflect disappointed expectations in life. Another 9
per cent of the childless couples feel especially frustrated when they
look at other families and see what experiences they are missing.

Deviant cases are the 3 per cent of all Detroit wives who wouldn't
want any children if they had their life to live over again. Most of
these women have succeeded in avoiding childbirth in actual practice.
They can see nothing bad in not having children and usually give economic reasons for their abstention.

By contrast, women who cannot have children for physical reasons are the really frustrated ones. They overwhelmingly regret the companionship they have missed and almost unanimously feel that there are no good things about not having children.

Incidentally, not a single wife gives the trouble children cause as a reason for avoiding having children completely. On the other hand, 18 per cent of the women who have actually had children list anxieties and responsibilities as reasons for not having more. Perhaps childless women are not aware of the troubles children can cause. More likely, they are quite prepared to cope with the troubles for the sake of the rewards children bring.

WHAT CHILDREN MEAN TO THEIR PARENTS

Most married couples spend the bulk of their married lives with their children. Typically, only two years elapse between the wedding ceremony and the birth of the first child. After launching, there are fourteen years or so of "empty-nest" living. In between is generally a quarter century of living with children (Glick, 1955).

Table 61

Good Things about Having Children, in City and Farm Families

GOOD THINGS ABOUT HAVING CHILDREN	PLACE OF RESIDENCE	
	City	Farm
1. *Pleasure,* emotional satisfaction	48%	35%
2. *Companionship* for parents	18	24
3. Gives life *purpose,* meaning	16	17
4. *Strengthens family,* makes a real home	12	15
5. *Strengthens marriage,* brings husband and wife closer together	4	3
6. Children help parents, provide *security*	2	6
7. *Nothing* good	*	—
Total	100	100
Number of families	599	155

* One case.

Table 61 lists the kinds of answers wives give when asked "What have been some of the good things about having children?" The most common answers describe the emotional satisfactions in raising chi dren. Typical ways of expressing this are: "Children are a joy," "pure pleasure," "make you happy," "it is a joy to give and receive love, affection, and appreciation, and to do things for them," "children are fun, entertaining," "I enjoy watching them mature and relive my own childhood through them."

Children give life purpose through providing something to work for, plan for, look forward to. Wives sometimes say life wouldn't be worthwhile without children, they keep you going. Some wives suggest that their whole lives revolve about their children. Certainly most wives spend more time in the housewife-mother dual role than any other, and may feel that being a housewife without children isn't sufficiently challenging. Indeed some say that without children they wouldn't know what to do with themselves.

Some purpose-mentioning wives value the contribution childrearing has made to their own maturity. They feel that it has helped them settle down and become more responsible persons. It has made them less self-centered and more considerate of others. They understand life better and are wiser individuals. Other purpose-mentioning wives stress the feeling of pride and accomplishment which they derive from raising children.

The kind of help and security parents find in children is not always financial. Such parents talk about how nice it is to be able to rely on children when you get old, implying that affection and companionship are involved as much as financial resources.

The city wives in Table 61 mention emotional satisfaction more often than farm wives, perhaps reflecting a more hedonistic philosophy of life. Farm wives are more apt to mention the companionship of children, whose presence or absence is more conspicuous on an isolated farmstead than in a city neighborhood. Perhaps much of the rural emphasis on security in old age also reflects a desire to avoid loneliness. Some of it, however, involves the tangible economic roles of children as members of the farm labor force. Similarly, two wives mention that it is good to be able to pass the family farm on to one's children.[5]

---

5. Such voluntary mentions would usually be echoed by many other wives if they were asked specifically whether or not such a factor was one benefit among many derived from children.

The one deviant wife, who complains that nothing is good about having children, would go through life childless if she had it to live over again. She is interesting because she is so typical of what might be expected of a woman sour on children: grade school educated, very dissatisfied with her marriage, her oldest child past age eighteen but still living at home. She is an extreme but symptomatic case of the mothers of unlaunched children.

Table 62

Good Things about Having Children, by Stage in Family-life Cycle

GOOD THINGS ABOUT HAVING CHILDREN	STAGE IN FAMILY-LIFE-CYCLE				
	AGE OF OLDEST CHILD				POSTPARENTAL
	Under 6	6–12	13–18	19+	
1. Pleasure	44%	46%	57%	43%	53%
2. Companionship	15	16	18	22	18
3. Purpose	17	17	13	17	16
4. Strengthens family	13	15	9	11	7
5. Strengthens marriage	10	4	3	—	1
6. Security	1	2	—	5	5
7. Nothing	—	—	—	2	—
Total	100	100	100	100	100
Number of families	126	137	101	63	83

Here Today, Gone Tomorrow. Table 62 shows that launching-stage wives especially value the companionship they derive from their grown children. In the next chapter, it will be apparent that such companionship with children may be a substitute for companionship with the husband. Wives past the age of sixty, especially those whose husbands are retired, tend to shift from mentioning companionship with the children to talking about help and security derived from them.

The husband-wife relationship, by contrast, is largely a concern of young wives. Newlyweds are both more interested and more successful in achieving a satisfying husband-wife relationship. Older wives either lose hope of finding satisfaction in marriage or else realize that children don't magically cement a husband and wife together.

Marriage vs. the Family. Children seem to have contrasting effect on different aspects of marriage, however. Young children may be associated with love and affection between the husband and wife but no with a nice home (in the sense of a high material standard of living) nor with unfettered leisure-time companionship. Indeed, wives who stress the companionship they derive from their children notoriously lack companionship with their husbands. Children, therefore, may draw a husband and wife closer together in love, but may also serve as a substitute source of love and companionship for wives who become estranged from their husbands.

Estrangement is often involved in the assumption of power by the wife. Hence, dominant wives are more apt than those who make fewer decisions to value the companionship of children (again as a substitute for the husband), and seldom mention that children strengthen either marriage or the family generally. Their submissive husbands are usually absentee husbands (absent in spirit if not in body) who leave their wives dependent on substitute sources of gratification.

In general, dependent young wives with happy marriages tend to see children as sources of strength in marriage. By contrast, dominant older wives with large families are often so alienated from their husbands that their marriages provide little satisfaction. They turn to their grown children for the love and companionship their husbands neglect to provide. After leaving home, children offer less companionship to their mother, but as she approaches aged dependence, they seem an increasingly valuable source of economic and emotional security. This need for security is manifested primarily in low-status wives with relatively little education. Not a single wife who has completed high school or gone to college mentions depending on her children for security. This may be because education creates a feeling of competence or because such wives place more emphasis on the pleasure and meaningfulness that children add to life.

The Costs of Having Children

With the very positive attitude that most wives have toward children, it is not surprising to find that many wives decline to say that there are any "bad things about having children," (just as many childless wives feel that there are no good things about *not* having them). Nevertheless, a majority of the city mothers and even more of the farm mothers specify at least one area in which children have created problems (see Table 63).

Table 63

Problems Children Present in City and Farm Families

PROBLEMS CHILDREN PRESENT	PLACE OF RESIDENCE	
	City	Farm
1. None	29%	18%
2. Financial problems	17	18
3. Illness	15	17
4. Childrearing difficulties and burdens	15	23
5. Worries and anxieties	12	12
6. Restrictions on freedom	11	11
7. Husband-wife conflict	1	1
Total	100	100
Number of families	584	149

Financial troubles are mentioned most often. Usually wives frame their remarks in terms of not being able to give the children as much as they would like to. Less often, the financial repercussions on the parents' own standard of living are mentioned.

The illnesses wives mention are also primarily those of the children, but a number of wives mention that their own health suffered during pregnancy, childbirth, or childrearing.

Childrearing difficulties fall on the mother herself. Farm wives often mention the extra work involved in caring for children. Since farm women do so many household tasks and farm tasks, the extra burden of caring for children is especially noticeable. More than a third of the childrearing burdens deal with getting children to behave correctly, i.e., questions of discipline and control.

Worries and anxieties are emotional reactions which for farm wives often center around either the fear or the actual experience of losing a child through death. Relatively few wives mention the irritation or nervousness which childrearing creates in them—mostly they are concerned about the children's welfare.

Restrictions on freedom involve being tied down at home and unable to participate in outside activities. Very few wives complain that children interfere with marriage, although the evidence later in this book suggests that such is often the case.

In general, both the city and the farm wives are primarily concerned about the hardships experienced by their children, secondarily by the extra burdens they have incurred personally, and hardly at all by the repercussions on their relationship to their husbands. The latter are more apparent to the sociological observer than to the participants in marriage.

Table 64

Problems Children Present, by Stage in Family-life Cycle

PROBLEMS CHILDREN PRESENT	STAGE IN FAMILY-LIFE CYCLE				
	AGE OF OLDEST CHILD				POSTPARENTAL
	Under 6	6–12	13–18	19+	
1. None	21%	22%	36%	39%	54%
2. Financial	14	19	10	17	10
3. Illness	15	19	12	9	10
4. Burdens	21	13	16	20	9
5. Worries	10	11	17	8	12
6. Restrictions	19	15	9	5	5
7. Conflict	—	1	—	2	—
Total	100	100	100	100	100
Number of families	127	137	101	64	79

Table 64 suggests that saying "nothing is bad about having children" may sometimes be a nostalgic remark. Most often, it is made by wives who no longer have any children left at home. Prior to that point it is made largely by women who are too old to have any more children. The number of wives making this remark almost doubles around age forty when most wives are either experiencing menopause or consider themselves too old to make further childbearing advisable. Furthermore, wives who have been unable to have any children or have severe deficiencies due to physical difficulties overwhelmingly express this attitude. Clearly, absence of children makes the heart grow fonder!

What about a surfeit of children? Which problems bother women who would drastically scale down their family size if they could wave a magic wand? Primarily, they complain of the burden of caring for so many children, secondarily of the financial cost. Saddled with these tangible responsibilities, they seldom mention the more esoteric loss of social life or merely worrying about children.

Being tied down at home understandably results from having young children who must be watched after. Teen-agers tie the mother down less but worry her more as they move into the outside world.

A syndrome of burdensomeness, worrying, and restrictions characterizes high status wives. They are the three top-ranking problems for college-educated wives and for families in the top category on the general Social Status Index.

Conversely, financial problems and illness plague low status wives, especially Negro wives. Thirty-nine per cent of all Negro wives refer to the economic hardships involved in raising children. For many people, the most troublesome aspect of illness is the medical bills which follow. At least this interpretation seems consistent with the fact that wives who specify health problems are especially apt to have husbands who work overtime (20 per cent vs. 8 per cent), perhaps earning the money to pay the doctor.

How much income does it take to overcome the economic burden which children present? Apparently a minimum of $10,000. As shown in Table 66, financial problems are not mentioned by a single wife with that much income. At the same time, only one of the wives in this income bracket mentions illness as a problem. The net effect of eliminating these two problems is to leave high-income wives concerned primarily about problems of their children's behavior.

Table 65

Problems Children Present, by Husband's Income

PROBLEMS CHILDREN PRESENT	HUSBAND'S INCOME				
	Under $3,000	$3,000 –4,999	$5,000 –6,999	$7,000 –9,999	$10,000+
1. None	38%	34%	28%	28%	40%
2. Financial	25	15	15	15	—
3. Illness	12	13	17	19	2
4. Burdens	12	14	14	14	31
5. Worries	6	12	10	15	18
6. Restrictions	6	12	15	9	8
7. Conflict	1	—	1	—	—
Total	100	100	100	100	99
Number of families	48	151	171	80	48

The decrease above $7,000 in the percentage mentioning being tied down probably indicates that funds for baby-sitting and other time-releasing help become more generally available at this income threshold.

CHILDREN AND MARRIAGE

To most American women, children and marriage go together as much as love and marriage. Indeed love, marriage, and children are what most young girls look forward to as the three great chapters in their lives. Of the three, perhaps their childbearing experience will be the most disappointing. At least, for the whole generation of women who married in the Depression years, disappointment was the order of the day.

Since the end of the Depression, husbands and wives have been able to afford more children and the number of disappointments has decreased correspondingly. Nevertheless, many Americans seem destined even in prosperous times to be physically unable to have as many children as they would like to have.

The number they would like to have is a matter of increasing concensus: not less than two and not more than four. Reasons for wanting families of this size are primarily child-oriented: (1) an only child leads a lonely existence, and (2) a fifth child gets less affection, attention, and education than he deserves.

Similarly child-oriented are the reactions of parents to questioning about their experiences with children. The problems involved focus around the children themselves—their needs, their troubles, their futures. The benefits derived are primarily the enjoyment of having children around and watching them grow up, rarely the security-oriented motives of more precarious societies.

Many women disappointed in childbearing can think of no benefits from the lack of children but only of what they have missed. Despite the headaches, the hard-work, the expenses, and the confinement which children bring, it is a rare mother who wishes she hadn't gotten into the business of reproduction, and who wouldn't do it again if she had her life to live over.

COMPANIONSHIP

MARRIAGE NORMALLY INVOLVES the coming together of a man and a woman into a common household. In so doing, the two partners commit themselves to a life-long companionship. Henceforth, two people who grew up in separate families live together under one roof. From this point of view, marriage has always been based on companionship.

THE EMERGENCE OF COMPANIONSHIP

In the past, the companionship element was often taken for granted and the emphasis placed elsewhere. If marriages were arranged, the partner was rarely selected on the basis of leisure-time interests or personal attraction. Bride and groom were sometimes complete strangers to each other. They began their life together wondering what the partner was like but submitting dutifully to what parents and culture had ordained. The parents were concerned with finding a daughter-in-law to bear male children to continue the family line and maintain the family shrine.

Even in societies where men and women chose their own partners, the emphasis in the past was often on what the partner could *do* rather than on who the partner *was*. In primitive societies, where the margin of protection against starvation is narrow, a man is valued for his hunting prowess or agricultural skill, and a woman prized for her good health, her culinary arts, and whatever else she can contribute to the division of labor. In short, a primitive economy focuses the attention of its members on the economic resources which a potential partner can bring to marriage. The focus is away from personality characteristics. Life is so preoccupied with staying alive that little time or energy is left over for anything else.

Romance. The modern concept of companionship differs sharply from the utilitarian yoking-together of fellow "work-horses" in primitive marriage. Companionship today has two essential components: (1) free choice of partner as a unique personality and (2) enjoyment of leisure time with that person.

Both components were made possible by the rise of mercantilism and the industrial revolution in an urban environment. The specter of starvation recedes whenever facilities arise for the storage of grain against lean years (like Joseph in Egypt). Security and prosperity are enhanced when the surplus of one community can be exchanged for the products of another through trade. Finally, the standard of living leaps ahead as industrial technology increases the output of the individual worker.

The dawn of Western civilization in the Middle Ages brought the age of chivalry and romance (Beigel, 1951). At first, only noble ladies were idealized—and not by prospective husbands. Everyone took it for granted that no man could ever prize his wife's companionship, nor she his. But gradually what began as a leisure-class phenomenon spread to the merchants, the new middle class in the cities. Gradually, too, romantic idealization shifted from somebody else's wife to prospective brides. Finally, the industrial revolution increased productivity so fast that the hours of labor for even the working man could be shortened and leisure time became available to every man for the first time in history.

In the past, what little leisure men had was spent chiefly in the company of their own sex. If female companionship was desired, it could hardly be obtained from one's wife since she dwelled in a different world—uneducated in the ways of men, and too submissive to achieve the equality which companionship requires.

To fill the gap, special women were often available—the *heterae* of ancient Greece and the *geisha* of Japan—unmarried women, trained to please men with their intellectual, aesthetic, or sexual skills.

When leisure is universal, however, the supply of female specialists becomes exhausted. If every man desires feminine companionship, then every woman must learn how to provide it. Fortunately, the same economic developments which made leisure available to men also made education available to women. And the shift from patriarchate to equality in decision-making broke down the barriers of reserve and respect between men and women, enabling them to enjoy each other as persons.

Dating. This shift in the marital relationship was accompanied by corresponding changes in the nature of courtship. Where previously courtship had sometimes not even existed (with arranged marriages) or was telescoped into introductory meetings which rapidly committed the participants to marriage, now dating arose. Dating differs from courtship in stressing the immediate satisfactions of the participants. Regardless of what tomorrow may bring, tonight we will have fun. A good date depends primarily on who the partner is. Not just any person will do. The partner must be a person who is likable, whom it's fun to be with, in short, a good companion.

In adolescence, dating is the chief form of leisure-time activity. In their dating careers, the average American boy and girl experience companionship with literally dozens of partners. When love blossoms from one of these friendships, it intensifies the desire to be together. Companionship is regularized in going steady, then intensified as young lovers spend every spare minute together. Modern courtship thus involves selecting a preferred companion from the panorama of dating partners. It also accustoms the partners to joint leisure-time activity. Companionship in marriage is partly the goal of courtship, partly the culmination of increasingly firm habits of spending time together.

Primary Relations. Companionship is more than just a habit made possible by the existence of leisure time. Companionship fulfills a basic human need—the need for response from another person, for what sociologists call "primary relations."

A primitive community consists exclusively of primary relationships. Everybody knows everybody else and the same group share life together from birth to death. The rise of cities shattered this communalism. With increasing size, knowing the whole group became impossible. With specialization of function, interpersonal contact is segmented into small fragments of activity—a transaction here, an encounter there, but seldom the establishment of encompassing primary relationships.

Personal friendships do not cease altogether in an urban environment. They sprout in some of the unlikeliest places. Corporation organizational charts are fouled up by interoffice friendships. Even on the assembly line, cliques arise to frustrate the time-and-motion-study boys by controlling output. The difficulty with such friendships is mobility. Differential promotion rates take old pals out of contact with each other in the administrative hierarchy. More disruptive than vertical mobility is geographical mobility. The route to the home office leads via the branches. And skilled workers, too, search the city, the county, sometimes the nation for better jobs.

Mobility severs the ties of old friendships. Sometimes they continue a truncated existence via letters and occasional visits. Mostly they wither and die. The only friendship which is guaranteed to survive mobility is marriage. Because husbands and wives move together, they can count on each other in strange communities. So the need for the primary relations, formerly provided by the local community, gives impetus to the valuation of companionship in marriage.

His wife has become a man's best friend. A man chooses his friends carefully; so he chooses this best friend with special care, knowing he is likely to spend more leisure time with her than with anyone else. To many a modern man, his leisure is the best time he has. If he works on an assembly line, his working time may be boring —something to be endured until 5:00. Then comes the time when he can really live. Then is the time for real companionship.

Without a wife to return to after work, city life can be awfully lonely. In fiction, the bachelor leads a gay life—but in practice, gay bachelors are few. Eating alone is dreary. Roommates can substitute, but marriage is the real thing. Surely this is one of the main reasons why more Americans are marrying today than ever before.

This is the kind of background against which companionship has risen to become the single most valued aspect of marriage.

The Pre-eminence of Companionship

In Detroit, 48 per cent of the wives choose "companionship in doing things together with the husband" as the most valuable aspect of marriage. This far outstrips the other four aspects—love, understanding, standard of living, and the chance to have children. The latter is a poor second with only 27 per cent first choices. In addition to being overwhelmingly popular as a first-choice item, companionship is chosen second by 21 per cent more and third by 16 per cent, leaving only 14 per cent who do not choose it as one of the three most valuable parts of marriage. This compares with 30 per cent not choosing children and still more neglecting the less popular aspects of marriage.

These figures show that when modern Americans think of marriage, they think of companionship more than anything else.

In the case of farm wives, this emphasis on companionship is accentuated even further, with 53 per cent making it their first choice, and only 9 per cent not choosing it at all. This means that the contemporary American farm must be distinguished from the primitive community which was described earlier as providing a broad network of primary relationships. Primitive communities usually consist of households close together, often containing extended families of relatives who co-operate in many activities.

The farm villages of Europe and Asia consist of cottages clustered together in the midst of surrounding fields. By contrast, the American pattern of isolated homesteads, each on its own farmland, results in a physical isolation from neighbors and friends which may be equivalent to the social isolation imposed by mobility on city people. Unable to chat over the back fence or have morning coffee with the girl next door, the farm wife needs companionship from her husband correspondingly more. The main point, however, is not the marginal difference between city and farm wives, but the fact that both stress companionship as the chief end of marriage.

TYPES OF COMPANIONSHIP

The broad definition of companionship, as leisure time spent by the husband and wife in joint activities, covers a wide gamut of activities. Unfortunately, we have no measure of pure "dating companionship." However, the selected types to be reported here illustrate the broad range of variation.

Table 66

Organizational Companionship and Satisfaction with Companionship

Number of Types of Organizations to which both Partners Belong	Proportion of families	Wife's Mean Satisfaction with Companionship
(0)* None	63%	3.70
(1) One	9	4.09
(2) Two	15	4.04
(3) Three	9	4.30
(4) Four or more	4	3.78
Total	100	
Number of families	731	

* The numbers in parentheses show the basis for computing mean intensities of organizational companionship in later tables.

Organizational. One type of companionship involves joint husband-wife participation in formally organized groups of various kinds, or "organizational companionship." This is rather rare in Detroit. Since 19 per cent of the husbands and 42 per cent of the wives belong to no formal organizations whatsoever (except perhaps a church), even separate organizational activity is limited. When the additional criterion of *joint* membership is added, the number of nonparticipants rises still further to 63 per cent. This leaves hardly more than a third who belong to even one organization together.[1]

Although the number of couples who participate in organizations

---

1. Primarily these are youth-serving organizations like P.T.A. (22 per cent of the couples), church-connected organizations (16 per cent), and neighborhood improvement associations (14 per cent). Since organizational companionship refers to the number of *types* of organizations, two youth-serving organizations would count as only one joint membership. The full list of types (plus church membership) appears as question 39 in the questionnaire (see Appendix B).

together is relatively small, those who do engage in such activity experience a form of companionship quite different from many leisure-time activities. Organized interest groups flourish more in the United States than anywhere else in the world, so organizational companionship is especially interesting to observe in a study of American marriage.

Informative. A second type of companionship doesn't involve time spent outside the home. Rather, it deals with communication to each other about things which happen while they are apart. The following question represents a measure of this "informative companionship": "When your husband comes home from work, how often does he tell you about things that happened there?" Informative companionship is quite common in Detroit (see Table 67).

Table 67
Informative Companionship and Satisfaction with Companionship

Frequency Husband Tells Wife about Events at Work*	Proportion of families	Wife's Mean Satisfaction with Companionship
(0) Never	7%	3.56
(1) Occasionally*	5	3.44
(2) Monthly	11	3.54
(3) Weekly	37	3.74
(4) Daily	40	4.04
Total	100	
Number of families	731	

* "Occasionally" includes a few times a year and less often. "Monthly" indicates once a month and a few times a month. "Weekly" includes from once a week up to almost every day. The numbers in parentheses show the basis for computing mean intensities of informative companionship in later tables.

The importance of informative companionship to the wife lies in giving her a sense of vicarious participation in the husband's life away from home. She can seldom share in the husband's day directly but feels less isolated if she hears about interesting events that happen to him.

Such information-giving strengthens the wife's feeling of companionship with her husband, just as joining the same organizations does. The norm of information-giving is so high that satisfaction with companionship slumps rapidly when the frequency drops much below daily.

Colleague. A third type of companionship involves more direct contact with the husband's work role. Getting together with work colleagues has been singled out as an aspect of general sociability. Visiting with neighbors may occur by chance, but visiting with work-mates requires more initiative. This form of companionship involves the wife in more of her husband's life. As she gets to know the men who share his work role, a crucial area of his life becomes more meaningful to her.

Table 68

Colleague Visiting and Satisfaction with Companionship

Frequency of Getting together with Work mates*	Proportion of families	Wife's Mean Satisfaction with Companionship
(0) Never	41%	3.65
(1) Occasionally	30	3.81
(2) Monthly	20	3.96
(3) Weekly	8	4.04
Total	99	
Number of families	731	

* The frequency categories are defined the same as for Table 67 except that so few couples visit colleagues oftener than once or twice a week that the most frequent categories are combined under the heading "weekly." The numbers in parentheses show the basis for computing mean intensities of colleague visiting in later tables.

Colleagues are the least frequent target of visiting, lagging after relatives, neighbors, and other friends. Though infrequent, "colleague companionship" presents another facet of the total picture of companionship.

Friendship. A fourth type of companionship consists in sharing friendships. The question involved is, "About how many of your husband's friends are men that you personally know quite well?" This is a product of joint visiting such as that specified in colleague companionship. However, friends may come from many sources in addition to work contacts. Other ways of assessing this sort of companionship would be to discover *how many* friends a husband and wife have in common or *how much time* a couple spend with friends. The aspect used here is the *proportion* of the husband's friends whom the wife knows well.

Detroit wives vary a great deal in their "friendship-companionship" as thus measured. Some know all and some know none but most wives fall between these extremes.

Table 69

Friendship Companionship and Satisfaction with Companionship

Proportion of Husband's Friends Whom Wife Knows Quite Well	Proportion of families	Wife's Mean Satisfaction with Companionship
(0)* None	11%	3.54
(1) Some	27	3.58
(2) About half	14	3.93
(3) Most	28	3.99
(4) All	20	4.04
Total	100	
Number of families	731	

* The numbers in parentheses show the basis for computing mean intensities of friendship-companionship in later tables.

Interrelationships

Organizational companionship, informative companionship, colleague companionship, and friendship companionship—all four are particular aspects of companionship in marriage. Highly companionable couples tend to engage extensively in all four types, except that those with the most joint memberships often get so involved in organizational activity that they have less time to visit work-mates or for the husband to tell about what happened during the day. Indeed, Table 66 shows that such couples have very little satisfaction with companionship in general. Perhaps these "over-organized" couples escape into the outside world from boredom with each other. Up to that point, however, couples who have more of any one kind of companionship usually have more of other kinds, too.[2]

Perhaps this interrelationship reflects a generalized sociability. Some couples seem to socialize a lot with each other and with others as well. This is visible in the fact that wives who get a lot of love and affection from their husbands also tend to know most of their husbands' friends. Sociability with each other does not prevent a couple

---

2. Sharing tasks in the division of labor is, like belonging to organizations, correlated with companionship satisfaction up to a certain point. However, when more than half the tasks are shared, satisfaction with companionship drops, presumably because housework isn't perceived as a leisure-time activity. Most couples share that many tasks only under heavy time pressures which would prevent them from enjoying leisure together. In any case, shared housework is arbitrarily excluded from the definition of what is meant by companionship in this chapter.

from being sociable with others—nor vice versa (up to the point of organizational satiation). At the other extreme, some couples are unsociable in many different ways. For instance, couples who have no organizational companionship are significantly low on all three other types of companionship.

A second irregularity in the relationships between types of companionship correlates with intensive knowledge of the husband's friends. Wives who know *all* of them visit with colleagues less often than wives who know most or half of them. Such irregularities suggest that knowing all his friends often reflects a smaller *number* of friends—and correspondingly less sociability. A complete picture of friendship companionship would have to take into consideration the number of joint friends as well as the proportion. Selective friendship sometimes yields more aggregate companionship than complete knowledge of a narrow circle, though over-all satisfaction continues to increase slightly with inclusiveness of friendship (see Table 68).

In general, however, all four types of companionship are interrelated with each other and can be looked at as different aspects of a single marital function, each in its own way adding to the loneliness-combating value of marriage.

CONDITIONS OF COMPANIONSHIP

What are the circumstances under which husbands and wives spend a lot of time together?

Novelty

If companionship in marriage is at least partly a carryover from dating and courtship, newly married couples should be more companionable than others. This hypothesis is confirmed by the fact that no matter how old they are, new brides tend to be especially satisfied with the companionship of their husbands. When newlyweds of various ages are compared, those most enthusiastic of all are the handful past fifty (mostly widows?) who have recently married. In fact, the older the woman is, the more this differential satisfaction manifests itself, suggesting that marital companionship may be valued not only as a continuation of adolescent dating but also as an escape from the specter of elderly loneliness. It seems doubtful that husbands behave more companionably in later marriages but they apparently are appreciated more.

Table 70

Satisfaction with Companionship, by Stage in Family-life Cycle

WIFE'S MEAN SATISFACTION WITH COMPANIONSHIP		STAGE IN FAMILY-LIFE CYCLE			
Childbearing stages:		Preschool	Preadolescent	Adolescent	Unlaunched
		3.99	3.91	3.76	3.50
		(128)	(140)	(98)	(62)
Childless stages:	Honeymoon			Postparental*	Retired
	4.26			3.83	3.80
	(19)			(87)	(10)
Childless couples:		4.09	3.93	4.00	
		(11)	(29)	(9)	

* Mean satisfaction for the 14 postparental couples married less than 27 years is 4.07.

Childlessness

That young childless couples should be most satisfied with companionship fits the notion that their life is a continuation into marriage of patterns of dating and courtship. With no children to alter their life styles, with both partners usually still working, weekend dates may be quite similar to premarriage dating.

The surprise in Table 70 is the limited degree to which the arrival of children interferes with companionship. The preadolescent stage in the family-life cycle is sometimes referred to as the Golden Years of family interaction, when parents and children picnic and vacation and generally spend their leisure time together. Perhaps such total-family activities bolster up the wife's satisfaction with companionship at this stage.

Family-type activities may even be enhanced by enlarging the size of the family group, at least up to the point where age diversity prevents joint activity. This may explain why the most satisfied wives have three children whereas the least satisfied have four or more. Three children will typically be fairly close together in age, perhaps

five years from oldest to youngest. This means they have similar recreational interests. When the number of children increases to four
and more, the age gap from oldest to youngest widens so much that
recreational interests tend to differ. It may be necessary for the husband to take the older kids on a hike while the wife stays home with
the baby, cut off from companionship with him.

However, activities within the family are not alone in accounting
for peak satisfaction with three children. Even colleague companionship is higher in this size family, too. The decline beyond the three-
child level reflects not only the fact that the children are a less compact
unit, but that parents have been married longer with a consequent
deterioration of companionship.

Table 71

Organizational Companionship, by Stage in Family-life Cycle

MEAN ORGANIZATIONAL COMPANIONSHIP		STAGE IN FAMILY-LIFE CYCLE			
Childbearing stages:		Preschool	Preadolescent	Adolescent	Unlaunched
		0.65	1.13	1.35	0.98
		(130)	(141)	(102)	(66)
Childless stages:	Honeymoon			Postparental	Retired
	1.10			1.35	0.73
	(20)			(86)	(11)
Childless couples:		1.82	1.21	0.30	
		(11)	(29)	(10)	

Organizational companionship declines to a low ebb when the wife
has only preschoolers on her hands—partly because she must baby-
sit at home, partly because the children themselves require little organizational activity. The latter notion is implied in rising organizational participation in the grade school and high school segments of
the cycle. The peak is hardly more than one organization per couple
on the average—often such a youth-serving organization as the P.T.A.
Nevertheless, it reflects the ability of the wife to move out of the
home into evening activities again once the children can be responsible
for themselves in the evening.

There is one form of companionship which childlessness does not
promote, namely informative companionship (see Table 72). Although the novelty factor wears off during the first three years of

Table 72

Informative Companionship, by Stage in Family-life Cycle

MEAN INFORMATIVE COMPANIONSHIP		Preschool	Preadolescent	Adolescent	Unlaunched	Honeymoon	Postparental	Retired
		STAGE IN FAMILY-LIFE CYCLE						
Childbearing stages:		3.19 (129)	3.10 (138)	3.15 (98)	2.45 (60)			
Childless stages:	Honeymoon					3.60 (20)	2.77 (86)	2.00 (7)
Childless couples:		2.91 (11)	3.17 (29)	3.20 (10)				

marriage, fathers of preschool children tell their wives more than non-fathers married the same length of time. Perhaps young housewives are especially eager to hear about the outside world they left behind for child-rearing. Undoubtedly these new mothers have far more to tell their husbands each evening than wives who have undergone no new role transition since marriage.

Informative companionship therefore is partly stimulated by role differentiation. The separation of the partners' lives gives a special incentive to listen to the other's story in order to participate vicariously in another world of activity. Children interfere relatively little with such conversation within the family in comparison to the impediments they present to social activity outside the home.

Table 73

Colleague Companionship, by Stage in Family-life Cycle

MEAN COLLEAGUE COMPANIONSHIP		Preschool	Preadolescent	Adolescent	Unlaunched	Honeymoon	Postparental	Retired
		STAGE IN FAMILY-LIFE CYCLE						
Childbearing stages:		1.20 (130)	1.44 (139)	1.10 (101)	0.84 (63)			
Childless stages:	Honeymoon					0.84 (19)	0.99 (88)	0.55 (11)
Childless couples:		1.45 (11)	1.45 (29)	1.30 (10)				

Getting together with work-mates is less hampered by babies than organizational participation, especially if children can be brought along, even more when it involves entertaining other couples at home. This total-family or home-based companionship rises during the pre-school stage and crests in the preadolescent stage of the family-life cycle. Perhaps many family picnics of the Golden Age are two-family affairs with relatives and friends.

Table 74

Friendship Companionship, by Stage in Family-life Cycle

MEAN FRIENDSHIP COMPANIONSHIP		STAGE IN FAMILY-LIFE CYCLE					
Childbearing stages:		Preschool	Preadolescent	Adolescent	Unlaunched		
		2.32	2.24	2.38	2.17		
		(129)	(140)	(101)	(66)		
Childless stages:	Honeymoon					Postparental	Retired
	1.68					2.42	2.64
	(19)					(88)	(11)
Childless couples:		2.73	2.45	2.80			
		(11)	(29)	(10)			

Friendship companionship is the only type which rises throughout the life cycle. This reflects partly the gradual introduction of the wife to the husband's friends, but also the gradual restriction of the husband's associates to a narrower circle whom the wife can more easily encompass. "Friendship companionship" is therefore a poor measure of the absolute number of shared friendship which the wife experiences. This explains why it can run counter to the general tendency of companionship to decline with the passing years.

Satisfaction with the husband's companionship declines to its lowest ebb in unlaunched families. To some extent, this is the culmination of long-term trends: familiarization with one another sometimes to the point of boredom, decreasing energy with the passing years, resignation to frustrated mobility aspirations which means the wife is no longer a partner in helping the husband get ahead. But there must be factors more specifically associated with having grown children in the home. Does the mother find actual companionship with her children instead of with the husband? Or does she vicariously relive her own youth through their dating experiences? Does the father feel threatened by his strong young sons and his daughters' dates? Or feel neglected and turn outside the family for solace? Whatever the causes, this is clearly the period when the estrangement of husband and wife is most complete.

Against this background, what happens after the children leave home gains special interest. Though postparental couples participate more actively than parents of unlaunched children in all four types of companionship (Tables 71–74), they rarely equal and never exceed the adolescent childrearing stage. Why, then, does postparental satisfaction with companionship increase, especially among those whose children have recently left home? Our guess is that pure dating companionship (going out together just for a good time) does increase right after that last child departs. If so, there may be such a thing as a second honeymoon where couples recapture the unmitigated companionship which has been difficult ever since the children arrived. Now winter vacations in Florida become possible and travel may be taken up with renewed enthusiasm. The home may have its emptiness but it also has a freedom comparable only to the freedom of young childless couples—freedom to do what you want to when you want to, without having to cope with baby-sitters, chauffeuring schedules, and other conflicting responsibilities.

Like the first honeymoon, the second one has its early glow and then subsides. As old age comes on, the husband and wife may not do much apart from each other but neither do they have the energy to do much together. The wife may know more of her husband's friends than ever but she sees them less often. Satisfaction with companionship tapers off again since companionship is defined as *doing things* with the husband. Since women retain their vitality longer than men, it may be that husbands feel that this activity is quite adequate but the wife is not ready to give up as fast as he. However, it should be remembered that these are marginal trends which are being discussed. Even at low ebb, a majority of wives are still satisfied. And in old age it is not so much complaints which are voiced as resignation to a can't-complain level. In any case, companionship in marriage does have at least the possibility of a secondary upswing at the beginning of the postparental stage to offset the long term decline which comes with the passing years.

Salience

Old families differ from young families. But not all old families are uncompanionable, nor all young ones enthusiastic. Some people value companionship more than others of the same age. If ranking companionship high among the valuable aspects of marriage is an indication of this, not all types of companionship are equally salient. Wives who value companionship highly belong to more organizations with their husbands and make better listeners (at least their husbands tell them about work events more often). But the most getting together with work-mates is done by couples who rank companionship second rather than first. Whether the wife happens to know more than half of the husband's friends is hardly associated with companionship rank at all.

Homogamy

Religious wives tend to rank companionship especially high, the more so if their husbands fail to go to church as often as they do. By contrast, wives who don't go to church as often as their husbands are uniquely apt to omit companionship from their three choices—perhaps if they valued companionship more, they would make more of a point of going to church with him. Valuing companionship apparently doesn't prevent a woman from marrying someone of another faith, but it usually produces equality of religious participation or of nonparticipation by the two partners.

Mixed marriages consist of two quite divergent categories—those with equal versus those with unequal church attendance. Mixed couples who go to church equally seldom rank companionship very high. Conversely, if one partner to a mixed marriage goes to church

Table 75

Satisfaction with Companionship, by Religious Homogamy

	CHURCH PREFERENCE AND ATTENDANCE				
	SAME CHURCH			DIFFERENT CHURCH	
	Husband more	Equal	Wife more	Equal	Unequal
Wife's mean satisfaction with companionship	3.93	3.99	3.70	3.61	3.52
Number of families	14	355	79	66	76

but the other doesn't, companionship is ranked quite low. In the religious area, the latter marriages have the least companionship since they share neither a common faith nor a common degree of interest.

Table 75 shows how religious homogamy conditions companionship or perhaps is a form of companionship. The more homogamous the marriage, the more satisfied the wife is with marital companionship generally.[3] Belonging to the same church contributes to a sense of joint participation more than an identical frequency of attending, but among unmixed marriages as among mixed marriages, similar frequency yields greater satisfaction.

Satisfaction declines as the degree of religious mixing increases. Where both partners grew up in the same church, the wife's satisfaction is highest (3.90), declining to 3.78 where the partners came from two different Protestant churches, and to 3.64 where one partner was brought up Catholic and the other was not. The satisfaction scores of mixed marriages in Table 75 are even lower because these refer to continuing religious differences between husband and wife, not just to differences in the way they were brought up.

It has often been suggested that mixed marriages work better if only one partner is devout and the other has largely abandoned his faith and become indifferent. However, this does not appear to be true as far as feelings of companionship are concerned. The two categories of mixed marriages in Table 75 differ considerably in the frequency with which the wife goes to church. The equal frequency group contains an unusually large proportion of couples (29 per cent) who never go to church, suggesting that the wife may have sacrificed attending church for the sake of equality. The husband apparently makes this up to her by going out of his way to provide other forms of companionship. By contrast, wives who continue going to a different church appear to retain their faith at the expense of companionship. In both cases, differential religious affiliation creates a barrier to complete companionship which compensatory efforts in other leisure-time activities only partially overcome.

Religious homogamy, then, provides a basis for companionship,

---

3. Perhaps the comparative frequency of church attendance is a form of companionship subject to the individual's voluntary control, but since church affiliation is usually a product of childhood socialization, it is more of an *a priori* condition affecting the possibility or impossibility of companionship.

doubly so if the partners not only belong to the same church but go to it together. Homogamy in irreligiosity, however, is a negative affair, a lack of going to church together which adds less to the feeling of companionship. Where differential attendance exists, the partner who feels the loss the most is the one who is active alone, not the one who stays home alone. Stay-at-home wives do not sense a loss of the husband's companionship nearly as much as wives who go to church while the husband sleeps, golfs, or reads the Sunday paper. The norm governing church participation requires joint attendance, so the attending partner is the one who feels deprived of companionship.

Age Compatibility. If homogamy in religious backgrounds creates a feeling of companionship, what about homogamy in other respects? This depends on the extent to which the characteristic affects the present life of the couple. For instance, differences in family occupational backgrounds affect satisfaction with companionship relatively little. Similarly, differences in age must be rather substantial before they create a barrier to companionship. Where the husband is much older than the wife (ten years or more), there is a slight decline in her satisfaction with companionship, but a larger drop (to 2.81) occurs where the husband is appreciably her junior (four or more years younger). These are the same husbands who provide an unsatisfactory standard of living for their wives. Perhaps for the same reason (i.e. passive dependency), they aren't good companions either. Few of these husbands give informative companionship to their wives, perhaps because they're not very proud of their occupational achievements. (Downward mobile husbands similarly are conspicuously apt never to tell their wives about work events and never to visit workmates). On the other hand, these over-mothered husbands may duck out of the home to find more satisfying companionship elsewhere.

Table 76

Satisfaction with Companionship, by Comparative Education of Husband and Wife

	COMPARATIVE EDUCATION		
	Wife more	Equal	Husband more
Wife's mean satisfaction with companionship	3.76	4.01	3.81
Number of families	185	189	217

Many of their wives complain that they know few or none of the husband's friends.

Educational Similarity. Educational differences interfere with companionship more consistently than age differences. Even a one- or two-year difference in education creates a marked decline in satisfaction. Educationally homogamous families include remarkably few wives who feel shut out completely from the husband's friends and correspondingly many who fit the norm of knowing most of his friends.

Where differences in education exist (as with religion), it is the wife with more interest who feels most deprived because the husband is unable to keep up with her. Wives who have been to school without their husbands regret his inadequacies.

By contrast, wives who marry men from a higher occupational background are extra satisfied with his companionship. Perhaps if we were to ask the husband, the reverse would be true. Women who marry up provide their husbands with power and a feeling of superiority which he may appreciate, but power and companionship may be somewhat difficult to maintain in the same husband-wife relationship.

Equality

Power tends to decrease companionship because it creates psychological distance between the partners. On the other hand, mere equality between the partners is not enough if it involves separate-but-equal decision-making. Companionship consists in doing things together. Hence, it is related to sharing in decision-making, not simply to the absence of inequality in power. Table 78 shows how satisfaction with companionship is geared to the number of joint decisions in marriage.

Table 77

Satisfaction with Companionship, by Sharing in Decision-making

	NUMBER OF SHARED DECISIONS		
	0–2	3–5	6–8
Wife's mean satisfaction with companionship	3.68	3.96	4.26
Number of families	218	266	60

In one sense, shared decision-making is a kind of companionship in itself. To sit down and talk over problems is to do something together. More importantly, perhaps, to arrive at mutual decisions is to be sure that both partners' wishes are taken into consideration. When leisure-time activities are planned jointly, they are most likely to please both partners.

The differences in Table 77 affect primarily the extreme cases. Where nearly all decisions are made jointly, dissatisfaction with companionship is almost nonexistent and enthusiasm extremely common. At the other extreme, unilateral decision-making is not quite so strongly associated with dissatisfaction. It is possible but not usual for a couple to share leisure and not share power.

As might be expected, sharing in decision-making correlates especially closely with informative companionship, since both involve communication. Couples who share power also tend to belong to the same organizations. But sharing power fits in with only a moderate level of colleague companionship, and many wives who share decisions know as few as half of the husband's friends.

Table 78

Companionship Intensities and Satisfaction, by Nature of
Wife's Economic Role

MEAN INTENSITY OF COMPANIONSHIP	WIFE'S ECONOMIC ROLE*			
	Hostess-Companion	Collaborator	Working Wife	Residual
Organizational	1.43	1.29	1.18	0.78
Informative	3.42	3.30	3.05	2.96
Colleague	1.12	1.12	1.03	0.94
Friendship	2.57	2.65	2.32	2.25
Wife's mean satisfaction with companionship	4.26	4.05	3.97	3.79
Number of families	56	52	149	502

* These categories are not mutually exclusive in all cases but reveal an interesting pattern. The working wives consist of all those who are actually working outside the home, some of whom may be collaborating with their husbands. Hostess-companions, collaborators, and the residual wives are defined by their answers to the question, "How do you help your husband get along in his work?" These three categories are exclusive divisions of the entire urban sample.

Economic Co-operation

Shared earnings are also conducive to a sense of companionship (see Table 78). It is interesting to note that working wives not only leave home for jobs but also belong to a substantial number of organizations with their husbands. Yet it is not the working wives who find the most companionship as a total group. They are exceeded in enthusiasm by wives who collaborate with the husband in his work and even more by wives who help the husband get ahead by entertaining clients, acting friendly to business associates, and understanding his business problems.

The latter activities were grouped together as *a priori* companionable ones which show that companionship in marriage can be found within the framework of the traditional division of labor. That is, a wife does not have to go to work or participate directly in her husband's business in order to achieve a high sense of companionship with him.

These "home-based" companionable wives receive unusually regular reports of work-events from their husbands and join their husbands in extensive organizational companionship after working hours. Wives who work in the family enterprise, on the other hand, are understandably more apt to know all the husband's friends and to get together frequently with their mutual colleagues. Home-based companions are particularly apt to know many (but not all) of the husband's friends and do their entertaining at more judicious intervals than every week.

Rural Collaboration. Farm wives are a prime example of collaborative wives but their situation is affected by special characteristics of the farm. For instance, colleague companionship is low (0.59), because most farmers work alone or utilize only neighbors or relatives as colleagues. Knowledge of the husband's friends is reciprocally high for the same reason (2.95). The isolation of the farmer and his wife from other human contact may account for the very high level of informative communication between husband and wife (3.58). If they don't talk to each other, they won't have anyone to talk to. (Urban collaborative wives frequently deal with customers and other employees.) Organizational participation similarly is high, because informal social contacts are rare, making organized excuses for getting together more imperative. The over-all satisfaction of farm wives is depressed (3.79) by the fact that they average ten years older than city wives. Matched on age, their satisfaction with companionship would probably equal that of urban collaborative wives. Farm wives necessarily have a different pattern of companionship from urban collaborative wives but it adds up to similar satisfaction.

From the standpoint of the wife's economic role, then, a hierarchy of bases for companionship can be erected. Lowest of all is the wife who "sticks to her knitting" while the husband is absorbed in his own business. This traditional-type marriage involves relatively little companionship.

If the wife goes to work, she usually experiences more shared decision-making, shared household tasks, and shared leisure-time activities. But her work partly separates her from her husband.

By contrast, the wife who works directly with the husband shares especially fully in work-oriented types of companionship. But a family business sometimes consumes so much time that it gets in the way of leisure-time companionship. So the wife who finds the most companionship in marriage is the one who concentrates on entertaining and organizational activity. This is the wife who most often and most enjoyably finds the modern type of husband-wife companionship: recreational togetherness.

Leisure Time

Male roles vary, too. Husbands who work overtime are often too busy to find time for much organizational activity with their wives. On the other hand, overtime husbands whose wives stay home all day are particularly companionable in telling about work events. They also manage to get together with work-mates more than other husbands, with the result that their wives know more of their friends. In general, these overtime husbands appear to be a particularly work-involved group of men.

In similar fashion, husbands with mobility aspirations tell their wives more about work events than nonmobile husbands, although not as much more as might be expected. Whether the partners want to get together with colleagues depends a good deal on the type of mobility desired. Those hoping to be promoted visit most often, while those who want to get away from their work-mates and become independent entrepreneurs have correspondingly little to do with them in their leisure time.

Organizational Men. Many of these differences are due not so much to the occupational goal as to the husband's present occupational framework. Colleague-companionship, for example, is primarily a white-collar-bureaucratic type of activity—especially at moderate frequencies. These captive professionals and executives differ most from other families in the rarity with which they *never* get together with work-mates (only 25 per cent compared to 43 per cent of all others). These bureaucrats reflect the stress on getting along with colleagues which characterizes the "organization man" (Whyte, 1957). Within this group, the most intensive getting together with work-mates (at least once a week) involves top executives rather than management personnel as a whole.[4]

Table 79

Companionship Intensities and Satisfaction, by Husband's Occupation

MEAN INTENSITY OF COMPANIONSHIP	HUSBAND'S OCCUPATION			
	BLUE COLLAR		WHITE COLLAR	
	Low	High	Low	High
Organizational	0.60	0.77	1.00	1.18
Informative	3.09	2.78	3.03	3.21
Colleague	1.38	1.54	1.60	2.09
Friendship	2.01	2.31	2.37	2.64
Wife's mean satisfaction with companionship	3.81	3.81	3.92	3.87
Minimum number of families	170	170	87	161

Telling his wife what goes on in the business, on the other hand, is more characteristic of junior executives than of the head man. Fifty-five per cent of total management personnel always provide feedback to their wives, but only 36 per cent of the top executives are this regular, showing an "almost everyday" pattern instead. Could they be too busy to talk to their wives?

---

4. Data are available in this study for an adequate number of heads of small businesses (with less than 100 employees). Presumably, colleague visiting characterizes heads of large businesses as much or more.

The chief differences in Table 79 in intensity of companionship are between high-white-collar occupations and all others. High-status jobs involve so much responsibility and variety that they provide more news for the wife. In addition, off-hours contact with work-mates pays off financially and promotion-wise at this occupational level—hence the frequency of getting together with colleagues. How-ever, job-oriented visiting should not be attributed to mercenary mo-tives alone. Top occupational personnel have such specialized occupa-tional roles that congenial companions are apt to be found only within their select group. Where almost any neighbor will do for a factory worker, specialists tend to be choosier and may go long distances for leisure-time companionship.

At the same time, business and professional men are more apt to take their wives with them in leisure-time activities of various sorts, with the result that their wives know most of their friends quite well. This acquaintance is gained partly while entertaining in the home, and partly through joint activities elsewhere. In general, co-educa-tional leisure-time patterns characterize high-status marriages whereas sex-segregated patterns are found especially in low-blue-collar mar-riages.

Busy Businessmen. In view of the fact that all four types of com-panionship reach their highest level in high-white-collar families, it is surprising to find that over-all satisfaction with companionship de-clines slightly in this stratum. This may be due to the fact that these four types of companionship tend to be occupationally-relevant. Probably more frivolous, pure-enjoyment types of companionship are neglected by these husbands.

Such neglect seems to be especially common among success-ori-ented husbands (the same husbands who are least available to help around the house with household tasks). One symptom of this is the fact that men who have moved ahead of their fathers occupationally make less satisfying companions than non-mobile husbands. Simi-larly, high-income husbands (especially in the $7,000 to $10,000 bracket) have conspicuously dissatisfied wives (see Table 80). Ap-parently these husbands are so tied up with their occupations that they are too busy both for housework and for leisure-time companionship.

Since satisfaction always depends on how the husband's actual behavior measures up to the wife's expectations, it may be that higher

Table 80

Companionship Intensities and Satisfaction, by Husband's Income

MEAN INTENSITY OF COMPANIONSHIP	HUSBAND'S INCOME				
	Under $3,000	$3,000 –4,999	$5,000 –6,999	$7,000 –9,999	$10,000+
Organizational	0.38	0.61	0.94	1.11	1.77
Informative	2.89	3.31	3.11	2.89	3.08
Colleague	1.09	1.42	1.85	1.78	2.18
Friendship	2.44	2.11	2.29	2.36	2.82
Wife's mean satisfaction with companionship	3.67	3.94	3.93	3.69	3.87
Minimum number of families	59	177	194	87	56

expectations also make wives in this next-to-the-top income bracket more dissatisfied. If such wives expect as much companionship as top-income husbands give, their husbands don't show up very well in comparison. Since these are often upward-mobile families, conflicts emerge between the husband's involvement in occupational advancement and the wife's desire to have more companionship from him. Table 80 suggests that earning money and being a good companion are partially incompatible roles for the husband, depending on how hard he has to work for the money.

Table 81

Companionship Intensities and Satisfaction, by Wife's Education

MEAN INTENSITY OF COMPANIONSHIP	WIFE'S EDUCATION		
	Grade School	High School	College
Organizational	0.34	0.87	1.70
Informative	2.76	3.10	3.15
Colleague	1.15	1.82	2.22
Friendship	2.38	2.39	2.41
Wife's mean satisfaction with companionship	3.72	3.86	4.21
Minimum number of families	141	386	62

The Good Life. Income rolls in most easily for men who have inherited high-family position in the community, sometimes along with ancestral wealth. It also comes to those who have been well educated. For such reasons, more education is not associated with the ambivalences about companionship that often occur when high income is secured the hard way (see Table 81). College-educated wives —who are usually married to college-educated husbands—experience not only more of every kind of companionship but also are more satisfied with the husband's over-all leisure activities with her. Indeed their satisfaction far exceeds that of any occupational or income category of wives.

Where college education and superior family background occur in combination, top occupations and incomes usually follow, too. These indices combine in the Social Status Index to produce high satisfaction with companionship in the top-ranking group (see Table 82). However, the next to the top social-status group is relatively dissatisfied because it contains many upward mobile husbands who are striving to get ahead at the expense of companionship with their wives. Typical of this group would be a self-made businessman who works long hours at his managerial responsibilities to earn $7,000 to $10,-000 a year—self-made in the sense that he comes of lower-prestige ethnic stock and never had a chance to go to college. The previous chapter suggests that his efforts may pay off in a better life for his children than he has known himself—and that they may enjoy more marital companionship than he can afford to steal from the business.

Table 82

Companionship Intensities and Satisfaction, by Social Status

MEAN INTENSITY OF COMPANIONSHIP	PERCENTILE RANKING ON SOCIAL STATUS INDEX				
	0–19	20–39	40–59	60–79	80–99
Organizational	0.33	0.50	0.73	0.92	1.47
Informative	2.79	2.81	3.07	3.05	3.07
Colleague	1.48	1.42	1.66	1.72	2.26
Friendship	1.83	2.08	2.30	2.30	2.70
Wife's mean satisfaction with companionship	3.40	3.82	3.92	3.77	4.02
Number of families	18	99	215	191	95

To be a good companion after marriage doesn't cost much money (indeed it may cost less than dating during courtship!) Perhaps this helps to explain why Negro wives, though seldom enthusiastic, are not as far below white wives in their satisfaction with companionship as they are with respect to their standard of living. With a mean of

3.51, they exceed the lowest-status white couples shown in Table 82. Moreover, extreme dissatisfaction is more common in $7,000–$10,000 income white wives than among Negro wives generally.

This is not to say that Negro marriages achieve a great deal in absolute terms when it comes to companionship but that they suffer less extreme deprivation here than in most areas of life. At least, a good many Negro wives say they are quite satisfied in this area.

Commuting Time. A suburb's intensified separation of the occupational and residential spheres of life interferes with the ability of the wife to know all her husband's friends. On the other hand, it increases the likelihood that the husband will report his far-away adventures when he returns from the daily expedition to work. The suburban wife's satisfaction with companionship tends to suffer, however, under the stress of commuting time and geographical separation which create some sense of being cut off from the husband.

Urbanity

Of all the wives living in the Detroit metropolitan area, those who find the most satisfaction in doing things together with their husbands live in the central part of the city nearest to the bright lights. Most satisfied, too, are couples who were city born and city bred— presumably they know their way around in the maze of city affairs.

The dissatisfaction of migrants from small towns and Northern farms is countered by unusually extensive participation in organizations. This appears to be a carry-over of the farm wife's need for organizational contacts and the town resident's sense of involvement in local affairs. By contrast, the native Detroiter seems to be the true "mass man," unmoved by organizational efforts but participating in urban recreational facilities. Immigrants from abroad, on the other hand, have little companionship of any type. Presumably, this reflects the advanced years of most Detroit Poles and Italians.

COMPANIONSHIP BETWEEN HUSBANDS AND WIVES

Companionship has emerged as the most valued aspect of American marriage today. In this sense, the family has undergone a transition "from institution to companionship" (Burgess and Locke, 1953). But what is meant by companionship is not necessarily what some- times comes to mind. The primary emphasis is on companionship in leisure-time activities, not on merging every aspect of married life. In this respect, a wife can be enthusiastic about companionship even though she stays home while her husband goes to work, does most of the housework without his help, and in general plays a quite different role in life. In other words men and women don't have to be identical in order to have a good time together.

On the other hand, couples must take time to do things together if companionship is to exist. Such time is short if the husband works overtime, if he is obsessed with getting ahead in life, and if the wife is tied down with a large number of children.

Just having time available to spend is not enough. The enjoyment of leisure is heightened by education which may enlarge one's sphere of appreciation in life. Similarity in education provides the two part- ners with a common outlook on life, and common tastes for leisure- time activities. Similarity in religion furnishes an important leisure- time activity in itself—going to church together. Moreover, most churches are the focus of a host of auxiliary activities which provide companionship to joint members which is lacking in interfaith mar- riages.

Even with similar tastes and common backgrounds, however, companionship is not universal. Primarily it is characteristic of young couples, but even more so of newlyweds, regardless of age. This may be because companionship in marriage carries over from premarital dating. Indeed, Englishmen sometimes refer to marital companionship itself as dating, though the term sounds a bit strange to American ears. Couples discover each other through dating and look forward to the sense of mutual acceptance and response gained in dating situa- tions. Their appreciation of each other's company reaches a peak in the honeymoon—a time of pure companionship. In subsequent years, satisfaction declines as the two partners come to take each other for granted, to deplete the stock of new experiences which they can share together, to find companionship vicariously in children repeating the cycle of romance—or even less directly in TV.

The ebb tide of companionship can be reversed in second honey- moons when the kids depart, and in second honeymoons when people remarry. This is one reason why some couples divorce—because leisure together has lost its kick—and why second marriages, too, sometimes end in boredom.

However, these are tendencies, not iron laws. As life's end approaches, one wife in four is still enthusiastic about the companionship she finds in marriage and a second is still quite satisfied. For the individual couple, companionship doesn't have to lose its savor. But for American marriages as a whole, the trend is unmistakable: during the childrearing years, husbands and wives often cease doing things together, and grow apart from each other. When they are left with only each other again for company, their losses are only partially recouped. For many couples, the estrangement is permanent and the second opportunity comes too late to catch fire. Such couples live the later years as relative strangers under the same roof, searching elsewhere for companionship or resigned to a life of increasing loneliness.

This is the loneliness that marriage is designed to prevent. This is the need that companionship is supposed to meet. Companionship is above all what marriage is supposed to provide—but the wedding ceremony does not guarantee it. Companionship is available for the taking—for all except the most badly mismatched couples. But companionship requires taking time and making a little effort. Most couples do—but not all.

CHAPTER

7

UNDERSTANDING AND
EMOTIONAL WELL-BEING

HOW DO YOU FEEL about the understanding you get of your problems and feelings? The way a woman answers this question shows what her husband is contributing to her emotional well-being. The purpose of this chapter is to discover how marriage contributes to the mental health of the participants, especially of the wife.[1]

This "mental-hygiene" function of marriage seldom appears in the standardized lists of family functions. Sometimes a term like "emotional security" is mentioned, usually referring to something parents give their children rather than an exchange between husband and wife.

To a considerable extent, therefore, mental hygiene is what sociologists call a "latent" function of marriage, i.e., one which people are seldom aware of, even though it exists, one which they don't consciously perform, but which occurs nevertheless.

---

1. It would be equally desirable to study the wife's contribution to the husband's mental health. The most relevant data in this book involves the wives discussed in Chapter Four who help their husbands get ahead through providing emotional support, understanding and encouragement. However, the context of that chapter is different, and fuller information must await other studies.

175

It is also an emerging function of marriage, since concern for mental hygiene is new in the life of the world. The more dramatic forms of mental illness have plagued the earth for eons and mobilized the services of witch doctors, shamans, and their successors. But mental hygiene is concerned not so much with the cure of mental illness as with its prevention. It involves the emotional well-being of everyday people. To this end, mental-hygiene lectures are given in schools, educational movies shown, and child-study classes held. To this end, earnest parents strive to love their children so that they will be emotionally secure.

Frustration and Recuperation

The creation of mental well-being does not end with graduation from school nor with launching from home base. Adults have emotional needs, too. They have emotional problems to be solved. What sort of needs and problems? Needs for acceptance as a person, for a sense of belonging, for knowing someone understands how they feel, for sympathy and empathy.

The emotional problems of everyday living often stem from frustration. A businessman goes in the red, a worker loses his job or fails to get the expected promotion, a baseball game is washed out by rain, a cake falls in the oven, the kids act up in church. The list is endless of humiliating, embarrassing situations which may overwhelm an individual and "get him down."

It's bad enough when these circumstances are outside one's control—like rain on the Fourth of July. Hardest to take are the difficulties which are of one's own making—the frustrations caused by personal inadequacy. These are depressing occurrences because they threaten the basic foundations of self-confidence by undermining the conception of the self.

Another word for the self is the ego. The ego is that aspect of the personality which constitutes the sense of self. Its function is to mobilize and direct the activity of the individual. Where the ego is weak, passivity or even paralysis ensues as the person finds it difficult to act. Some adults have stronger egos than others—derived from their childhood experiences. But the ego of every normal adult is subject to change, is affected by new experiences. The problem facing the individual is to cope with experiences which are ego-threatening and to find ones which are ego-enhancing.

Every individual needs to see himself as somehow adequate to the demands of life. If not, he may be able to plunge doggedly ahead for a while, but eventually he will falter, pull his head back into his shell, or even commit suicide. How can a man face the world if he cannot face himself? How can he face himself if the world seems against him, if the boss says he's no good, if he fumbles the ball every time it is passed to him?

What can restore his shattered self-confidence?

Psychologists have concluded that self-confidence is created in the first place not simply by the achievement of goals but by the approval of others. It is not enough to be able to jump five feet if the audience considers nothing short of six satisfactory. Standards of achievement do not originate in ourselves but in the expectations of others. Nor are standards fixed and immutable. One solution to frustrated ambitions is diminished expectations for ourselves. Lowering one's sights, however, accentuates the humiliation of defeat unless accompanied by new definitions from the environment—or by definitions from new persons in the environment.

Sometimes self-confidence can be restored if only someone else will say he knows that we can do the job. Perhaps he will reinterpret our defeat as only a temporary setback to be overcome by renewed effort—"if at first you don't succeed. . . ."

This doesn't always work. Everyone has limits. When they are reached, it will only intensify the disappointment to continue to expect success. Then the only avenue to peace of mind is acceptance, resignation, acquiescence.

Either way out of defeat—confidence in the new possibilities of the future or acceptance of the worthwhileness of the present—depends on the attitude of "significant others." Those are the people whose opinions matter most to us. If this "board of judges" agrees that we have been a success, there is no problem. If they feel unanimously that we have failed, there is no solace. But if they are divided, then the encouragement of some (perhaps of only one) may offset the discouragement of the rest.

If the boss thinks a man is expendable, what about his wife? Does she agree, plunging him into deeper gloom? Or does she see in him values the boss overlooked or qualities which don't matter on the job —assets which, if appreciated, will help her husband realize he is not a total failure and that someone cares for him.

If she has a bad day when everything seems to have gone wrong, does he make matters worse by blaming, critizing, I-told-you-so-ing, or does he find ways of restoring her morale?

Clearly the "marriage partner" is a "significant other" person. One reason people marry in the first place is the fact that they find each other's company rewarding. Rewards come not simply in good times together but in mutual acceptance, appreciation, and confidence.

Just how significant the spouse is depends partly on the issue at hand. If the husband's frustration reflects a technical area the wife knows nothing about, it is harder for her to bolster his confidence than in an area she understands. Nevertheless, any wife can appreciate her husband as a father, a sexual partner, a good companion, or whatever his domestic strong points are. She can appreciate such talents even if she can't appraise his technical competence. Even there she can assess the intelligence, the ambition, and the effort which he devotes to the task.

The Patriarchal Tradition. Past American tradition provided a limited place for such emotional support. A patriarchal family system inherently requires faith in the abilities of the patriarch because the family is expected to depend on his competencies. Yet the patriarch is not really expected to rely upon his wife's support for emotional sustenance. A real he-man (pioneers are all supposed to be he-men) does not depend on petticoat encouragement. He gets it—to be sure—but only because it is his due, not because he needs it.

As long as things go well, this arrangement is fine. But what good is compulsory confidence when one has just met defeat? Doesn't the naive confidence of dependent loved ones intensify the agony? This audience which expected to applaud is now baffled into silence by the failure of the leading man. How difficult it is for the patriarch to admit defeat to those he loves! Patriarchs aren't supposed to have problems (so they tend to deny their existence even from themselves, to say nothing of their loved ones). Faced with problems, they are supposed to be able to solve them on their own, or else suffer them out in heroic silence.

Within this tradition stood the legendary Spartan soldier, uttering no cry while the fox within his tunic devoured his innards. Bravery, courage, fortitude, stamina—these badges of an inner-directed civilization extolled the merits of the man who met trouble magnificently alone (Riesman, 1954). To cry out, to appeal for help, to turn to the weaker sex in time of trouble would be disgraceful, adding shame to defeat.

In the patriarchal family, the expectations of the community plus the status of the husband prevented him from turning to his wife for real assistance in time of ego-need. Were he to do so in private, he could escape community opprobrium but not the accusations of his own superego. Moreover, what help could be expected of a wife accustomed to being a clinging vine?

To reverse the viewpoint, however, the American tradition also contained barriers to the reliance of the wife on the husband for help with emotional problems. Her right to have problems was fully accepted—for the weaker sex was by definition subject to limitations. To cry was an acceptable symbol of her inability to cope with difficulties, and the appropriate place for crying was on her husband's brawny shoulder.

Yet the difference between a good wife and a troublesome wife was whether she "bothered" her husband. The Puritan tradition in American Protestantism valued the self-sufficient ego—male or female. The expression of weakness to the husband was a form of self-indulgence akin to self-pity and equally sinful in the sight of God. The ideal woman was a stalwart mother who coped with the problems of her brood on her own, giving her mate no cause to worry about her sphere of things.

After all, he was too busy to be bothered. The previous chapter recalled the lack of leisure under pioneer conditions. Is it more important for a husband to save his family from starving or to listen to his wife's woes? Mental hygiene is a luxury which few societies in the past have been able to afford. Pioneer America wasn't one of them.

The Modern Attitude. Today's climate of opinion is different. One hundred years of psychology have altered our view of emotional problems. Something of the cost of silent suffering is now appreciated—the cost in unhappiness, immobilization, and sometimes insanity. We are more aware of what goes on behind the mask of simulated adequacy, what goes on inside a man who tries to pretend that all is well when all is not. Such knowledge makes help more urgent.

We are more sensitive, also, to the fluctuations in life. As more is learned about individuals and groups, the complexities of human existence emerge. The ups and downs of life are more apparent than they once were—menstrual cycles in women, the temporary influence of fatigue and hunger, the sequence of frustration and aggression. This close-up view of the irregularities of life makes the admission of trouble seem less catastrophic. One can admit difficulty today without necessarily implying that all is lost. If life has innumerable downs as well as ups and other people have their troubles too, it is less embarrassing to confess a failure.

Embarrassment has diminished, too, as social psychologists have demonstrated the power of the group over the individual, making individual defeat at the hands of the group seem less avoidable than it once did. The whole emphasis on noble independence in America has weakened, giving way to "other-directedness" as a basis for guides to conduct, and to reliance on specialists for a multitude of services. Psychology has contributed not only knowledge of the difficulties people face but evidence of the difficulty of curing oneself. Psychotherapy has demonstrated how helpful it is to people in trouble to have someone else to share their burdens with. The concept of catharsis has given dignity to the notion of getting something off one's chest. Such developments make it seem easier and even desirable to unburden oneself of inner troubles.

Psychotherapy is not for everyone, nor forever. Yet it provides an analogy for the help which everyone needs with ordinary emotional problems. People need opportunities for catharsis, for ventilating their feelings, for help in interpreting their difficulties, for emotional support and encouragement. Where can such lifetime therapy-as-needed be found better than in marriage?

The changing alignment of the two sexes has eased their communication with each other. Now that husbands and wives are more nearly equals than they once were, they can experience more interdependence. Partners who consult one another about decisions smooth the way to trouble-shooting. Companionship in happiness provides a basis for sharing unhappiness, too.

To be able to help each other, certain prerequisites are needed.

For one thing, the partners cannot be the main source of difficulty for each other (else an outside counselor will be needed). More positively, they need to have a generally beneficent relationship, a background of marital strength. But advanced degrees in psychology are not necessary to understand emotional problems. So here is one of the services which modern marriages can and do provide for their members.

THE IMPORTANCE OF UNDERSTANDING IN MARRIAGE

In the past, physical problems preoccupied the energies of husbands and wives. Today, the rising standard of living and the falling work week are subordinating material concerns and enabling attention to new dimensions of married life. How much importance do contemporary women attach to the mental hygiene-function, in comparison to other new and old aspects of marriage?

In Detroit, understanding ranks a poor third after companionship and the chance to have children. However, it edges out the more traditional function of affection (leaving the standard of living last of all). In view of the fact that the world has heard about love so much longer, the mental-hygiene function has achieved surprising prominence. Perhaps the time has come when it should become a recognized part of marriage rather than a latent function of which married people are relatively unaware.

Understanding typically comes third in the Detroit popularity contest, but there is very little concensus among the women interviewed in their personal rankings. A full third see it as more important than the average group (15 per cent ranking it first; 20 per cent, second). This reflects considerable variation between different segments of the community in the amount of emphasis attached to marital understanding.

Women with Problems. In general, wives with serious problems are the ones who most want them understood. In other words, the relative importance given to this function is often a measure of felt need. Probably awareness of this aspect of marriage is most acute among wives whose need for their husband to understand their frustrations is itself frustrated.

Table 83

Relative Importance of Understanding as an Aspect of Marriage, by Race

RELATIVE IMPORTANCE OF UNDERSTANDING	RACE		
	Negro	White	Total
First choice	29%	10%	13%
Second choice	18	20	20
Third choice	26	31	30
Not chosen	27	39	37
Total	100	100	100
Number of families	114	602	716

The Negro-white contrast in Table 83 results primarily from the severity of the problems which confront the average Negro wife. So acute are those problems that she is three times as apt as a white wife to give first place to this aspect of marriage. Negro husbands fail on many counts to meet their wives' needs, but other evidence shows they do rather well on this emotional one.

Among white wives, there are two subgroups who rank understanding high because of the problems they face. One is wives who come into conflict with their husbands over personality issues, a type of disagreement which tends to cut to the quick. Fifteen per cent of them rank understanding first, compared with 8 per cent of those who disagree about as impersonal an issue as finances. Even more problem-laden is the middle-aged woman, though her high valuation of understanding also reflects alienation from her husband. Menopause, the loss of her children at launching—such factors produce 22 per cent first choices among women in their fifties—far more than the mere 4 per cent among confident young women in their twenties.

As for unresponsive husbands, perhaps they are indicated in marriages which rate low on marital cohesiveness (16 per cent of these wives put understanding first compared to only 4 per cent of the wives in highly cohesive marriages). Similar differences occur between wives at the two extremes on marital satisfaction in general and on satisfaction with understanding in particular.

Women Who De-emphasize Understanding. Less apt to choose understanding as a valuable part of marriage are wives who depend on their husbands for most decisions (48 per cent of whom omit understanding completely from their three choices compared to only 33 per cent of the dominant wives). Forty-eight per cent of the wives whose husbands aspire to be promoted also omit understanding whereas only 35 per cent of the wives of men with no mobility aspirations pass this over. Partly, these are younger compared to older marriages, but they are likely also to involve they-shouldn't-be-bothered attitudes toward husbands preoccupied with more important affairs.

A quite different group which also de-emphasizes understanding is composed of working wives, 45 per cent of whom omit this item from their three choices compared to 39 per cent of non-working wives. Again, there is some bias toward a younger age group but certainly no correlation with the preceding group of unbotherable husbands. Here, perhaps, the wife's social contacts on the job decrease her dependence on her husband for sympathetic ears. If this interpretation is sound, working wives have less need, not in the sense of smaller problems but of less reliance on the husband's mental hygiene services.

To summarize, wives tend to stress the importance of husbandly understanding of their problems and feelings if their problems are more serious than usual and/or their husbands fail to deal adequately with their needs. Conversely, understanding seems relatively unimportant to wives who accept their husbands' involvement in alternative roles and to wives who have alternative resources outside the home for meeting their emotional needs.

THE MENTAL-HYGIENE ENDEAVORS OF MARRIED WOMEN

The mental-hygiene function of marriage can be understood best within the context of the total mental-health functioning of the person involved. What proportion of her emotional problems does the typical wife lay before her husband? If she doesn't utilize her husband for therapy, to what other resources does she turn?

Emotional problems come in various shapes and sizes. Presumably, the more serious the problem, the more apt the wife is to call upon her husband for help with it. The more serious the problem, the more likely he is to know about it in the first place and to be able to respond spontaneously. Most husbands probably respond if the wife loses a parent by death, is locked in conflict with a child, or the victim of uncomplimentary gossip.

But what about the little emotional crises which arise periodically? Here the daily separation of husband from wife creates a private life for the wife. Many frustrations encountered by mothers and housewives are transitory in nature and occur when the husband is not present. A broken milk bottle on the front steps, burning grease on the kitchen stove, bawling kids—if these crises occur in mid-morning, the wife will hardly phone her husband at work to unload her troubles.

Perhaps because the role of housewife cuts women off from adult contact during the day, they learn to fend for themselves emotionally as best they can. With no one at hand to hear their grievances, they develop other ways of alleviating inner tension. Confined to the home and separated from their husbands, they discover ways of "detensifying" themselves which utilize the only resources at hand—TV, reading, a hot bath, sleep.

As problems accumulate in a crisis-filled "bad day," the husband's return from work becomes more imminent and his pending availability more pertinent. Yet there are still obstacles to utilizing his therapeutic capacities. One is habit—wives who have learned to be self-reliant earlier in the day may continue to depend on their own devices. A second is the husband's own problems, preoccupations, or known incapacity to help, which discourages the wife from turning to him. A third is lack of opportunity, especially if there are children in the house. Supper tasks, childcare tasks, and "little pitchers with big ears" may block effective access to the husband. Nevertheless, a bad day is more apt to come to the husband's attention than a component problem, but less so than an enduring, recurrent problem.

Urban and Rural Resources. Such bad days are the focus of interest in this chapter. The phraseology in the questionnaire is: "Every wife has some days when things go so badly that she gets pretty tense and upset. After you've had a bad day, what do you do to get it out of your system?"

Table 84

Wife's Therapeutic Endeavor after a Bad Day, in City and Farm Families

WIFE'S THERAPEUTIC BEHAVIOR	PLACE OF RESIDENCE	
	City	Farm
Get away from house	14%	14%
Housework	9	10
Solitary distraction at home	10	11
Passive relaxation at home	23	38
Oral indulgence	2	3
Turn to religion	3	4
Positive interaction with husband	5	3
Positive interaction with others	7	6
Negative interaction with husband	3	0
Negative interaction with others	18	9
Other or N.A.	6	2
Total	100	100
Number of families	731	178

Table 84 shows how few city or farm wives mention their husbands in response to this question. A few more may actually interact with their husbands, but only 8 per cent of the city wives and 3 per cent of the farm wives specifically mention him.

It is questionable, moreover, whether city wives who name him as the target of their anger or aggression are being helped by him. More likely such husbands caused the bad day in the first place. Certainly, they are liable to react so negatively to being attacked that the wife will end up no more relaxed.

Other people are referred to about as often as the husband. Children are the target of aggression for 2 per cent of the city wives, relatives a distraction for 3 per cent, friends and neighbors turned to by 4 per cent.

Much of the generalized anger, crying, and pouting of 15 per cent of the city wives and 6 per cent of the farm wives is undoubtedly directed toward the family as an audience. Refusing to eat or to talk is meaningful only in the presence of "significant others" who can receive the message that the wife has had a bad day, is upset and disturbed, wants sympathy or relief from the pressure upon her.

Somewhat analogously, turning to religion through prayer may be thought of as utilizing an audience or resource outside the self.

When positive interaction, negative interaction, and religion are added together, hardly more than a third of the city wives and even fewer farm wives normally turn outside themselves for assistance. When listing more than one therapeutic endeavor, only 3 per cent more urban wives (and no more farm wives) mention their husbands as a secondary resource and less than 1 per cent as a tertiary one.

Clearly, most housewives cope with bad days on their own. Their most characteristic device is to go to bed early, to sit down and relax, or just try to forget about their troubles. Reading and TV are common distractions at home, going for a walk the favorite way of getting out of the house.

Such activities (or inactivities) reflect the housewife's lack of meaningful alternatives at home. From one point of view, they sound like escaping from the problem rather than solving it. But bad days often reflect the pressures of living with children, so withdrawing from the stimulus situation may at least temporarily relieve the problem.

The Rarely Mentioned Husbands

In this pattern of therapeutic endeavors, the husband does not seem to be a very salient resource. Nevertheless, it will be useful to learn which wives do turn to him under these circumstances.[2]

Status Differences. In many respects, positive interaction and negative interaction with the husband characterize opposite groups of people. For instance, talking and doing things with the husband tend to be characteristic of high-status people, whereas low-status wives more often confess that they take out their feelings angrily or aggressively against their husbands. Middle-class children learn to inhibit and control their aggressiveness toward the ones they love, whereas work-

---

2. The striking differences between the urban tendency to express tension and the rural tendency to passive relaxation (sitting down or going to bed) are tangential to the present concern with husband-wife relationships; they will be discussed in detail in a companion volume, to be published by The Free Press under the tentative title, *Friends and Relations.* Significant differences also exist between religious groups and ethnic groups, suggesting that this is one area where value patterns affect the wife's activity through the medium of differential socialization in childhood, i.e., some people learn to express their tensions whereas others learn to inhibit them.

Table 85

Spontaneously Mentioned Interaction with Husband after a Bad Day, by Social Status

WIVES SPONTANEOUSLY MENTIONING HUSBAND BY TYPE OF INTERACTION	PERCENTILE RANKING ON SOCIAL STATUS INDEX				
	0–19	20–39	40–59	60–79	80–99
Positive	—	4.5%	3.4%	6.5%	8.0%
Negative	7.1%	6.7	3.9	2.7	3.4
Husband not mentioned	92.9	88.8	92.7	90.8	88.6
Total	100.0	100.0	100.0	100.0	100.0
Number of families	14	89	206	186	88

ing-class children grow up in an atmosphere where anger is less restrained. Differences in childhood socialization affect not only the willingness of women to confess aggression against their husbands but also their willingness to *be* aggressive.

Differences in aggressiveness are tied most closely to the wife's ethnic background and education, since these reflect her own upbringing. The husband's occupational status and income less directly affect the wife's behavior. One exception to the general status relationship is a decline in positive interaction in high-income families, especially above $10,000. Are such husbands too occupationally preoccupied to be bothered by their wife's troubles?

In general, however, the higher the wife's social status, the more apt she is to turn explicitly to her husband for help in trouble, and the less apt she is to turn her negative feelings against him.

Table 86

Spontaneously Mentioned Interaction with Husband after a Bad Day, by Marital Decision-making Pattern

WIVES SPONTANEOUSLY MENTIONING HUSBAND BY TYPE OF INTERACTION	MARITAL DECISION-MAKING PATTERN			
	Husband-Dominant	Syncratic	Autonomic	Wife-Dominant
Positive	6.5%	6.6%	3.1%	6.1%
Negative	5.6	3.3	3.7	2.0
Husband not mentioned	87.9	90.1	93.2	91.9
Total	100.0	100.0	100.0	100.0
Number of families	124	122	191	98

Power Differences. With respect to decision-making, the relationships are interesting but not opposites. Wives who make decisions jointly with their husbands also tend to share their problems with them. But syncratic marriages are not as low on aggression toward the husband as wife-dominant marriages. Is a dependent husband not a solid enough target for aggression? The extremes of decision-making power are related to aggression in an unexpected fashion, suggesting that a dominant wife may feel she has only herself to blame when she gets into trouble, but a dependent wife can find something worth attacking in a husband who makes most of the decisions.

Working wives, incidentally, more often mention their husbands as negative targets than housewives do (7 per cent vs. 3 per cent). Part of the difference reflects the lower social status of the average working wife, but part may also express the resentment which some wives feel over having to supplement an inadequate income.

Table 87

Spontaneously Mentioned Interaction with Husband after a Bad Day, by Family-life Cycle

WIVES SPONTANEOUSLY MENTIONING HUSBAND BY TYPE OF INTERACTION		STAGE IN FAMILY-LIFE CYCLE				
Childrearing stages:		Preschool	Preadolescent	Adolescent	Unlaunched	
Positive		9.4%	4.3%	2.0%	1.6%	
Negative		2.4	5.7	—	—	
Neither		88.2	90.0	98.0	98.4	
Total		100.0	100.0	100.0	100.0	
Number		127	140	100	62	
Childless stages:	Honeymoon				Postparental	Retired
Positive	5.0%				3.5%	—
Negative	25.0				2.3	—
Neither	70.0				94.2	100.0%
Total	100.0				100.0	100.0
Number	20				86	10
Childless couples:						
Positive		9.1%	6.9%	10.0%		
Negative		9.1	10.3	—		
Neither		81.8	82.8	90.0		
Total		100.0	100.0	100.0		
Number		11	29	10		

Life-cycle Differences. The biggest differences in husband-mentioning involve the decline in husband-wife interaction with the passage of time and the interference of children. Age, number of children, and stage in life cycle are interrelated variables which show similar rather than opposite trends on positive and negative interaction. Young wives turn to their husbands unusually often both for sympathy and in anger. As time passes, and with the interposition of large numbers of children, the husband assumes a less significant role as audience, being replaced by such alternatives as God, other people, and housework. Table 87 shows the prominence of the husband-wife relationship in the absence of children.

As might be expected, wives who turn to their husbands for talk and activity after a bad day are extraordinarily enthusiastic about the husband's ability to make them feel better. Equally understandable is the tendency of aggressive wives to report that they often feel worse when the fight is over. Such wives eventually learn to curb their aggressiveness, so that by age sixty no wives any longer try to reduce tensions in this boomeranging fashion.

Naked aggression occurs chiefly among the divorce-prone working class. Therefore, an additional reason why marital aggressiveness disappears among older couples is that battling couples have often gone to the divorce judge for a peace settlement.

The number of wives who mention the husband at all after a bad day is so small that the preceding insights should be treated tentatively. Only when women are specifically asked how their husbands fit into the picture is it possible to uncover the subordinate but significant mental-hygiene role they play. As long as the wife is queried only about her own resources, the husband seldom appears among them.

THE USE OF THE HUSBAND

FOR MENTAL-HYGIENE PURPOSES

When wives are asked directly whether they ever tell their husbands their troubles on bad days, the mental-hygiene function of marriage comes into sharper focus. Even so, "husband-therapy" is utilized less than "somno-therapy" and half a dozen other devices more accessible for ordinary troubles.

Rural-urban Frequencies. Despite their comparative unimportance, husbands are called in rather often as part of the total therapeutic process. A typical Detroit husband hears about his wife's troubles about half the time. The median farm husband hears of them a shade more often, perhaps because he's in earshot more frequently.

Table 88

Therapeutic Utilization of Husband after a Bad Day, in City and Farm Families

FREQUENCY WIFE TELLS HUSBAND HER TROUBLES*	PLACE OF RESIDENCE	
	City	Farm
(4) Always	21%	22%
(3) Usually	24	31
(2) About half the time	27	21
(1) Seldom	18	18
(0) Never	10	8
Total	100	100
Mean	2.28	2.41
Number of families	731	178

* Numbers in parentheses show the weights used in computing means.

Table 88 shows that the chief rural-urban difference is the larger proportion of farm wives who "usually" tell their husbands. Both groups turn to the husband selectively, the wife choosing to tell her troubles on some occasions and keeping them to herself on others. The most unusual cases are the few who never tell; secondarily, those who always do.

Some confidence that answers to this question weren't put into the respondents' mouths by the form of the question comes from their close-relationship to spontaneously mentioned therapeutic activities (see Table 89).

Table 89 shows that wives who mention positive interaction with the husband in response to an open-ended question have an extraordinarily high frequency of telling the husband their troubles (57 per cent always tell him, none never do). Mention of the husband as a target of aggression is also associated with frequent telling (38 per

Table 89

**Therapeutic Utilization of Husband after a Bad Day, by
Wife's Preferred Therapeutic Endeavor**

	PREFERRED THERAPEUTIC ENDEAVOR						
				POSITIVE INTERACTION		NEGATIVE INTERACTION	
	SOLITARY*	HOUSEWORK	RELIGION	Husband	Others	Husband	Others
Mean frequency wife tells husband her troubles	2.17	2.20	2.06	3.26	2.40	2.81	2.49
Number of families	304	59	16	28	35	21	113

* Includes getting away from home, solitary distraction, passive relaxation, and oral indulgence.

cent always, zero never). The latter supports the idea that the expression of tension is often designed to produce an audience reaction.

Declining Frequencies. Conspicuously less verbal are the great majority of wives who find their solace in solitary patterns and housework. Resort to religion cuts the husband out most completely—or, more accurately, reflects the severed lines of communication between husband and wife in old age.

In general, the longer the couple live together, the less often the wife turns to her husband with her troubles. The honeymoon period has an unusually high proportion of wives who always tell their husbands (34 per cent), a very small number who seldom do (7 per cent), and not a single one who never does. This dramatizes the pattern of interdependence which characterizes young couples during their engagement and honeymoon periods.

A steady decline in frequency occurs throughout the family-life cycle, with a corresponding increase in the number of wives who no longer ever share their emotional burdens with their husbands. Older wives depend increasingly on their own solitary resources for coping with emotional crises, achieving a remarkable degree of independence of other people.[3]

Should this independence be described as "emotional maturity"?

---

3. This agrees with the findings of the Kansas City Study of Adult Life reported by Neugarten (1956).

Sometimes it is, but much of it is a lonely independence correlated with a feeling of separation from her husband and dissatisfaction with her marriage. Early in marriage, the typical wife interacts frequently with her husband, subsequently with no one, ultimately sometimes with God, while the husband slips further and further into the background.

Table 90
Therapeutic Utilization of Husband after a Bad Day, by Stage in Family-life Cycle

MEAN FREQUENCY WIFE TELLS HUSBAND HER TROUBLES		STAGE IN FAMILY-LIFE CYCLE			
Childrearing stages:		Preschool	Preadolescent	Adolescent	Unlaunched
		2.58	2.43	2.34	1.78
		(128)	(139)	(100)	(64)
Childless stages:	Honeymoon			Postparental	Retired
	2.65			2.31	2.22
	(20)			(81)	(9)
Childless couples:		2.27	2.48	2.44	
		(11)	(29)	(9)	

Although external companionship tends to be reduced by the advent of children, mental hygiene reliance upon the husband apparently is not (see Table 90). If anything, the presence of preschool children seems to increase the wife's dependence on the husband for emotional support, just as it increases her dependence in decision-making. This increase is not quite enough to offset the corrosive effects of being married as many as seven years, but reduces the drop which would otherwise occur from the honeymoon to the preschool stage.

A more detailed analysis would undoubtedly show an actual upsurge in therapeutic utilization of the husband at the time of the transitional experiences of pregnancy, childbirth, and infant-care. This dependence is shown in the extraordinarily high frequency (mean 2.86) with which the teen-age brides in our sample tell their husbands their troubles (43 per cent always, zero never). These 13 cases combine newness of marriage with acuteness of need in the form of dependent young children. As a result, these young brides are more emotionally dependent than either honeymooners or mothers of young

children generally. Perhaps, in addition, their own youthfulness involves emotional immaturity and a transfer of dependence from parents to husband without an intermediate "weaning" to adulthood.

As wives recover from the crisis of bearing the first child, reliance
on the husband gradually decreases. Rather than shifting their preferred therapeutic reliance from the husband to the children, most
wives turn to impersonal or external resources. For example, mothers
of unlaunched children (who least often utilize the husband therapeutically) throw themselves more than other wives into housework (19
per cent) and religion (11 per cent). Apparently, the declining reliance on the husband during the child-rearing years is an alienation
or emancipation from the husband, rather than a shift from depending on him to depending on the children for emotional support.

The general trend toward decreased therapeutic utilization of the
husband could also be interpreted as the manifestation of an historical trend toward more mental hygiene functioning in marriage in recent decades. Perhaps, both historical and life-cycle factors are at
work. If so, it means that although today's young couples may provide
more mental hygiene services than ever before in history, nevertheless they, too, will probably drift toward silence as the years go by.

Status Differences. The relationship between social status and utilization of the husband for mental hygiene purposes is so complex that
only the distribution of percentages reveals the counter-trends involved.

Table 91 shows an erratic relationship between mean frequencies
and the husband's occupation. However there are regular trends in
three distinctive frequencies. At both extremes, the percentages
steadily decrease with higher occupational status, whereas the middle
category correspondingly increases. The result is that low-status
groups tend to be split into wives who always tell and those who never
do, whereas high-status wives are more selective. Why so? Are they
better able to inhibit their impulses, waiting for times when they need
help most and excluding those when the husband is too busy to be
bothered? Low-status wives, on the other hand, exhibit less emotional
restraint, turning to their husbands more indiscriminately. Or if re-
buffed too often by unsympathetic responses, they withdraw from contact altogether. They may also decline more steeply with length of

Table 91

Therapeutic Utilization of Husband after a Bad Day, by Husband's Occupation

FREQUENCY WIFE TELLS HUSBAND HER TROUBLES	HUSBAND'S OCCUPATION			
	BLUE COLLAR		*WHITE* COLLAR	
	Low	High	Low	High
Always	25%	23%	19%	17%
Usually	23	20	34	24
Half the time	23	26	30	32
Seldom	16	21	10	21
Never	13	10	7	6
Total	100	100	100	100
Mean	2.32	2.24	2.49	2.26
Number of families	173	173	88	157

marriage—starting out especially uninhibitedly but later losing contact more completely.

The ability to retain minimal contact with the husband is shown most remarkably in top-income families (over $10,000) and top social-status families, only 2 per cent of whom report no therapeutic use of the husband.

Selectively telling the husband half the time is commonest among wives who have been to college (40 per cent). Does their education increase their skill in discriminating between important and unimportant occasions for burdening the husband? Conversely, wives who never finished the eighth grade are especially apt never to tell their troubles to their husband (27 per cent). Poorly educated wives are often old immigrants affected by many years of marriage, but they may have been rather non-verbal in the first place.

Despite the irregularity of mean frequencies in Table 91, white-collar workers as a whole have a slightly higher average than blue-collar workers. Similarly, with total social-status scores, higher-status couples communicate more often than their social inferiors.

The higher the husband's income, the more often the wife tells her troubles, except above $10,000 where fifty-fifty selectivity gives way to seldom telling the husband. Perhaps he is too busy earning money for the wife to bother him with her little troubles. As with some other forms of interaction, high-status-index couples often find more time than high-income couples, suggesting the more leisurely life of the well-bred.

One other group, besides high-income families, seldom communicates, but for different reasons. The Negro average of 2.00 is lower than any white social-status group. Does the Negro man have troubles enough of his own, or has the wife learned not to depend on him for much of anything? At least she is left to her own devices.

Seldom telling one's troubles may also be a regional pattern. White wives who lived most of their lives on southern farms before migrating to Detroit have an even lower mean (1.89). Since most Negro migrants come to Detroit from the South, it may be that southern farm families generally neglect the mental-hygiene function. This is not a general rural-urban difference, however. Migrants from northern farms score relatively high (2.58).

In general, high-status wives share their troubles more often but also more discriminately.

Power and Interdependence. Table 92 shows that white matriarchs score almost as low as Negro wives. Presumably, this is caused by the same thing that makes the decision-making pattern wife-dominant in the first place, namely the withdrawal of "no-good" husbands from participation in family affairs.

Table 92

Therapeutic Utilization of Husband after a Bad Day, by Marital Decision-making Pattern

	MARITAL DECISION-MAKING PATTERN			
	Wife-Dominant	Autonomic	Husband-Dominant	Syncratic
Mean frequency wife tells husband her troubles	2.09	2.26	2.33	2.69
Number of families	98	192	127	125

Autonomic and husband-dominant marriages differ little in reliance on the husband. It would be interesting to know how they compare when the tables are turned. Could it be that dominant husbands are as independent as dominant wives, whereas autonomic couples are more symmetrical in their interdependence?

Symmetry combines with intensity in syncratic marriages. Such couples undoubtedly often act as therapists for each other. An appropriate motto for syncratic couples might be "Marriages at Work." Syncratic couples exploit the husband-wife relationship for all it is worth. Compared to other decision-making types, they have the most wives who always or almost always turn to their husbands for help with their troubles.

Companionship and Accessibility

The high mental-hygiene score of syncratic couples stems from their shared decision-making and correlates with other joint activities. Telling one's troubles to the husband isn't a form of companionship since it isn't exactly fun. Instead of doing something *with* the partner, it involves doing something *for* him (her). Nevertheless, both joint fun and therapy are types of off-hours interaction between the partners. A wife can't tell her troubles if no one is around to listen. Hence the high correlation between companionship and understanding.

Spending time together provides a framework which makes the husband more accessible for mental hygiene purposes. A wife who regularly joins her husband in other activities can catch his ear more easily.

News—Good and Bad. The type of companionship which should correlate most closely with telling troubles is informative companionship. Both involve verbal communication, and both occur at the end of the day. Informative companionship covers both positive and negative events which occur during the husband's day. Telling troubles involves only negative events but may reciprocate troubles the husband himself has told.

Table 93

Therapeutic Utilization of Husband after a Bad Day, by Informative Companionship

	FREQUENCY HUSBAND TELLS WIFE ABOUT WORK EVENTS				
	Daily	Weekly	Monthly	Less Often	Never
Mean frequency wife tells husband her troubles	2.61	2.15	2.00	1.81	1.69
Number of families	247	210	58	27	36

In the light of the parallels, it is not surprising to find that husbands who give their wives more news are more apt to hear the wife's troubles in return. (The only surprise relevant to Table 93 is that many of the Negro wives in our sample tell their troubles even though the husband never tells any news in return. This reflects the assymmetry often found in Negro marriages.)

Informative companionship is not the only type which makes the husband's therapy more available. Fifty-nine per cent of those wives who never trouble their husbands never visit work-mates with him either, and 80 per cent of them belong to no organizations together. To some extent, they also tend to know none of his friends and to work together on no household tasks.

Homogamy. By providing the conditions for companionship, compatible characteristics in general encourage the wife to turn to her husband after a bad day. This is most conspicuously true of similarity in age. Partly this is because age discrepancies occur chiefly among couples marrying at an age when dating cuts across wider age ranges. Wives who are four or more years older than their husbands tell their troubles less often than any age group of wives (mean 1.68). This involves fewer wives who always tell their troubles (6 per cent) and more who seldom or never do (52 per cent). Men who are attracted to older women are often too dependent to make good therapists for anyone else.

Another type of homogamy with a built-in age bias is work-homogamy. Working wives are younger on the average than house-wives and turn to their husbands with their problems more often (2.53 vs. 2.26). However, stay-at-home wives who serve as hostess-companions in helping their husbands get ahead utilize their husbands most of all (2.62). Collaborators, incidentally, fall between residual stay-at-home wives and working wives with a mean of 2.40.

Compensating for Religious Differences. Unlike most other forms of homogamy, religious homogamy is associated with less rather than greater trouble-telling to the husband. Chapter Six suggested that many interfaith couples have chosen companionship in preference to religion, and the same difference applies to mental hygiene as well.

Table 94 shows that as long as both partners belong to the same church, companionable joint attendance makes the husband more available to the wife in time of trouble. Recourse to the husband falls

Table 94

Therapeutic Utilization of Husband after a Bad Day, by Religious Homogamy

	CHURCH PREFERENCE AND ATTENDANCE				
	SAME CHURCH			DIFFERENT CHURCH	
	Wife More	Equal	Husband More	Equal	Unequal
Mean frequency wife tells husband her troubles	2.04	2.32	2.27	2.52	2.24
Number of families	78	353	15	65	76

off sharply, however, when the wife disdains her less devout husband.

When the husband and wife belong to different churches, the wife who goes to church alone utilizes her husband more than if the husband belongs to the same church. The "equal" group who suspend church attendance in order to avoid conflict, lean over backwards to make their marriages work best of all in this area.

Moreover, the greater the difference in religious backgrounds, the greater the effort. Mean score for couples with the same denominational background is 2.21, for couples from different Protestant churches a bit higher (2.31), for Catholic-Protestant couples much higher (2.53), and for four Jewish-Gentile couples sky high (3.25). Religious differences may create problems in themselves, but they don't prevent the average wife from communicating her feelings to the husband. But do they *cause* her to do so? Perhaps they do, as an effort to compensate for the dangers involved in mixed marriages. Perhaps also, couples who marry across religious lines are an unusually select group. Perhaps the strain of religious difference gets rid of mixed dating couples least suited in other respects, leaving behind a picked group who are unusually compatible, who love each other so much that they can't let religion stand in the way of getting married. Be that as it may, interfaith marriages are a conspicuous exception to the general rule that heterogamy inhibits therapeutic use of the husband. Similar attendance, however, among unmixed marriages, as well as similar nonattendance among mixed marriages provide companionship which increases the accessibility of the husband to the wife in need of solace.

Companionship, in the much broader sense of marital solidarity, also gives the wife a feeling that she can turn to her husband in time of trouble. Wives who feel that they are closer to their husbands than other wives utilize their husbands relatively often, while wives who confess to less than average closeness seldom get his help, nearly half of them never telling their troubles at all.

Of course it works both ways: wives who feel close to their husbands find it natural to turn to him, while the act of turning to him makes her feel closer still—provided his response is positive.

Rationales for Bothering the Husband

When women are asked why they tell their troubles to their husband as often or as little as they do, they do not find it difficult to give reasons for their behavior. A simple "why" question was asked which leaves it up to the respondent to choose, as her frame of reference, whether to justify why she doesn't tell him more or why she does tell him so much. About half the wives react from each point of view, 46 per cent giving reasons why they don't tell him more often, and 47 per cent giving reasons why they do (with 7 per cent not ascertained).

Table 95

Rationale for or against Therapeutic Utilization of Husband after a Bad Day

Rationale	Mean Frequency Wife Tells Husband Her Troubles	Per Cent of Total Sample
A. For Not Telling Husband (more)		
1. It *wouldn't help* or he would *react negatively*	.94	9%
2. He *shouldn't be bothered,* I should solve my own problems	1.25	23
3. I only tell the *main troubles*	1.79	5
4. Depends on his *mood* or my mood, etc.	1.87	9
B. For Telling Husband		
5. That's what marriages are for, I *ought to be able to tell him*	3.05	6
6. *He wants me to tell him*	3.05	4
7. If I tell him, *he can share* the problem	3.10	5
8. It makes me *feel better*	3.26	25
9. Convenience, *habit,* etc.	3.33	7
N.A.	—	7
Total	731 families	100

Their reasons are listed in Table 95 in order of the frequency of telling the husband. Wives with negative reasons ordinarily tell their husband less than half the time, whereas the mean frequencies for positive reasons are in excess of "usually" telling him. Asking why therefore effectively separates the silent sheep from the aggressive goats.

Many wives say their reason for not telling the husband more is that he shouldn't be bothered with her troubles. This sounds very much like the old-fashioned viewpoint of noninterference and Puritan-inspired self-dependence. Wives who hold this philosophy are seldom absolutists, however, vowing never to approach the husband with their troubles (only 18 per cent of them never bother him at all). Mostly this is a counsel of not bothering him excessively, not a monastic vow of perpetual silence.

Wives who never utilize the husband are apt to have found through actual experience that it doesn't work, either because he reacts negatively or because he is ineffective. After trying to get help early in marriage, they gradually learn it doesn't pay to try. They keep silent not from a conviction that the husband deserves respect, but from the bitter knowledge that it would be futile to try anything else.

Wives with Table 95's first reason modally "never" tell the husband while non-botherers "seldom" do. Those who select out the main troubles for therapeutic relief overwhelmingly report "about half" the bad days. By contrast, those who rely on their moods to guide them have a similar average but spread across the entire range of possible frequencies.

On the positive side, relatively few wives have an ideological argument to correspond with the noninterference philosophy. Only a few wives reason that the mental-hygiene function properly belongs in marriage. Most give pragmatic arguments for turning to their husbands—it pays off just by being able to tell someone or the husband actively relieves her blue mood and cheers her up. Despite the rewarding reinforcement of their behavior, such wives modally exercise it "usually" rather than "always."

Wives who list convenience or habit as their reason, show little discrimination between occasions. More than half of them always tell their troubles no matter what the husband's circumstance may be.

One wonders how sensitive such wives are to the husband's own mental hygiene.

The rationales can be summarized in three main attitudes: (1) if my husband responds negatively, I'm better off to keep quiet completely; (2) if he responds positively, that's reason enough to keep on telling him; but (3) he may believe or I may believe that I should solve my own emotional problems, in which case I'll do my best on my own, turning to him only as a last resort.

Table 96

Rationale for or against Therapeutic Utilization of Husband after a Bad Day, by Wife's Education

RATIONALE	WIFE'S EDUCATION		
	Grade School	High School	College
A. For Not Telling (more)			
1. Would not help or react negatively	13%	8%	3%
2. Shouldn't bother	27	23	33
3. Main troubles	4	8	5
4. Mood	14	8	5
B. For Telling			
5. Ought to	5	7	5
6. He wants	3	4	5
7. So he can share	4	5	11
8. Feel better	21	29	32
9. Habit	9	8	3
Total	100	100	102
Number of families	138	379	62

Educated Rationales. Table 96 shows that some rationales are given more commonly by educated wives, especially the contradictory philosophies of not wanting to bother the husband and wanting him to share her burden. Women with little education are apt to act on impulse or by habit. Feeling better rather than worse is also related to education but reflects the husband's behavior more than the wife's attitude.

Reason and Power. Couples who make their decisions jointly are less contradictory than college-educated wives. They feel strongly that problems as well as decisions should be shared and hence seldom say that husbands shouldn't be bothered. Equalitarian couples, whether syncratic or autonomic, less often argue that it wouldn't do

Table 97

Rationale for or against Therapeutic Utilization of Husband after a Bad Day, by Marital Decision-making Pattern

RATIONALE	MARITAL DECISION-MAKING PATTERN			
	Husband-Dominant	Syncratic	Autonomic	Wife-Dominant
A. For Not Telling (more)				
1. Would not help or react negatively	13%	2%	6%	12%
2. Shouldn't bother	24	17	26	28
3. Main troubles	7	7	9	3
4. Mood	6	9	9	12
B. For Telling				
5. Ought to	4	6	9	5
6. He wants	3	4	5	3
7. So he can share	8	10	5	1
8. Feel better	26	35	22	30
9. Habit	9	10	9	6
Total	100	100	100	100
Number of families	122	123	187	98

Table 98

Rationale for or against Therapeutic Utilization of Husband after a Bad Day, by Family-life Cycle

RATIONALE	STAGE IN FAMILY-LIFE CYCLE						
	Honeymoon	Preschool	Preadolescent	Adolescent	Postparental and Retired	Unlaunched	Childless Couples
A. For Not Telling (more)							
1. Would not help or react negatively	5%	8%	8%	6%	15%	16%	2%
2. Shouldn't bother	20	19	22	27	29	30	31
3. Main troubles	5	7	9	4	5	8	7
4. Mood	5	6	11	5	12	12	4
B. For Telling							
5. Ought to	10	6	7	10	3	3	9
6. He wants	5	4	5	3	1	3	7
7. So he can share	10	4	8	7	7	2	—
8. Feel better	40	36	25	32	20	17	29
9. Habit	—	11	5	4	8	9	11
Total	100	101	100	98	100	100	100
Number of families	20	123	138	96	89	64	45

any good or would provoke retaliation than couples dominated by one partner.

Time and Reason. The most striking life-cycle change is the steady increase in not-botherers with the lapse of time, paralleled by a decreasing number of husbands who want to hear.

Feedback

The pragmatic positive reasoning for telling the husband is echoed in the wife's report of how she feels after she has told the husband her troubles. Wives who get the most relief tend to tell the husband most often, and those who feel worse tell him hardly ever, if at all. How the wife feels after he reacts also correlates highly with her general satisfaction with his understanding of her problems and feelings. If the husband is to achieve such understanding, he has to know what her problems are. So, communicating her troubles usually results in greater emotional support.

How often she will continue sharing her troubles subsequently depends on the kind of reaction she gets. If the husband criticizes her for getting into trouble in the first place, she has little incentive ever to tell him again. But wives who get sympathy or practical advice, in response to their tale of woe, have rewarding memories to encourage them to come back for more.

If the wife's stimulus produces a positive response, her behavior pattern, as the learning theorists say, is reinforced. If the response is negative, her habit will tend to be extinguished. Marriage is an interactive process of action and reaction in vicious or beneficent cycles. Responsive husbands produce satisfied wives. But a wife who encounters only negative responses to her overtures will eventually either leave the field of battle through divorce or call a cease-fire by living alone in the same house with an unutilized husband. The human spirit cannot stand being caught in a vicious cycle forever.

THE HUSBAND'S THERAPEUTIC RESPONSE

It is apparent that the wife's decision to resort to her husband is greatly affected by her prediction of his reaction. Even at the beginning of marriage, she should be able to predict quite well from their previous experience together. One characteristic of courtship as distinguished from casual dating is the willingness of the lovers to bare their souls and share their troubles. Hence, engaged couples characteristically achieve considerable emotional interdependence.

The crucial question after marriage is not how much understanding will be achieved, but how much will survive the withering influence of children under foot and the passing years. This is not to say that married couples don't increase their knowledge of each other as a result of living together. Few couples interact intimately enough before marriage to gain the familiarity with each others' mood fluctuations and vulnerable spots which old married couples have. This increased knowledge comes simply from scrutinizing the partner microscopically. It is the kind of knowledge any observer would acquire from years of close-at-hand observation.

Understanding means something more than mere knowledge. To be understood requires response from the partner. Nor will just any response do. Critical, rejecting responses are worse than none at all as far as understanding is concerned. To be understood means to have one's feelings accepted. Acceptance involves both knowing what the feelings are and communicating a judgment that they are legitimate. By what he says or does, the husband shows that it doesn't make him mad to discover how she feels. He doesn't attack her for feeling blue or criticize her for being down in the dumps. To discover that she has had a bad day doesn't make him wish he had never married her. He doesn't feel sorry for himself for being saddled with such a sob-sister but feels sorry for her for having to go through such an ordeal.

This kind of understanding of the other's feelings is often called empathy. I know how you feel—and you know that I know—and the burden of sorrow is lightened by the knowledge that such empathy exists between us.

What are the conditions which promote empathy in marriage? Presumably the first requisite is the wife's willingness to communicate her feelings. If she keeps her thoughts and experiences bottled up inside of her, the husband will have very little to go on except perhaps facial expression, tone of voice, and other indirect clues.

The second condition for empathy is the willingness of the husband to listen to the tale of woe, to notice the facial cues, to receive the wife's message. Finally there is the factor of acceptance. Messages can be received but repudiated. Empathy fails not only when wives are uncommunicative or husbands inattentive but when husbands reject what they hear because it bothers them or makes them think less of their wives. Attention can be expected of husbands who love their wives—provided competing demands upon the husband don't get in the way. Acceptance is even more a product of love, since love involves concern for the welfare of the partner.

Faced with an unhappy wife, the husband has a series of alternatives. He can notice or disregard her feelings. If he notices, he can accept or repudiate them. If he accepts them, he can undertake an active effort to make her feel better. By listening and accepting, he has already contributed to her recovery, but he can clinch it by more tangible measures. These will vary with the source of the wife's frustrations. If it was an unavoidable accident, sheer sympathy may be all that is called for. If child-care pressures accumulated, the husband may be able to take over the kids to relieve the pressure or he may reach the same goal by taking her to a movie. If the crisis seems preventable, anxiety about future recurrences may be diminished by practical advice about preventive measures.

What the husband can do depends on the nature of the problem and on the resources at his disposal. What matters is that he become aware of the problem and respond in whatever way will most effectively meet the wife's needs. The goal is the restoration of her emotional equilibrium—whatever means will achieve this end with the minimum cost to the husband is the appropriate one.

Given the wide variety of circumstances which can create a bad day for old wives or young wives, working wives or housewives, child-ridden wives or childless wives, it is to be expected that therapeutic reactions will take many forms—and that many activities will be equally effective in meeting the wife's emotional needs.

Seven major ways in which husbands respond to the wife's troubles are shown in Table 99. These classifications were developed from the various activities wives report in answer to the general question, "When you do tell him about your troubles, what does he say or do?"

Active help includes such examples as helping with the dishes,

Table 99

Husband's Therapeutic Response, Its Contribution to the Wife's Immediate Relief and to Her General Satisfaction with His Understanding of Her Problems and Feelings

Husband's Therapeutic Response	Per Cent of Total Sample	Effect on Wife of Husband's Response*	Wife's General Satisfaction with Understanding
1. *Help toward solution* of problem	6%	3.31	3.83
2. *Help in withdrawing* from the situation	3	3.80	3.70
3. *Sympathy, affection*	28	3.63	3.59
4. *Advice, discussion* of how wife can solve problem	20	3.53	3.54
5. *Passive listening*	18	2.92	3.27
6. *Dismissal as unimportant*	7	2.79	3.27
7. *Criticism and rejection*	6	1.89	2.90
Wife never tells her troubles	9	—	3.22
N.A.	3	—	—
Total	100		
Number of families	731		

* Code: Wife feels "much better"—4 points; "a little better"—3 points; "sometimes better-sometimes worse"—2 points; "about the same"—1 point; "worse"—no points.

repairing the damage, or putting the kids to bed. Help in withdrawing involves taking her out of the house to dinner or a movie, etc. Typical examples of advice are to "get out for a while and forget it," or not to try to do so much. A dismissing husband often refuses to take her troubles seriously, telling her it's all her imagination or just laughing at her. A critic characteristically tells his wife her troubles are her own fault, while rejection is the masculine counterpart of feminine noninterference, saying not so much that he shouldn't be bothered as that he doesn't want to be.

The Effectiveness of Various Therapies

The seven response types are listed in Table 99 in order of their contribution to the wife's general satisfaction with her husband's understanding of her problems and feelings. In every case but one, this is the same order as the amount of immediate relief the wife feels.

The exception is active help toward solving the problem. This is less effective in the short run than in the long run. It focuses on preventing the recurrence of difficulty rather than on relieving the wife's feelings. In this sense, it seeks to cure rather than palliate the disease. At the moment, it doesn't help the wife as much as if the husband had whisked her away from it all in his chariot. However, in the long run, it not only decreases the likelihood of recurrence but provides a tangible demonstration of the husband's sympathy. When he rolls up his sleeves and pitches into the work himself, the wife can be very sure that he understands her problem. Such husbands have more enthusiastic wives than any others (21 per cent compared to only 13 per cent for the sample as a whole). By contrast, not a single husband, whose characteristic response is to help her withdraw, produces enthusiasm about his mental hygiene function, although satisfaction is common.

Expressions of sympathy seem to be just as effective as withdrawal in the short run but perhaps not as long remembered, decreasing the over-all satisfaction. Advice and discussion are positive verbal responses similar to sympathy and affection—in the long run, they all produce moderately satisfied wives.

Far lower in effectiveness are sheer listening without response and refusal to take troubles seriously. In the long run, these hardly leave the wife feeling better understood than if she had never told her troubles in the first place. The husband who just sits and listens is not responding at all in the active sense of the term while the one who laughs it off is making an irreverent response. Few wives under the latter circumstance say they actually feel worse—nevertheless they don't feel as good as they would if he gave no response at all.

Of the fifteen white wives in the total sample who usually feel worse after telling their troubles, two-thirds are the recipients of criticism or outright rejection. The others have either passive or dismissing husbands. To continue approaching such husbands is self-defeating—in the long run, such wives usually quit trying altogether. They might well feel better understood if they told him nothing.

How effective is the average husband in providing emotional relief? Only 2 per cent of the wives feel worse afterwards; 8 per cent feel about the same; 33 per cent a little better; and 55 per cent, much better. The remaining 2 per cent sometimes feel better, sometimes worse. Most of the latter receive advice from their husbands, so their feeling probably depends on how appropriate the advice seems to be. Feeling no better and no worse is understandably often a product of passive husbands who give little basis for change in either direction. Nevertheless, even more wives of passive husbands feel somewhat better for having poured out their troubles to someone, passive as he may be. Even with critical husbands, more wives who still tell their troubles feel better than feel worse. In general, a majority of wives find their efforts to get emotional relief at least partially rewarded, regardless of their husbands' responses. Otherwise, they would quit trying.

Conditions for Empathy

Because understanding is related to companionship and to love, marriages which are generally satisfactory to the wife or which are rated by outside observers as very cohesive tend to be characterized by the same patterns of therapeutic response. Not a single husband who actively helps his wife solve her problem or helps her withdraw from the situation has a poor marriage from either point of view. These active husbands go to the most trouble to free their wives from the burdens they are carrying. Either they take part of the load upon themselves, or they go out of their way to give their wives a popularized form of play therapy. The latter may not prevent the recurrence of the problem in the future, but it gives her hope that if things get as bad again, she can count on a recreative break whenever she needs it.

Sympathy provides the most explicit ego repair as such. It is the commonest form of therapy in Detroit, unusually common in the most satisfactory marriages (40 per cent, compared to 28 per cent for the total sample). Getting sympathy or affection in return for a recital of troubles proves for sure that the wife is still loved and appreciated—vigorous tonic for a wilted ego.

Advice and discussion is not always directed at improving the wife's competence. Sometimes the problem can be solved only by lowering the wife's expectations about herself to more reasonable levels. Whether by lowering standards or raising competence, advising husbands try to enable the wife to close the gap between her standards and her achievements so she won't feel frustrated any more.

Passive husbands may not give the wife much feeling of understanding, but they have better marriages in other respects than poohpoohing husbands. Criticism and rejection are liable to leave the wife's ego feeling even more deflated than it was in the first place. After all, she already had troubles enough without the husband adding to them. A full third of the really poor marriages in the sample (as rated by the wives themselves) contain criticized wives, and an equal number have already lapsed into silence. From every point of view, criticism and rejection represent failure to fulfil the wife's need to be rescued from her fix.

Confronted with a drowning ego, some husbands do nothing. As if that weren't cruel enough, others answer her cries with the cavalier comment that she couldn't possibly be in trouble. Worse yet are those who criticize her inability to swim and tell her she deserves to drown anyway since she's so dumb.

The Husband's Ego Resources. Since the husband's response is his own affair, one would expect it to be predictable from his occupational role or other personal characteristics. Yet there are relatively few consistent differences between occupational, income or educational groups.

Sympathy is purveyed more often by high-status husbands, and criticism by low. Perhaps a man who is secure in his own ego can afford to be generous with his wife, whereas an insecure man is more apt to feel threatened when his wife begins recounting her troubles, thinking perhaps she is blaming him.

The husband's childhood experience affects his response to trouble just as it affects the wife's preferred therapeutic endeavor after a bad day. For instance, farm husbands tend to be passive listeners, whether they still live on the farm or have moved to the city. Those still engaged in farming are also more inclined than city husbands to dismiss the wife's troubles (perhaps because they have troubles of their own). Their failure to help the wife in crises often corresponds to their slight participation in ordinary household tasks.

Young childless husbands married only a year or two are especially sympathetic (45 per cent), carrying over into marriage the emotional support characteristic of engagement. Sympathy decreases rapidly as the couple move into the next few years of marriage and acquire an infant or two. It is replaced by an upsurge in the proportion of merely passive listeners. Is it easier for childless husbands to understand their wives' problems than for any man to comprehend what a young mother has to go through?

Table 100

Husband's Therapeutic Response and Its Effectiveness, by Comparative Work Participation of Husband and Wife

HUSBAND'S THERAPEUTIC RESPONSE	COMPARATIVE WORK PARTICIPATION			
	WIFE NOT EMPLOYED		WIFE EMPLOYED	
	Husband Employed*	Husband None	Husband Overtime	Husband Full-time
1. Help solve	7%	7%	2%	3%
2. Help withdraw	3	4	4	3
3. Sympathy	30	22	39	21
4. Advice	17	11	29	31
5. Passivity	19	19	12	16
6. Dismissal	8	7	2	10
7. Criticism	6	11	4	10
Wife never tells troubles	10	19	8	6
Total	100	100	100	100
Husband's mean therapeutic effectiveness	3.27	2.95	3.48	3.21
Number of families	441	27	49	62

* Since there are no significant differences between husbands who work overtime and those who work full-time, they are combined into one column. The cases in which only the wife is employed are too few to express in percentages.

Overtime husbands of working wives are quite sympathetic, but husbands who work no more than their wives are unsympathetic and critical (see Table 100). Their egos may be threatened by the wife's competition in the bread-winning role, leaving them unable to respond generously to her troubles. The same concept may account for the similar pattern among retired husbands.[4] Husbands of working wives are generally prone to give advice but rarely offer active help. If the wife's bad day occurs at work, the husband can hardly pitch in to help out, but his occupational experience gives him a basis for making suggestions.

Equalitarian Marriages. The husband's response can be predicted better from the kind of marriage he has. Like the wife's decision to tell her troubles, his response is influenced by feedback from their mutual interaction and by other aspects of their relationship.

---

4. Where the roles are completely reversed, the three non-working husbands in our sample show nothing but sympathy for their working wives' bad days. Since so few cases are involved, it is difficult to know how generally the threat to the masculine ego is overcome by other factors under these circumstances.

Table 101

Husband's Therapeutic Response and Its Effectiveness, by Comparative Age of Husband and Wife

HUSBAND'S THERAPEUTIC RESPONSE	COMPARATIVE AGE		
	Wife Older 4+ Years	More or Less Equal	Husband Older 11+ Years
1. Help solve	—	6%	—
2. Help withdraw	—	4	3%
3. Sympathy	19%	30	35
4. Advice	12	18	32
5. Passivity	19	18	11
6. Dismissal	6	8	3
7. Criticism	25	7	3
Wife never tells troubles	19	9	13
Total	100	100	100
Husband's mean therapeutic effectiveness	2.92	3.26	3.65
Number of families	16	538	37

One aspect of the husband-wife relationship which affects the husband's response is their comparative ages (see Table 101). Extreme age differences have been highlighted by classifying the intermediate cases together. Men often marry much older women as mother-substitutes upon whom they would like to depend for emotional support.[5] Under these circumstances, their own egos are easily threatened. Chapter Four showed that these men are unable to provide their wives with an adequate standard of living. According to Table 101, they are equally unable to meet her emotional needs, often reacting negatively.

It must be anxiety-provoking to a dependent husband to find that his source of emotional security can't meet her own needs. Having married her in the hope that she would be able to succor him, he took for granted that she could take care of herself, too. On occasions when a mother-wife does meet with frustration, she cannot turn to her "little boy" and expect him to nurture her. If she does, she is bound to be disappointed or even hurt, since his precarious ego defends itself against its inadequacy by lashing back at her.

---

5. The reason why women only four years older than the man are classified as "much" older, whereas the converse difference is eleven or more years is that the typical American husband is several years older than the wife. Hence the cutting points must be skewed in the husband-older direction.

At the opposite extreme are father-daughter type marriages. Older husbands also seldom pitch in and help solve the problem, not because they are incompetent but because it's beneath their dignity to do housework. On the other hand, they can be sympathetic with their "poor young wives" in a paternal sort of way. Their paternalism tends to go beyond mere sympathy into directive advice about how the wife can solve her problems. Such husbands play the role of "big strong men" on whom the wife depends for emotional support and decisions but aren't likely to work beside her. They are good at doing things *for* their wives, not *with* them.

Table 102

Husband's Therapeutic Response, by Informative Companionship

HUSBAND'S THERAPEUTIC RESPONSE	FREQUENCY HUSBAND TELLS WIFE ABOUT WORK EVENTS				
	Daily	Weekly	Monthly	Less Often	Never
1. Help solve	7%	4%	7%	4%	5%
2. Help withdraw	6	2	—	—	3
3. Sympathy	34	32	26	12	19
4. Advice	23	16	16	23	14
5. Passivity	13	23	20	20	11
6. Dismissal	6	9	9	12	8
7. Criticism	4	7	12	12	14
Wife never tells troubles	7	8	10	19	27
Total	100	101	100	102	101
Number of families	251	206	58	26	37

In sharp contrast to dependent husbands or dependent wives are marriages in which the partners share their lives with each other through such media as informative companionship. Table 102 shows that men who always tell their wives what went on during the day are particularly sympathetic and uncritical. Perhaps their empathy for the wife's needs is one reason they share their experiences with her so often.

Even more sympathetic are husbands who share not only news but power with their wives (see Table 103). Syncratic husbands also conspicuously often co-operate in solving the wife's problems. Since they team up with their wives in many different ways, such husbands do not hesitate to plunge whole-heartedly into therapeutic endeavor.

In their passivity and lessened sympathy, autonomic husbands are at the opposite extreme from syncratic husbands. Autonomic

Table 103

Husband's Therapeutic Response and Its Effectiveness, by Marital Decision-making Pattern

HUSBAND'S THERAPEUTIC RESPONSE	MARITAL DECISION-MAKING PATTERN			
	Wife-Dominant	Autonomic	Husband-Dominant	Syncratic
1. Help solve	3%	5%	5%	11%
2. Help withdraw	5	4	2	4
3. Sympathy	29	24	29	43
4. Advice	14	20	21	17
5. Passivity	20	23	18	11
6. Dismissal	10	7	10	6
7. Criticism	5	8	10	3
Wife never tells troubles	14	9	5	5
Total	100	100	100	100
Husband's mean therapeutic effectiveness	3.24	3.18	3.17	3.52
Number of families	99	192	126	125

marriages stress the separateness of the husband and wife, with little emotional or functional dependence of either partner on the other. Under these circumstances, lack of sympathy and lack of responsiveness are dual symbols of their *apartheid*.

The differences between wife-dominant and husband-dominant marriages coincide with those for wife-older and husband-older marriages in the case of advice-giving, but reverse the relationship for criticism. Since the number of cases involved in Table 103 is much larger than the analogous categories in Table 101, this is not necessarily a contradiction. Husbands who make many decisions may provide both positive advice and negative criticism. However, a fatherly husband's criticisms may be softened into advice by his sympathy. The defensive origin of a dependent husband's criticizing is different from the decision-making origin of a dominant husband's.

Although autonomic and dominant husbands are about equally effective on the average, the latter have much more divergent effects on their wives. Dominant husbands help their wives feel "much better" more often than any other group except syncratics, but they also leave more wives feeling worse from their criticisms than any other group. Autonomic wives, by contrast, are unusually apt to feel just the same or only a little better after attempting to communicate with their passive-distant husbands.

The slightly higher mean effectiveness of wife-dominated husbands is offset by the large number of such wives who find it useless even to approach their husband with problems.

In general, it takes a strong ego to repair a weak one. Where both partners' egos are basically sound, they can easily help each other when an occasional bad day comes along. Especially if they are accustomed to joint communication, is it easy to turn to each other in times of trouble and get the desired response.

SATISFACTION WITH THE HUSBAND'S UNDERSTANDING

The immediate reaction of the wife to the husband's therapy can be predicted from the type of treatment he gives her. If he is sympathetic, she feels much better; if he just listens, it still helps some; but if he is critical, she may wind up wishing she had never approached him.

Table 99 demonstrated, however, that the wife's satisfaction with her husband's over-all understanding of her problems and feelings cannot be derived completely from the nature of his response, although the one certainly contributes to the other. Additional factors which must be considered include (1) the husbands' ability to pre-

Table 104

Satisfaction with Understanding, by Race

DEGREE OF WIFE'S SATISFACTION WITH HUSBAND'S UNDERSTANDING OF HER PROBLEMS AND FEELINGS	RACE		
	Negro	White	Total
(1) Pretty disappointed	5%	4%	4%
(2) Would be nice to have more	16	9	10
(3) All right—can't complain	40	29	31
(4) Quite satisfied	32	45	43
(5) Enthusiastic	7	13	12
Total	100	100	100
Mean satisfaction	3.19	3.54	3.49
Number of families	113	603	716

vent the recurrence of her problem. This is what makes active help in solving problems so rewarding in the long run. (2) Wives have other types of problems beside those which produce a bad day—bigger problems that mar a whole year or even a lifetime. Therapy for bad days is only one segment of the husband's total mental-hygiene task. (3) Satisfaction with his performance depends on what the wife expects of him. If she expects a lot, a better than average performance may produce only satisfaction, not enthusiasm. But if she feels he is busy with more important things, she may be satisfied with tiny scraps of attention.

Problems: Simple or Acute

Negro wives, as usual, can be cited as a group with severe problems. Their extremely low satisfaction with the understanding they get is unusually striking in view of the fact that Negro husbands do not differ significantly from white husbands in their pattern of responding to bad-day troubles, except in their predilection for giving advice. Hence, the wife's dissatisfaction may be due primarily to the severity of the problems she faces.

Expecting Little or Much

Differential expectations may account for the fact that farm wives are just as satisfied as city wives in spite of their husbands' passivity. Farm wives typically are only slightly helped by unburdening themselves, but this is all they apparently expect. City wives would react much more negatively if their husbands were as passive.

A similar factor may account for the greater enthusiasm of high-status wives. Their husbands, being busy men preoccupied with the world outside of marriage, can't afford to devote as much time as middle-status husbands to marital therapy. As a result, they are less often able to help directly with the solution of the wife's problem and are more apt to dismiss her troubles out of hand. The wives, consequently, often feel no better after telling their troubles. They also are especially apt to be selective in the times they bother the husband at all with their troubles. Yet despite this combination of self-discipline in utilizing the husband for therapeutic purposes and his relative ineffectiveness in providing immediate relief, these wives are the most enthusiastic of all about the understanding they get (see Table 105).

Table 105
Therapeutic Utilization of Husband after a Bad Day, His
Therapeutic Effectiveness, and Wife's General Satisfaction
with Understanding, by Husband's Education

	HUSBAND'S EDUCATION		
	Grade School	High School	College
Frequency wife tells husband her troubles			
Over half	42%	48%	45%
Half	23	27	32
Under half	35	24	23
Total	100	99	100
Husband's mean therapeutic effectiveness	3.31	3.39	3.26
Wife's mean satisfaction with understanding	3.65	3.59	3.72
Minimum number of families	123	297	101

Perhaps this enthusiasm means either (or both) that educated husbands convey understanding even when they can't help directly, or that their wives are satisfied with less attention in view of the husband's responsibilities outside the family. Whichever it is, high-status marriages clearly produce more satisfaction per husbandly favor than any others.[6] Satisfaction, therefore, is clearly a relative matter—if you get more than you think you deserve, you will be enthusiastic, but if you think what you get is less than your husband ought to provide, dissatisfaction will emerge.

Working wives illustrate the same phenomenon. They get lots of mental-hygiene servicing by their husbands, but since they feel they deserve it, they are less satisfied than wives who stay home. If the husband works harder than the wife, she doesn't resent it so much, but none can compare with the stay-at-home wife of a successful husband for a sense of feeling appreciated and understood.

The Accumulation of Understanding

In view of the previous relationship, it is to be expected that childless wives will be less enthusiastic than young mothers.

---

6. The pattern in Table 105 is similar to relationships by occupation, income, and the social-status index.

Table 106

Satisfaction with Understanding, by Stage in Family-life Cycle

WIFE'S MEAN
SATISFACTION
WITH
UNDERSTANDING   STAGE IN FAMILY-LIFE CYCLE

Childrearing stages:		Preschool	Preadolescent	Adolescent	Unlaunched	
		3.75	3.58	3.40	3.18	
		(129)	(140)	(100)	(66)	
Childless stages:	Honeymoon				Postparental	Retired
	3.60				3.67	3.30
	(20)				(85)	(10)
Childless couples:		3.90	3.48	3.60		
		(10)	(29)	(10)		

Table 106 shows that satisfaction with understanding increases during the early years of marriage, despite the fact that the wife's frequency of turning to the husband and his therapeutic effectiveness both decline. This surge in satisfaction is sufficient to prolong the honeymoon phenomenon past the first three years of marriage until a full decade of interaction has been completed. Perhaps this continuity reflects to some degree the cumulative aspect of understanding—it takes a while to get to know a woman and her problems. Such understanding persists until he becomes noticeably disinterested.

As with many other aspects of marriage, disinterest manifests itself increasingly as the children grow older, reaching its peak when the children are young adults themselves. The degree of recovery after the children leave home is surprising, however. This occurs despite the fact that older wives tell their troubles to their husbands less often than young ones and that the husbands fail to give as much immediate relief. Nevertheless, the declining intensity of marital interaction appears to be more than offset by the cumulative sense of the husband's understanding and perhaps also by the resumption of a similar stance in life with the termination of the wife's special child-rearing responsibilities. At least the general pattern of Table 106 suggests that childless women feel better understood than those with children in the home. If this interpretation is correct, we might expect retired couples to have even more understanding (since the husband has then dropped out of his special occupational role). However, the effect of retirement is likely to be asymmetrical: it should enable the wife to understand the husband better, but it undermines the husband's self-confidence so that he has fewer resources for expressing sympathy (or for decision-making).

THE MENTAL-HYGIENE FUNCTION IN MARRIAGE

Companionship may wane and love may wither but the typical American wife can count on more lasting understanding from her husband. The passing years sap the energy which joint activities require and calm the fires of passionate love—but sheer living together provides the basic condition for understanding another person. The longer a man lives with a woman, the greater his accumulated store of memories of how she behaves, what upsets her, and what will make her feel better. The wisdom of experience enables him to read her facial expressions more accurately, to sense her silences, to interpret her sighs. Hearing her troubles becomes less necessary, since he can read her thoughts without words.

Similarly for the wife, the sense of being understood and accepted depends less and less on words—though words never become completely superfluous. As long as the wife faces the same problems, the memory of previous sympathy from her husband is reassuring. New problems require fresh feedback, however, to be sure the ego still has its partner. Especially is this true when new problems involve the ego's vehicle—the human body. When that vehicle begins to show signs of wear and tear, the threat to the ego is acute. Old cars are junked—why not old wives? The fact that some American wives *are* replaced with newer models heightens the anxiety. Fortunately for the wife, most are not. Fortunate, because there is no companion for the older years who compares with an equally aging one.

Second wives in polygynous societies may renew the old man's sex life and rejuvenate the female work force. But it is hard for the young to empathize with the problems of the old. Old men and old women need each other for mutual understanding and that companionship of the spirit which revives the drooping ego.

Old people are not the only ones with problems. Life always has its downs as well as its ups. Young wives quite rightly tell their troubles often to their husbands, for they are news to him and help him get acquainted with her. As time goes on, most wives become more selective and many cease sharing their burdens altogether.

It seems doubtful that complete withholding can ever be considered therapeutic. Where silence is prolonged, it usually signifies failure for this aspect of marriage. Selectivity, on the other hand, seems to be the mark of maturity. A mature wife is able not only to consider her need for therapy but to predict her husband's ability to give it. If he seems depressed or preoccupied with other things, it may be wise to leave him alone. More than that, a mature wife considers not only her own needs but his, and not only his needs but his responsibilities elsewhere. If he has important duties outside the family, they deserve to be balanced against the wife's problems. High-status men have more taxing outside responsibilities and high-status women tend to have the ability—learned in childhood and perfected in marital interaction—to refrain from telling all their troubles, waiting instead until their gain will exceed the price asked of the husband.

Once the wife has revealed her need, the husband's responsibility is to do whatever he can to meet it. How much time he can devote to ego repair depends on the other pressures he is under. The least he can do—if his own emotional resources are adequate—is to listen sympathetically to her statement of the problem. Better yet, he can discuss it with her, help her find new insights, communicate to her the knowledge that he still loves and respects her. Most effective of all is taking time to solve the problem, contributing his own strength to make up for her deficiencies. Then he really makes his marriage work to the best of his ability.

If he is inadequate in other respects, however, the chances are he won't be much of an ego-repairman either. Men whose egos are incapacitated may be familiar with the feelings afflicting the wife but too wrapped up in their own problems to be able to say so. Just as psychiatrists need to be freed of their own problems through didactic analysis, husbands must have emotional resources of their own to be able to respond therapeutically to their wives.

In most marriages, therapy for bruised feelings is provided by the husband on request (and presumably by the wife in return). Perhaps more than ever before in the history of the human race, the average man meets this particular need. Not that men have suddenly become angels, but marital therapy has been facilitated by the American Federation of Labor and the American Psychological Association —one providing the necessary leisure time, and the other improved understanding.

As modern marriages restrict their functioning in other respects, ego therapy for the participants becomes more possible and more salient. Today, the mental-hygiene function is valued enough to be recognized as an important family function and effective enough to be a source of genuine satisfaction to most wives.

CHAPTER

8

LOVE

MOST AMERICANS believe that people should marry only for love. Many Americans even believe people should *stay* married only for love. The latter view is more controversial, however. Marriage vows don't say "so long as we both shall love," but talk about "for better or for worse." One of the turns for the worse that marriage may take is the cooling off of love. When this occurs, some couples feel disillusioned and run to the divorce court. Experts like Levy and Munroe (1938), however, stress the inevitability of the transformation of love from the feverish excitement of courtship to the calm security of marriage.

What is love? From a theoretical point of view, it is the feeling accompanying an interpersonal relationship that is mutually ego-enhancing. It is the good feeling which results from past need-satisfactions received, the anticipation of future gratifications, and the sense of fulfillment that comes from being able to meet another's needs.

To a considerable extent, love is linked to the attainment of other marriage goals. Love is strengthened by appreciation for companionship, a pleasant home, enough but not too many children, emotional support, and sexual fulfillment. Love is undermined when couples fail to achieve these satisfactions and lose hope for their future together. To some extent, however, love is a separate aspect of marriage—ex-

221

pressed in the language of affection, a language both of words and gestures.

In any case, it is important to marriage in the Western world—although sometimes viewed askance elsewhere. In Japan, love-matches are considered beautiful but tragic, often leading to the fiery pit of a volcano. Love in many societies is considered too ephemeral for building a lasting marriage. Better to have the solid foundation of social and economic ties in a negotiated marriage. But not for Americans—by comparison we are incurably romantic, committed to the importance of feelings, unwilling to settle for anything less idealistic.

The American system is not pure madness. Personal choice is appropriate in a country as mobile as ours, where children leave their parents both before and after marriage. Moreover, most couples do not fall vaporously in love but test their compatibility through months of companionship. In effect, the American pattern of courtship stresses those luxuries of companionship, emotional support, and love, which a mature economy can afford.

To be loved does more for the ego than anything else in the world. To be loved means not only to be accepted but to be appreciated. Falling in love is one of life's most exciting experiences for this very reason. Unfortunately, it can't be repeated every day. But couples who marry for love can have their interest in each other renewed and their appreciation for each other strengthened as they encounter new experiences and reach new goals together.

LOVE IN MARRIAGE

Despite the prominence of love as a basis for marriage, the wives in this study rank the husband's expression of love and affection next to least valuable of five aspects of marriage. Only 10 per cent of the city and farm wives list love first of all and nearly half omit it completely from their three choices.

Could it be that love is more a prerequisite to marriage than a goal of marriage? Perhaps people don't marry in order to love each other but because they love each other. After marriage, they are more apt to stress doing things together and having children as values derivable from marriage.

Curiously enough, young wives are especially apt to skip over love on their list of valuables. Forty and fifty year old newlyweds are far more romantic in this sense of the term. For young brides, does marriage bring more in the way of intensified companionship than of new opportunities for love and affection? Similarly, do children loom high because they can be had uniquely in marriage?

SATISFACTION WITH LOVE

Whatever the answers to the previous questions, one thing is clear: the wives in this study are seldom disappointed with their husbands, despite all the expert talk about disillusionment, cooling passions, and taking one another for granted. Table 107 shows more enthusiasm, more satisfaction, and less complaining about love than

Table 107

Satisfaction with Love in City and Farm Families, by Race

DEGREE OF WIFE'S SATISFACTION WITH HUSBAND'S LOVE AND AFFECTION	RESIDENCE AND RACE		
	CITY		FARM
	Negro	White	
(1) Pretty disappointed— I'm really missing out on that	2%	2%	1%
(2) It would be nice to have more	11	4	6
(3) It's all right, I guess—I can't complain	34	16	24
(4) Quite satisfied—I'm lucky the way it is	32	45	45
(5) Enthusiastic—it couldn't be better	21	33	24
Total	100	100	100
Mean satisfaction	3.59	4.03	3.85
Number of families	116	593	176

about any other aspect of marriage. The urban Negro-white average of 3.96 outstrips satisfaction with companionship (3.80) and leaves understanding and the standard of living far behind (3.49 and 3.43).

Negro wives are less satisfied than white wives with this aspect of marriage (as with all others) despite the occasional stereotype of the Negro male as a passionate lover. However, they complain less about this aspect of marriage than any other.

Down on the Farm. Between city and farm families (all of whom are white), this is the only aspect of marriage in which there is a significant difference in satisfaction. Farm wives are almost as seldom enthusiastic as Negro wives about the love and affection shown by their husbands. The previous chapter found farmers relatively taciturn in response to the emotional needs of the wife. Their taciturnity may inhibit the expression of love and affection as well.

CONDITIONS FOR LOVE

Communication

The expression of love is a form of communication between the husband and wife. Couples who communicate about other matters are more apt to express their love to each other, too.

Table 108
Satisfaction with Love, by Informative Companionship

	FREQUENCY HUSBAND TELLS WIFE ABOUT WORK EVENTS				
	Daily	Weekly	Monthly	Less Often	Never
Wife's mean satisfaction with love	4.15	4.01	4.00	3.48	3.70
Number of families	250	209	57	27	37

The mean satisfaction score for *never*-tellers doesn't show it, but they involve twice as many "pretty disappointed" wives (8 per cent) as among *seldom*-tellers. Despite the minor upturn among never-tellers, the communication of love and of news events are clearly related. The exceptions may be older husbands retired from work or with little newsworthy to report.

Since communication is usually reciprocal, it is not surprising to find the wife's feeling about her husband's expression of love correlated with her own frequency of telling him her troubles after a bad day. Wives who never tell their husbands are relatively dissatisfied (3.50), whereas those who usually or always turn to him are most enthusiastic (4.15).

Cause and effect in this area work both ways. Couples who are in love find it easy to share their troubles with each other. Conversely, the emotional gratification derived from mutual therapy strengthens the feeling of affection.

Companionship

Like other forms of communication, the expression of love is most common among couples who do things together. For instance, satisfaction with the husband's love is associated with friendship-companionship. This means that love and friendship are seldom contradictory but covariant. Husbands who let their wives in on their friendships tend to let their wives in on their feelings as well. But wives who don't know their husbands' friends, usually don't see much of their husbands either (see Table 109).

Table 109

Satisfaction with Love, by Type and Degree of Companionship

WIFE'S MEAN SATISFACTION WITH LOVE BY TYPE OF COMPANIONSHIP	DEGREE OF COMPANIONSHIP				
	None	Slight	Moderate	Considerable	Intense
1. Friendship*	2.43	3.83	4.16	4.20	4.12
	(56)	(141)	(84)	(184)	(125)
2. Colleague†	3.82	4.09	—	4.31	4.05
	(231)	(195)		(107)	(55)
3. Organizational‡	3.89	4.18	4.20	4.37	4.15
	(360)	(56)	(94)	(57)	(26)

* Proportion of husband's friends wife knows quite well: none, some, half, most, all. Numbers in parentheses are numbers of families on which mean is based.

† Frequency of visiting work-mates: never, seldom, monthly, weekly.

‡ Number of joint memberships: none, one, two, three, four or more.

The same is true of other types of companionship—up to a point. Visiting cronies and participating in organizations can be too much of a good thing if overdone. Sociable husbands are ordinarily affectionate, but shop talk and Roberts' Rules of Order can get in the way. The sociability of love requires privacy which some couples are too busy to find. Besides, visiting and attending meetings together need not always provide companionship. If the husband is more interested in the colleagues and organizational business than in his wife, such "companionship" may demote rather than promote love.

The decline in love for wives who know all the husband's friends may not be *caused* by her knowledge but be symptomatic of the fact that few wives have such exhaustive knowledge unless the husband's friends are limited to a narrow circle. Often this is found among old couples, especially when the husband has retired. The lesser love may show the kind of people involved, more than the effect of intense companionship.

It may be no accident, however, that love tapers off under extreme intensities of all three out-of-the home types of companionship. Perhaps it would be in order to generalize that external companionship can be detrimental to love when it engulfs so much leisuretime that the private "madness of love" (*folie à deux*) is interfered with.

Homogamy

Companionship may promote communication of love, and we know that homogamy promotes companionship. Therefore, homogamous marriages should yield more satisfaction with love than mixed marriages. Educational differences interfere with marital affection in

Table 110

Satisfaction with Love, by Comparative Education of Husband and Wife

	COMPARATIVE EDUCATION				
	WIFE MORE		EQUAL	HUSBAND MORE	
	3+ years	1 or 2 years		1 or 2 years	3+ years
Wife's mean satisfaction with love	3.88	3.92	4.18	4.06	3.93
Number of families	78	106	188	119	98

the usual way, i.e., more so when the husband is inferior than vice versa (see Table 110).

Age homogamy, similarly, is conducive to satisfaction with the husband's expressed love. There is no difference in the middle range of less than four years' difference in ages. Beyond this point, satisfaction tapers off, especially when the wife marries a man younger than herself.[1]

Table 111

Satisfaction with Love, by Comparative Age of Husband and Wife

	COMPARATIVE AGE			
	WIFE OLDER	MORE OR LESS EQUAL	HUSBAND OLDER	
	4+ Years		4–10	11+ Years
Wife's mean satisfaction with love	3.87	4.07	3.99	3.90
Number of families	15	332	206	39

Power and Love. Marriages with syncratic power relations combine both equality and a high level of communication. It is to be expected therefore that syncratic wives will be especially enthusiastic —as Table 112 shows they are. By contrast to the 42 per cent of syncratic wives who are enthusiastic, only 34 per cent of the husband-dominated wives are, and even fewer of the rest. Autonomic marriages involve a large cluster of simply satisfied wives. Their marital interaction is not sufficient to promote either great enthusiasm or negative reactions. Dominant husbands more often elicit either enthusiasm or complaints from their wives, twice as many of whom express dissatisfaction as in the rest of the sample. Dominant wives, on the other hand, are apt to say they can't complain about their husbands—faint praise at best.

Why should dominant husbands provide their wives with such little love and affection? After all, they contribute a great deal in the way of other resources to marriage. Probably their wives feel a great deal of affection for them because of what they represent in the way of community success. Apparently, however, the very imbalance in the

---

1. Interfaith marriages are an exception to the general rule that heterogamy interferes with love. Catholic-Protestant marriages are just as satisfied as un-mixed marriages or Protestant interdenominational marriages.

Table 112

Satisfaction with Love, by Marital Decision-making Pattern

	MARITAL DECISION-MAKING PATTERN			
	Husband-Dominant	Wife-Dominant	Autonomic	Syncratic
Wife's mean satisfaction with love	3.94	3.94	4.02	4.23
Number of families	127	98	192	128

husband-wife relationship impedes the husband's affection for her. If he has extra resources, it means that she has relatively few. Although he meets many of her needs, he gets less satisfaction in return. Expressions of love do not grow from one-sidedness despite all the talk about he-man lovers.

Social Status

As long as the husband and wife contribute reciprocally to each other, higher status results in greater expression of love and affection (see Table 113).

Table 113

Satisfaction with Love, by Social Status

	PERCENTILE RANKING ON SOCIAL STATUS INDEX				
	0–19	20–39	40–59	60–79	80–99
Wife's mean satisfaction with love	3.54	3.87	3.93	4.13	4.22
Number of families	13	92	206	189	91

Enthusiasm is five times as common among top-status wives as in the bottom group. A similar trend exists in relation to the husband's income (one of the components of the social status index) except that wives of men earning $7,000–$10,000 are less satisfied than would be expected. Since this group is also less satisfied with companionship, their inadequate affection may be further evidence of the husband's absorption in his job at the expense of his marriage. Occupations themselves differ only in the higher satisfaction of wives of business and professional men compared to all others.

Satisfaction with love is much more closely related to educational differences than to income or occupational differences (see Table

Table 114

Satisfaction with Love, by Husband's and Wife's Education

WIFE'S MEAN SATISFACTION WITH LOVE	YEARS OF EDUCATION					
	Under 8	8	9–11	12	13–15	16+
By husband's education	3.68	3.77	3.96	4.14	4.29	4.34
	(72)	(88)	(133)	(188)	(56)	(53)
By wife's education	3.55	3.81	3.98	4.15	4.33	4.36
	(62)	(81)	(140)	(245)	(40)	(25)

114). Hence, the greater satisfaction of high-status marriages is primarily a result of the educational factor.

People who go to high school and college develop skills in communication and habits of self-expression. Hence, it is easier for them to express affection as well as to communicate information and opinions. Love is, after all, a kind of opinion—a very favorable opinion of another person.

The secure community position of highly educated persons may also contribute to their ability to love. Emotional security is necessary to be able to give love to another person. Social status may contribute to emotional security if that status itself is secure and highly crystallized. Emotionally secure persons can give love to others as a rich man showers gifts on his friends.

Comparative Status. Ego-wealth can be gauged partly by looking at a man's standing in the community. But just as satisfaction with the standard of living is relative to reference group norms, so a man's ability to love is enhanced by favorable comparisons, and undermined by unfavorable ones. Comparisons may be made between a man and his own father or between a man and his wife's father. In both cases, extreme differences prey upon the husband's morale or boost it, as the case may be, affecting his affectionateness correspondingly.

Downward-mobile men have difficulty satisfying their wives' needs for love—the greater the decline, the worse matters become. Upward-mobile men, however, less consistently outshine occupationally stable men, perhaps because the personality and role requirements for getting ahead in the world shift their attention away from the family. The ego's added resources then become less accessible to the wife.

When a man gains his ego strength from comparison with the

wife's childhood social status, no such mobility complications are involved. Moderate differences in family background are not relevant enough to affect satisfaction greatly, but extreme differences do. A new complication is the differential expectations of the wife. If the wife comes from a low enough status, her high-status husband may give her more love than she was raised to expect. On the other hand, if his status is much lower than hers, this not only threatens his ego but means he has been socialized in affectional patterns below what she is accustomed to.

Urbanity

Formal and informal socialization affect the emotional life of the couple more than they do other aspects of marriage. Just as ethnic and religious subcultures affect the ways women deal with the frustrations of a bad day, the place where a man was raised affects his expression of positive feelings. Tables 115 and 116 suggest that expressiveness is an urban American characteristic.

Table 115

Satisfaction with Love, by Degree of Urbanization

	PLACE LIVED MOST OF LIFE			
	Southern Farm	Northern Farm	Town Under 50,000	City Over 50,000
Wife's mean satisfaction with love	3.67	3.91	3.99	4.07
Number of families	18	32	172	345

The taciturnity of Michigan farmers also characterizes men who grew up on farms and migrated to the city (see Table 115). The difference between migrants from northern and southern farms may be simply a regional variation, but more likely reflects the depressed economic and educational status of the latter. Families from small-town backgrounds (nearly half of whom are from villages less than 2,500 in size) are also appreciably less affectionate than people who have always lived in cities. Apparently, love and affection are expressed more openly in cities than elsewhere.

If we were considering only kissing in public places, many a city visitor would nod his assent. Casual observation suggests that affection is expressed more publicly in the anonymous environment of a large city than under the scrutiny of village acquaintances. However, the issue at hand is not expression in front of others but expression between husband and wife. Why should this be more common in the city than in the country?

Does the city husband's departure for work in the morning result in affectionate farewells (and subsequent reunions) which a farm couple has less occasion to experience? Do the contacts between people in urban jobs and neighborhoods accustom them to greater verbalization than the isolated rural wife and the farmer alone with his animals and his crops?

Table 116

Satisfaction with Love, by Degree of Americanization

PLACE OF BIRTH OF HUSBAND AND WIFE

	Both Foreign-born	One Foreign-born	Both Native-born
Wife's mean satisfaction with love	3.70	3.83	4.13
Number of families	66	72	371

What about foreigners? Many of them were raised in peasant families in the old country, so they often have a rural background. Their low enthusiasm (only 17 per cent) is partly a result of age, too, for most immigrants came to Detroit in the great wave of migration before World War I. Nevertheless, some of their dissatisfaction may be an international difference between the freedom and spontaneity characteristic of modern American lovers and the inhibition and reserve of other countries (continental stereotypes to the contrary notwithstanding). No differences exist, however, between Catholics and Protestant wives, although the lesser Jewish enthusiasm may reflect immigrant backgrounds as well as occupational preoccupation.

THE CYCLE OF LOVE

Love is most intense when it is new. Appreciation for the partner is keenest when the partner's presence has just been acquired. As marriage continues, the partner is taken more for granted and affection expressed less often. Vitality, energy, and sexual drive wane with age and length of marriage, leaving less physical impetus to express affection to the spouse. Accordingly, satisfaction with the husband's expression of love and affection declines steadily with the passing years.

Honeymooners. A majority of the new brides are "enthusiastic" about the love and affection they receive from their uncalloused husbands. But the honeymoon period passes quickly into moderate satisfaction in the middle years of marriage, while uncomplaining acceptance characterizes an increasingly large minority of those married more than twenty years.

Because people get married (or remarried) at different ages, age trends are not as clear as the processes which result once a marriage is set in motion. Indeed, some of the most enthusiastic wives in the entire sample are those past age fifty who have recently remarried. In general, the older the wife is when she gets married, the more enthusiastic she is about the affection she gets as a result.

Table 117

Satisfaction with Love, by Stage in Family-life Cycle

WIFE'S MEAN SATISFACTION WITH LOVE	STAGE IN FAMILY-LIFE CYCLE			
Childrearing stages:	Preschool	Preadolescent	Adolescent	Unlaunched
	4.26	4.13	4.01	3.48
	(129)	(139)	(98)	(63)
Childless stages:	Honeymoon		Postparental*	Retired
	4.21		3.89	3.70
	(19)		(84)	(10)
Childless couples:	4.20	4.07	4.10	
	(10)	(29)	(10)	

* Mean satisfaction for the 14 postparental couples married less than 27 years is 4.08.

Love and Children. Although children may depress the standard of living and the ability of the couple to find companionship outside the home, they increase the emotional bonds of understanding and love between the partners. Table 117 shows that mothers of preschool children are more satisfied with the husband's love and affection than any other group of wives. More detailed analysis suggests that this feeling of being loved is especially high when the first child is an infant. Perhaps babies are such lovable objects that they stimulate expressions of affection between the parents. Certainly one of the symbols of this phase is the proud young couple standing arm in arm gazing at their sleeping child.

Does this mean that couples on the verge of divorce should have a baby to save their marriage? Doubtfully—the marginal increase in the average wife's satisfaction with love is too slight to guarantee miraculous benefits to incompatible couples. Indeed, part of the increase could be due to the selective loss from the sample of the least compatible couples through early divorce. (Only a follow-up study over a period of time could ascertain the reason.)

Nevertheless, the new marital pattern of the child-bearing period seems to have greater inner strengths. The wife's withdrawal from her occupational and social roles outside the home leads to greater therapeutic and decision-making dependence on the husband, to which he responds with increased communication of information and affection.

How can this strengthening be reconciled with the fact that syncratic marriages in general are the most satisfactory? The answer seems to be that the appropriateness of a marriage pattern depends on the circumstances. Joint external participation and a syncratic family structure are ideal for young childless couples. Then the arrival of the first child entails a shift in the pattern toward greater dependence by the wife as she withdraws from the outside world. As the children grow up, we would expect the marital pattern to swing back in a more autonomic direction (equal again but less shared because the newness has worn off).

When the love-satisfaction of wives of all ages is analyzed by the number of children in the home, those with three children are most satisfied. So marital love tends to be strongest in homes with a moderate number of children, neither too few nor too many. Beyond this ideal number, the impact of more children on the husband-wife relationship seems to be deleterious. Sometimes child-bearing in families of four or more children is a substitute for marital gratification. Parent-child affection may offset the lack of love between husband and wife.

Length of marriage and number of children combine to leave mothers in the launching stage seldom enthusiastic and often bitter about the loss of the husband's affection and companionship. Whom should she sue for the alienation of his affections? Few husbands have been bewitched by other women. Rather, the internal dynamics of family living produce this disaffection between husband and wife.

Perhaps the depression of the wife is accentuated by the thought that soon she will have no one left for ego-support except her husband. Such anxiety for the future is unwarranted since the best way to revive the husband's interest is to get rid of the children. Once they are out of the way, the parents' appreciation of each other as persons is renewed. Some (but not all) of the novelty of the first honeymoon is recaptured in a second honeymoon period. After all, she is still the same old girl. But the ex-father takes a new look at her and resumes the role of husband which had fallen into disuse.

Second honeymoons, however, like first ones, don't last forever. The old-married-couple period is long enough in this era of increased life expectancy to allow ample time for a second settling down to occur. This time, however most wives are "quite satisfied" with what they have. The husband's love is not unusual enough to arouse admiration but is secure enough to create satisfaction. Old men are seldom ardent lovers, but they can be depended upon by the wife.

LOVE AND MARRIAGE

Cynics are wrong who say that love and marriage are incompatible. It is true that love is most intense and most satisfying in the earliest years of marriage. It is true, in a sense, that disillusionment occurs; but it seldom reaches the point where people wish they had never married—yet go on living together. Most of the really bad marriages break up during the first decade, leaving behind couples who are often more satisfied with the affectional aspect of their relationship than with any other.

Some people are better prepared for the art of love than others. Low-status urbanites love least and divorce most. Farmers express their love relatively seldom without correspondingly severe consequences. Farmers and immigrants come from environments which give low priority to the expression of love and higher priority to the economic and other functional interdependencies of husband and wife. Love is an artistic creation which reaches its widest perfection in the sophisticated upper reaches of American society. It is a boon which a more leisurely, better-educated society has conferred upon its members. The progressive urbanization, acculturation, and education of the on-coming generation suggests there is likely to be correspondingly more expression of love in the future.

Part Three

THE EVALUATION
OF AMERICAN
MARRIAGE

HAVING ANALYZED the structure of relationships between husband and wife and some of the key functions which marriage performs for both partners, what estimate can be made of the stability, the effectiveness, and the vitality of American marriage? Such an evaluation deserves to be made not only for marriages in general, but also for the many varieties which exist within our society. More specifically then, what are the conditions under which marriage flourishes or falters in America? Having looked at marriages from many different angles, the task now is to evaluate them as functioning wholes.

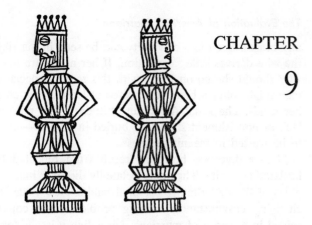

STRESSES AND STRENGTHS IN AMERICAN MARRIAGES

THIS BOOK began with the question, "What is happening to American marriages?" The purpose of this final chapter is to return to that question in terms of the weak points and strong points in contemporary married life. The weak points indicate where marriages are vulnerable, while the strengths resist the forces of decay and disintegration. In conclusion, an estimate will be given of the comparative potency of the negative and positive forces within American marriages.

DISAGREEMENTS AS STRESSES

As evidence of the stresses, we will study marital disagreements. These are not the only source of weakness in marriage. Sometimes couples simply drift apart, no longer drawn toward each other by any positive attractions, no longer dependent on each other for essential services. Such might be called decaying marriages, in which the meaningfulness of interaction departs, or interaction itself gradually ceases. Such loss of vitality can be seen in marriages from which the wife derives little satisfaction. If her needs are not being satisfied, why should she go on living with this man? Especially if some other man might offer a better chance or at least a new chance of meeting her needs. The usual American attitude is that marriages dead from lack of nourishment should be buried in divorce—life is too precious to be wasted in meaninglessness.

Other divorces, however, result from repeated battles between husband and wife. They may belatedly discover incompatible philosophies of life or irritating personal habits. New issues may arise from changing circumstances, posing problems that couldn't have been solved in advance of marriage. Disciplinary issues for children, what to do about financial set-backs, whether and how to get rid of boring visitors—there are endless new questions in married living which couples may see eye to eye on—or may not.

Disagreement isn't necessarily fatal. Some divergence is normal in any marriage. More crucial is what happens from there on out. Most couples achieve some agreement, or agree to disagree. Usually someone gives in or a compromise emerges.

Only a few couples are chronically unable to settle their arguments. In Detroit, 2 per cent of the wives say that no agreements are reached when they differ with their husbands, that neither partner gives in. Equally rare is total failure to reach agreement in farm families. For such marriages, disagreements are disastrous. Every additional issue alienates the couple further. Each disagreement is an open sore that never heals.

For most couples, disagreements are less threatening. Nevertheless, the kinds of issues which plague a marriage often reflect its weakest points.

Major Issues in City and Country

What are the main issues which crop up in modern marriages? Table 118 indicates the areas covered by answers to the question, "Since you were married, what are the main things you and your husband have sometimes disagreed about?"

With few exceptions, the proportions of couples disagreeing about general topics are similar for city and farm families. Only when spe-

Table 118

Major Areas of Disagreement in Urban Families

TYPE OF DISAGREEMENT	NUMBER TABULATED	
	Chief Disagreement	Total Disagreements*
1. Money	24%	42%
2. Children	16	29
3. Recreation	16	30
4. Personality	14	28
5. In-laws	6	10
6. Roles	4	7
7. Religion-politics	3	4
8. Sex	†	1
9. None	15	15
Not ascertained	2	2
Total	100	168‡
Number of families	731	731

* Most wives typically mention two areas of disagreement, while a few mention three or four. The right-hand column shows the total of all disagreements mentioned in each category, giving a rough idea of the proportion of all couples who ever have a major disagreement in that area. The first-mentioned disagreements are used as the basis for comparison in subsequent tables.

† Less than ½ of 1 per cent.

‡ Total adds to more than 100 per cent because many wives gave more than one response.

cific issues within topical areas are examined, do farm problems differ from city problems.

Table 118 shows that financial problems crop up in more marriages than any other category of disagreement. The proportions of city and farm families involved are practically identical, but their financial problems differ considerably when examined in greater detail. Urban disagreements are heavily concentrated around criticisms of the partner's extravagance, prices paid for particular purchases, and housing decisions. Rural Michigan wives move so seldom that housing is rarely an issue. Their chief disagreements reflect more difficult economic decisions, most often involving purchase of a major durable item, what the family can afford or will have to do without, and priorities for purchases. Often these rural issues involve struggles between the vested interests of the husband and the wife. Every expensive piece of farm machinery means postponing improvements for the house—and vice versa. In such a context, it is likely to be difficult for partners to compromise because their points of view differ so much.

The greatest conflict over children for both farm wives and city wives involves discipline. Child-rearing inevitably raises questions about how strictly the children should be handled—questions which differ little from city to country.

Recreational issues split into two main types: differing tastes in leisure-time activities and disagreements about the amount of companionship the partners have together. The latter is a typical feminine complaint because of the wife's need to get out of the home for a change of scenery. The chief rural obstacle to companionship in recreation is the husband's heavy work responsibility. When combined with physical isolation, this makes the farm wife twice as apt to complain of inadequate social life as the city wife (11 per cent vs. 5 per cent). She is so desperate for recreation that almost any activity will do—at least she disagrees with her husband about *what* to do less often than about the need to do *something*.

City husbands, too, are sometimes preoccupied with work responsibilities, but more apt to engage in separate recreation, leaving the wife to stew at home (5 per cent vs. 1 per cent). The fact that the husband is away from home during the day gives him contacts and friendships alien to the wife, which tend to involve him in after-hours activities apart from her. Sometimes this means coming home late from work because he has had some fun with "the boys." Other times, he goes out after supper to rejoin them. At least the farm wife has the advantage of being able to accompany her husband in his leisure time pursuits—if he can find time for any.

Personality clashes take many forms, only one of which differs by place of residence. City couples more often quarrel over acts or habits of one spouse which are morally disapproved by the other (6 per cent vs. 2 per cent for farm couples). Drinking and running around with other women (or men) are typical examples of this. The rural-urban difference could mean that rural consciences are better able to resist temptation. More tangible is the fact that rural environments present fewer temptations. The same separation of work-place from residence which causes urban husbands (and sometimes wives) to get involved in separate recreational activities also involves them in separate delinquencies. Indeed, except for the partner's moral disapproval, these delinquencies could be classified as recreational disagreements. What makes the husband come home late from work may just as well be a drink with the boys in the one case as in the other. If the wife disapproves of his drinking, the disagreement goes down as a personality issue. If she resents only his preferring the boys to her own company, the issue is recreational.

The journey to work is not the only urban factor in marital delinquency. The size of the community also contributes. In a small town, the average man is known by almost everybody, and this network of primary relationships reinforces his superego. In a large city (Detroit has two million people), the anonymity of the crowd invites deviant behavior unsanctioned by gossip. The big-city husband may feign work at the office while taking his young secretary to a show or cocktail lounge, and unless the wife's grapevine is unusually effective, nobody except the two delinquents will ever know the difference. Some urban escapades therefore fail to provoke conflict at home because they are unknown to the wife—but enough alcohol on the breath, lipstick on the collar, and mysteriously disappearing money become apparent to cause appreciable difficulty. Nor are husbands the only urban delinquents—wives, too, are sometimes influenced by the attractions and distractions of the urban environment, the more so as *they* journey to work.

Even more personality clashes, however, center around differing tastes, irritating (but not immoral) personal habits, temperamental quirks, and back-seat-driving-type criticisms of the other's skill. Such issues arise just as often in the country as in the city.

The remaining problem areas affect so few families that they can rarely be meaningfully subdivided. Role conflicts involve the wife's working (in city or country) and the division of labor in the home. City wives alone accuse their husbands of not working hard enough, not earning enough money, or otherwise neglecting their role, and some wives in both city and country come in for criticism about their housekeeping.

"Religion-and-politics" is mostly religion in both city and country. Ten per cent of the farm couples but only 3 per cent of the city couples report a major disagreement at some time or other about what church to go to, how often to go, or some other aspect of religion.

As for sex, not a single farm wife ventured to mention this private subject to our interviewers, despite the fact that most of the interviewers were married women. The handful of city wives bold enough to specify this area of disagreement unquestionably leads to an underestimation of the amount of sexual conflict in the general population. A better estimate might be secured by using a list of topics to be checked. Left to their own initiative, however, respondents probably hesitated to utter the three-letter word.

What about wives who say they never disagree about anything worth reporting? Are they hiding something? A few of them may be, but by and large they are consistent. In answering a related question, none of them says she and her husband disagree more often than other couples, and most of them say they disagree less often than others. Having no disagreements doesn't necessarily mean the best of all possible marriages; but, turned the other way around, it is safe to say that, in good marriages, disagreements get solved with relatively little difficulty.

Sources of Trouble

Disagreements may reflect characteristics of the wife alone, the husband alone, or the relationship between the two of them.

Table 119

Disagreements, by Education of Wife

DISAGREEMENT	EDUCATION OF WIFE		
	Grade School	High School	College
1. Money	17%	26%	18%
2. Children	16	19	21
3. Recreation	13	15	16
4. Personality	17	15	18
5. In-laws	3	7	2
6. Roles	2	4	12
7. Religion-politics-sex	4	3	5
8. None	28	11	8
Total	100	100	100
Number of families	147	391	62

Educated Sensitivities. Table 119 shows two ways in which the wife's education affects her disagreements. One is her readiness to report disagreements. Not a single wife among twenty-four college *graduates* fails to report at least one area of disagreement, and education generally is associated with fewer reports of no problem areas.

It may be inferred from the rest of this book that such a relationship does not mean that education ruins women for marriage (despite ancient fears). Rather, college alumnae are probably less apt to keep quiet when they disagree with their husbands, more anxious to work things through to a settlement, and more apt to recall such disagreements when interviewed subsequently.

Women who went only to grade school may have fewer disagreements because they are less verbally-oriented. Another factor involved is their greater average age. All women past fifty tend to report few disagreements, perhaps because they have been married so long. By that time disagreements have often been settled and forgotten, or else communication between the husband and wife has dwindled off, reducing the danger of disagreeing (or agreeing) about anything.

While educated wives tend to report more disagreements in general, they especially often disagree with their husbands about marital roles. Those who have been to college appear to be sensitive about the question of women's roles and to push for idealized husband-wife roles.

Money, Money. Disagreements about money are most pronounced among high-school educated wives. This may be primarily a question of income. Wives with only a grade-school education are usually married to husbands whose incomes are too low to offer much choice in how to spend it. Thus, only 19 per cent of city couples with below-average incomes have had memorable disagreements about money. Unlike farm families with equally little money (who have to make difficult choices between farm equipment and household expenditures), most city families face routine decisions about keeping the bills paid and the larder full. It takes at least a five-thousand-dollar income, apparently, for money to acquire live options in the city; 37 per cent of the disagreements of six- to seven-thousand-dollar-income couples are financial. Such couples have more than enough to subsist on, but not an inexhaustible supply of money—so financial choices loom large. Only above ten thousand dollars does the supply of money become generous enough to reduce financial disagreements to a low 9 per cent. In part, this reduction is achieved at the expense of increased complaints by the wife that the husband's "busy-ness" in making this money deprives her of his companionship.

Heterogamy. Quarrels over personal habits tend to occur in certain types of marital relationships. If the husband has had much more education than the wife, she seldom (11 per cent) mentions personality conflicts. However, as the balance of education shifts in the opposite direction, the percentage of disagreements rises steadily to a peak of 25 per cent when the wife has had at least three more years of schooling than the husband. When a man marries such a woman, he is likely to be in for considerable criticism from her about his uncouth ways.

Religious disagreements are more common in interfaith marriages than in homogamous ones, but not as much so as might be expected (6 per cent vs. 3 per cent). Personal criticisms loom largest (23 per cent) among couples who attend different churches at differential rates. Usually, it is the wife who is religious and the husband who seldom goes to his alien church, making him especially liable to criticism for his irreligious behavior.

Table 120

Disagreements, by Comparative Work Participation of Husband and Wife

DISAGREEMENT	COMPARATIVE WORK PARTICIPATION		
	WIFE NOT EMPLOYED	WIFE EMPLOYED	
		Husband Overtime	Husband Full-time
1. Money	23%	17%	27%
2. Children	21	17	11
3. Recreation			
a. Conflicting *interests*	10	11	16
b. *Amount* of companionship	5	6	2
4. Personality	15	15	15
5. In-laws	6	4	5
6. Roles	3	8	8
7. Religion-politics-sex	4	2	2
8. None	13	20	14
Total	100	100	100
Number of families	443	53	65

Role Problems. Table 120 reveals the role problems of working wives. Many of these couples undoubtedly disagree about the wife's employment itself. In addition, that employment requires drastic reshuffling of marital roles, most notably in the division of labor. This is reflected in the fact that couples who share the most household tasks have not the least but the most role disagreements. When the wife's employment involves both partners in overlapping responsibilities for household tasks, role conflicts are apt to occur. Questions of how much each partner should do crop up because of the lack of boundaries between tasks. In most households, such disagreements are settled by allocating tasks unilaterally in a specialized division of labor—but the time shortage of double-employment couples requires coparticipation at home with recurrent potential stress.

Table 120 also suggests that overtime work by the husband tends to cause disagreements over lack of companionship, but to reduce disagreements about money.

The differences between working wives and housewives in disagreements over children are a function of the number of children the latter have to care for. This can be seen more clearly in life cycle changes.

Table 121

Disagreements, by Stage in Family-life Cycle

DISAGREEMENT	STAGE IN FAMILY-LIFE CYCLE						
	Honey-moon	Pre-school	Preado-lescent	Adoles-cent	Postpar-ental and Retired	Un-launched	Child-less Couples
1. Money	10%	28%	24%	23%	21%	23%	18%
2. Children	—	13	29	32	10	20	—
3. Recreation							
a. Interests	20	8	8	9	6	—	14
b. Amount	10	9	5	7	11	3	6
4. Personality	20	14	16	11	14	23	12
5. In-laws	15	8	5	2	2	3	10
6. Roles	—	5	4	4	4	5	4
7. Religion-politics-sex	10	4	3	3	5	2	4
8. None	15	11	7	10	26	22	31
Total	100	100	101	101	99	101	99
Number of families	20	130	140	101	97	65	49

Changing Problems. From the previous discussion of working wives, one might expect role conflicts to be common among new brides, a majority of whom are working. The fact that none at all occur among our twenty "honeymoon" couples illustrates the extent to which working has become an accepted role for young women without children (see Table 121). With two incomes and no dependents, their money worries are few. Such couples are still at the dating stage as far as their main roles in life are concerned, disagreeing not about who should do the minimal housework but about what movie to see.

In-laws are an issue when the partners are young—indeed the younger the wife, the more often conflicts over relatives are mentioned. As young adult men and women transfer their loyalties from their parents to each other, some stress is inevitable and it shows in the concentration of in-law problems at the beginning of youthful marriages.

The biggest differences in Table 121 are between young couples without children and those with young children on their hands. If ever a transition from one life-cycle stage to another is a crisis, this is it. Suddenly the wife's employment shifts from being taken for granted to being controversial. Most wives, of course, quit work. The few who continue working under financial pressure tend to criticize their husband's economic incompetence, while the occasional middle-class career woman is apt to be criticized by him for neglecting her maternal and housekeeping tasks.

Money jumps into first place as a problem when the wife quits her job to have a baby. Belt tightening to accommodate reduced income and increased expenses requires choices that husband and wife may disagree about. The standard of living isn't necessarily worse at this point (dissatisfaction tends to intensify as more children are added and they develop more expensive appetites). Rather, the drastic shifts in income and expenditures require the most rethinking now.

As noted above, husbands who work overtime may provoke disagreements about the lack of joint recreation. During early childbearing, the complaints in this area undoubtedly reflect the wife's feeling of being tied down by dependent young children.

Children themselves do not become the chief bones of contention until they are old enough to get into "deliberate" trouble. Between the ages of six and eighteen, disciplinary questions are liable to divide the husband and wife even more than financial questions. Beyond age eighteen, children who still live at home become more responsible for themselves and create fewer issues for parents. They even become for many wives a substitute source of gratification, reflected in the rarity of disagreements about companionship in the unlaunched group. However, wives who no longer find their husbands very useful are still apt to snipe at them for personality deficiencies, the more so because of the gap between the two partners.

In the postparental period, the problems of companionship reassert themselves as joint use of leisure time resumes (or at least the wife wishes it would!). Also, the approach of death makes religious questions take on a new interest.

An unusually large proportion of the permanently childless couples report no disagreements whatsoever, reflecting the smooth continuity of their pattern of living. When they do conflict, they resemble childless "honeymoon" couples in disagreeing pre-eminently about their leisure-time dating.

Marital Interaction Patterns. Couples who disagree about companionship are not necessarily uncompanionable. Couples interested in recreation enough to disagree about it usually manage to get in a good deal of it as measured by frequency of joint activities. Despite this, they are least satisfied with the companionship they get, else they wouldn't disagree about it so much. They are not therefore objectively deprived couples but dissatisfied in relation to high expectations.

The two young wives who confess to disagreements about sex have highly companionable marriages. Least companionable are couples who disagree primarily about money. Sex is an interactive matter whereas money is a question of objects outside the interpersonal relationship—hence the differential relationship to companionship.

Highest on mental-hygiene functioning are wives who have no disagreements (because their husbands understand them so well?). However, they wish they had more companionship. Advice and active help are given most often to wives plagued with child-rearing problems. Least therapeutic are the relationships between husbands and wives who attack each others' personalities. Such wives are especially apt to get critical responses if they share their troubles with the husband after a bad day.

The Impact of Disagreements on Marriage

Rated especially incohesive are marriages where in-laws are a problem. Such marriages are usually in the early stages of being glued together.

When wives are asked how often they have disagreements, those whose chief problem is children report the highest frequency. From year to year, children present ever new disciplinary problems to be solved.

Couples with role problems also feel that they have more disagreements than the average family. Nevertheless, they manage to have cohesive, satisfied marriages. This combination illustrates how stresses can be taken in stride by a good marriage. A marriage need not be devoid of disagreements to be strong.

However, few marriages can stand attacks on a partner's personal behavior without serious consequences. Such attacks loom large in the alienation which leads to divorce (Goode 1956). Personal attacks hurt the ego too much to be easily repaired or easily forgiven. The damage they do lives after them to haunt attacker and victim alike. If any particular disagreements are symptomatic of crippling stresses in marriage, personality conflicts are the ones.

The Frequency of Disagreements. When Detroit wives are asked whether they disagree with their husbands more or less often than other families they know, most say less often. This is a logical absurdity—how can the average couple disagree less than the average couple? Nevertheless, a wife's answer to this question is symptomatic of her attitude toward her marriage and reflects a *relative* difference in the frequency of disagreements.

Wives who claim few disagreements are consistently more satisfied with the standard of living, the companionship, the understanding, and the love provided by their husbands. Conversely, the few wives who feel that they have more disagreements than other couples are conspicuously dissatisfied with their husbands. They also have the greatest discrepancies in their child-bearing experience, especially in the direction of unwanted children. Lack of enthusiasm for their children is partly a feedback from the unhappiness of their marriages, but the objective evidence shows that they average 2.34 children born compared to 2.19 for wives who claim average disagreement rates and 1.96 for those who disagree less than usual. In view of the fact that disagreements are most frequent among couples whose chief problem is children, it is difficult to escape the conclusion that children are a potent source of conflict between husbands and wives. Frequency of disagreeing is also related to mental-hygiene functioning. Husbands who give advice and sympathy have the fewest disagreements, whereas critical husbands have the most. Correspondingly, wives who experience few disagreements find the husband's therapeutic response most effective, whereas feeling worse is associated with many disagreements. Perhaps these are different ways of saying the same thing—husbands prone to disagree are likely to throw the wife's complaints back in her face. In any case, disagreements are not a form of communication which wives prize. Rather, they are both causes and consequences of marital alienation. In general, disagreements prominent enough to stick in the wife's memory reflect genuine stress.

THE STRENGTHS OF AMERICAN MARRIAGES

How strong are the marriages in a metropolitan community and on nearby farms? How vital, how meaningful? Are they hollow shells on the verge of collapse? Are they vestigial appendages of a changing civilization, soon to be cast aside?

There are two ways of determining answers to such questions. One is to ask the participants themselves how they feel about their marriages, the main approach in this study. The other is to ask outside observers to pass judgment on what they see in the marriage. This, too, has been done using the sociologists-in-training who coded each interview schedule as the observers. The cohesiveness shown in the *behavior* (not the self-evaluations) of the respondents was rated in this fashion.

If there were serious discrepancies between the wives' stated satisfactions and the coders' ratings of cohesiveness, it might mean that one of the measures doesn't mean much. Actually, there is a high correlation between the two (87 per cent of the dissatisfied wives being rated incohesive compared to only 1 per cent of the most satisfied wives, for example). Such results testify, at least, to the consistency between verbalized satisfaction of the wives and the rest of their interview responses. More likely, they indicate that wives who say they are satisfied with their marriages are not bluffing but really mean it.

From this point of view, the satisfaction of the interviewed wives is impressive. The vast majority of marriages fulfill the participants' expectations. Although very few wives feel that their marriages can't be improved in any respect, the average wife is not far from such enthusiasm. The old slogan urged skeptics to "Ask the man who owns one." We asked the women who own contemporary marriages, and they proved to be satisfied customers.

The objection might be raised that unhappy wives are rare because they have already become divorcees. This is less of a factor than might be imagined. While more than one-sixth of all first marriages do end in divorce, divorcees remarry so fast that they tend to be interviewed in their second marriage. Five per cent of the farm women and 11 per cent of the city women interviewed were remarried divorcees. This high rate of remarriage prevents the U.S. Census from finding more than 3 or 4 per cent of adult women in American cities at any one time who are unmarried divorcees. (Taeuber 1958). This means that a relatively small proportion of the satisfaction of Detroit wives can be attributed to skimming the cream off initial marriages.

Taken as a whole, these contemporary marriages appear quite stable from the standpoint of the participants. People who are satisfied are not likely to change partners or to give up married life for living alone. Only the few dissatisfied marriages are vulnerable to enticement from without and disintegration from within. The rest of the marriages meet too many of the participants' needs to be sacrificed.

All contemporary marriages are not equally satisfactory, however, so it will be useful to conclude this exploration of the dynamics of married living by reviewing the major sources of strength in marriage. There are four: (1) the family's social status, (2) the couple's homogamy, (3) the extent to which they meet each other's needs, and (4) children—in moderation. Against these, must be set a counter-agent: the corrosion of time.

The Family's Social Status

An important source of marital satisfaction for the wife is the husband's prestige or social standing in the community. Undoubtedly, many wives feel proud to be married to a man who is socially prominent or respectable and embarrassed if the husband is looked down upon by others. However, that is not what is meant here by marital satisfaction. Rather this term refers to how satisfied the wife is with the way her marriage functions, with the extent to which her husband meets her needs for companionship, children, understanding, love, and a comfortable standard of living. When the wife reports how satisfied she is with her husband *as a husband,* she is not simply duplicating the community's assessment of him if she rates a high-status husband tops.

Table 122
Marital Satisfaction, by Social Status

	PERCENTILE RANKING ON SOCIAL STATUS INDEX				
	0–19	20–39	40–59	60–79	80–99
Marital satisfaction	4.45	4.59	4.70	4.65	4.93
Number of families	11	80	198	178	88

Table 122 shows that high-status husbands do rate high with their wives. This means that the higher the husband's standing in the community the better he is able to play the role of husband. (Theoretically the wife's greater satisfaction could result from lowered expectations, too, but common-sense observation suggests that high-status couples expect a good deal of each other.)

The reasons why high-status marriages function so well can be illuminated by presenting the four component parts of the Social Status Index, namely the husband's occupation, income, education, and ethnic background.

Table 123 shows that education is most closely related to marital satisfaction. Occupation and income, on the other hand, although generally associated with satisfaction, incur slight declines in the upper brackets (occupation to a slight extent, income rather drastically). This difference suggests that a distinction must be made between settled, crystallized high status in which family position has been consolidated on a high plane for a generation back, and status currently being

Table 123

Marital Satisfaction, by Husband's Occupation, Income, Education, and Ethnic Background

MARITAL
SATISFACTION
BY

A. HUSBAND'S OCCUPATION:		BLUE COLLAR		WHITE COLLAR	
		Low	High	Low	High
		4.61	4.61	4.85	4.80
		(155)	(165)	(81)	(155)

B. HUSBAND'S INCOME:	Under $3,000	$3,000 –4,999	$5,000 –6,999	$7,000 –9,999	Over $10,000
	4.32	4.75	4.80	4.61	4.72
	(57)	(165)	(185)	(82)	(54)

C. HUSBAND'S EDUCATION:	Some Grade School	Grade School Graduate	Some High School	High School Graduate	Some College	College Graduate
	4.29	4.42	4.56	4.90	4.96	5.04
	(62)	(78)	(124)	(182)	(55)	(51)

D. HUSBAND'S ETHNIC BACKGROUND (MAJOR GROUPS):	Negro	Polish	Irish	German	British
	4.23	4.82	4.47	4.61	4.70
	(105)	(77)	(49)	(79)	(135)

struggled for, through earning money the hard way at the expense of the marriage (cf. Lenski 1954). If high income is earned through the husband's preoccupation with his job to the neglect of his wife, she feels dissatisfied. Indeed Table 123 suggests that comparatively little income is needed to satisfy the wife as long as it measures up to her expectations.

Education, by contrast, symbolizes a way of life involving a happy blend of companionship, love, understanding, and children, which at the same time provides an adequate standard of living without undue effort. These differences are analogous to the differences between aristocratic upper-upper class families and showy "nouveaux riches" but they extend well down into the middle class.

While its relation to satisfaction is not completely consistent, the prestige level of various ethnic groups depends to a considerable extent on the length of time they have been in the United States. Hence, marital satisfaction tends to be associated with the number of generations of American ancestry the couple have behind them (see Table 124).

Table 124

Marital Satisfaction, by Degree of Americanization

	DEGREE OF AMERICANIZATION			
	Both Partners Immigrants	One Partner Immigrant	Minimally First Generation	Minimally Second Generation
Marital satisfaction	4.31	4.56	4.73	4.93
Number of families	59	68	193	157

We believe that lengthy residence in the United States affects the family more by providing secure status in the community than by acculturation to American family norms. In any case, the process of Americanization doesn't seem to undermine family life as far as the participants are concerned.

To summarize, high social status provides a more satisfying marriage for the wife, insofar as it gives the husband the *savoir faire,* the emotional security, and the leisure to meet her needs, at the same time that he discharges his occupational role competently. Wives of men who are struggling to achieve such status can take comfort in the thought that their children will experience a more satisfying way of life than they have known. Families more moderately situated may find a pattern of living which suits their expectations eminently well. Dramatic evidence of this is the identical satisfaction scores of urban Detroit families and Michigan farm families who, on the whole, are far from prosperous. But bottom-status families, especially Negro families, are likely to find the going tough and married life just as dissatisfying as their life in the community. These are the weakest families in the community, most liable to divorce and desertion, for whom a satisfactory family life under adverse conditions is a rare achievement.

The Couple's Homogamy

How much a husband can satisfy his wife's needs depends not only on his standing in the community but also on his position relative to her. If his position is similar to hers, they tend to have compatible interests and expectations, and to share a common style of life. If his position is higher, he will be able to offer greater resources than she is used to which will partially offset the incompatibility of their backgrounds. However, if his position is lower than hers, the strain of incompatible outlooks is compounded by his inability to measure up to her expectations. Hence, homogamy normally produces the greatest satisfaction for the wife, husband-superiority gives lessened satisfaction, and husband-inferiority the least (see Table 125).

Table 125

Marital Satisfaction, by Comparative Age and Comparative Education of Husband and Wife

MARITAL SATISFACTION	HUSBAND SUPERIOR		EQUAL	HUSBAND INFERIOR	
	Markedly	Slightly		Slightly	Markedly
By Age*	4.23	4.74	4.79	4.65	4.00
	(35)	(193)	(256)	(57)	(14)
By Education†	4.55	4.73	4.89	4.62	4.51
	(93)	(115)	(180)	(94)	(71)

*Cutting points for age differences are as follows: husband 11 or more years older; 4–10 years older; 1–3 years older or equal; 1–3 years younger; and 4 or more years younger. Numbers in parentheses show the number of families on which means are based.

† The cutting point on education is 3 or more years for markedly different.

Usually, there is a limited range within which it matters little whether the husband and wife are precisely equal or differ slightly. This is especially true of age, since minor age differences signify little in terms of differential resources or differing interests. Moreover, the norm of current American practice is for the husband to be several years older than the wife—hence this "normal" group is the most satisfied maritally. Unlike superiority in education or occupational background, superior age is no guarantee that the husband will be able to offer the wife greater resources to compensate for differences in friends, interests, energy levels, etc. Indeed, since aging is so highly associated with declining marital interaction, an older spouse is very apt to function less adequately.

The mean scores regarding comparative education fit the theory of compatibility perfectly. Presumably, more extreme differences in education would depress satisfaction still further.

Other data show that marked superiority in the husband's occupational background increases rather than decreases the wife's satisfaction. Such husbands are able to offer sufficiently greater resources of family background, style of life, and money to offset the strains involved in a mixed class marriage. While the wife benefits from a discrepancy in this direction, correspondingly lessened satisfaction may be predicted for the husband.

Table 126
Marital Satisfaction, by Comparative Religious Background of Husband and Wife

	RELIGIOUS BACKGROUND		
	Same	Mixed-Protestant	Protestant-Catholic
Marital satisfaction	4.79	4.63	4.58
Number of families	258	144	125

Religious differences are a source of strain which lacks the invidious distinctions of age and status differences. Table 126 shows that the greater the difference in religious backgrounds, the less the satisfaction.

To summarize these comparisons, homogamy seems to make it easier for two people to achieve a better marriage. If the husband is superior to the wife, his additional resources may be sufficient to make up for the incompatibility, but if he is inferior, the wife's satisfaction normally suffers from his inability to meet her needs and expectations.

The Personal Needs Met by the Marriage Partner

Homogamy provides the foundation on which a strong marriage can be built. What the couple does with their potentialities determines how satisfactory the marriage really is. Thousands of people in the world are homogamous in age, education, religion, and social status, but homogamy alone doesn't guarantee satisfaction. Compatible individuals must go beyond choosing one another to loving each other and doing what love requires of them. Basically, love requires serving the partner in ways which satisfy his basic needs.

Marriage serves many needs—physical, emotional, and social. The following needs illustrate the contribution that particular services make to marital solidarity: (1) the need for self-esteem; (2) the need for companionship; (3) the need to be understood.

The Need for Self-Esteem. Everybody needs to respect himself and to feel that others respect him. The restoration of self-respect is a prime goal of the mental-hygiene function in marriage. It is accomplished, in part, by ego-repair from the partner, after injury has occurred at the hands of someone (or something) else.

To be able to repair his wife's ego, a man must have a sound relationship with her. He cannot be therapeutic if he offends her through neglect or ridicule.

But making a marriage work involves more than avoiding strain and providing therapy. Self-respect is also created through respect from the partner. Such respect is manifested through consultation over issues which concern both partners.

It is disappointing to discover that a major decision has been made without sounding out those involved. Unilateral moves produce feelings of not counting, of being a nonentity. By contrast, it is invigorating to feel that one matters to someone else—and no high-sounding words can prove this as much as inclusion in the decision-making process.

Table 127

Marital Satisfaction, by Decision-making Pattern

| | DECISION-MAKING PATTERN | | |
	Husband Dominant	Syncratic	Autonomic	Wife Dominant
Marital satisfaction	4.64	5.06	4.70	4.40
Number of families	120	120	187	91

Table 127 shows the conspicuous marital enthusiasm of wives who are counted-in on decisions. Equality between husband and wife is not the crucial factor—for autonomic couples are just as equal but much less enthusiastic. Equality combined with separate decision-making is a kind of not counting, not mattering to the other partner in his area of interest.

What about the dominant wife—doesn't she count? In the sense of having a voice in decisions, she obviously plays an even more central role than a syncratic wife. What matters is whether she counts in the eyes of her partner—and this is precisely where dominant wives get short-changed. The reason for their dominance is the husband's absention from the marriage. His marginality is evidence precisely of disrespect. Hence the wife who must "go it alone" in marriage feels dismayed rather than pleased.

The joint consultation of syncratic couples has instrumental value beyond undergirding the partners' self-respect. Decisions made jointly are most likely to represent the interests of both partners and therefore to meet other needs as well. Syncratic couples are likely to be unusually satisfied with the allocation of marital resources from the decisions actually made.

Table 128
Marital Satisfaction, by Sharing of Household Tasks

NUMBER OF SHARED TASKS*

	None	One	Two	Three	Four or more
Marital satisfaction	4.46	4.77	4.88	5.11	4.74
Number of families	171	166	103	53	27

* Number out of the eight major household tasks on which the wives were questioned.

It is important to note in passing that there is a significant difference between sharing power and sharing tasks (see Table 128). Being consulted in decisions is ego-reinforcing. Being helped with household tasks provides some companionship (and lack of mutual participation reduces satisfaction), but extreme sharing of this sort is not essential to knowing that one matters to the partner. Couples may specialize in tasks where each is most competent without feeling any loss of respect thereby. Indeed the recognition that one has a skill the partner lacks may be ego-enhancing in itself.

On the other hand, the decreased satisfaction which accompanies high sharing of home tasks probably doesn't result from sharing as such but from the stressful conditions under which pervasive help becomes necessary. Usually it is couples pressed for time by joint employment, many young children, etc. who share so much—and their marital satisfaction is impeded by the same stress-producing factors.

Some sharing of tasks is required for maximum satisfaction. The optimum pattern is neither complete sharing nor complete separation, but help as needed. Consistent sharing in work, then, is not essential to feeling respected. But shared decision-making is essential to mutual respect.

The Need for Companionship. People need people. Lack of contact with others is one of the symptoms of severe mental illness. But companionship is something more than just being near others. It involves appreciation for the presence of a particular person. It is the added enjoyment which comes from sharing experiences with a close friend, and the added satisfaction which comes from knowing that one's own presence is valued, too. The desire to spend life together is the essence of marriage. Cemented by religious and legal ceremonies, by social supports and inner functions, marriage is the most effective means ever devised for meeting man's need for companionship.

The close relationship between marital satisfaction and companionship reflects the high value which most wives place on this particular aspect of marriage (see Table 129).

Table 129

Marital Satisfaction, by Type and Degree of Companionship

TYPE OF COMPANIONSHIP	DEGREE OF COMPANIONSHIP				
	None	Slight	Moderate	Considerable	Intense
1. Organizational*	4.60	4.70	4.92	5.04	4.58
	(327)	(54)	(93)	(55)	(24)
2. Informative†	4.32	4.17	4.54	4.67	4.90
	(34)	(24)	(54)	(193)	(240)
3. Colleague‡	4.46	4.75	—	5.11	4.80
	(212)	(186)		(103)	(50)
4. Friendship§	4.22	4.54	4.84	4.87	4.76
	(50)	(128)	(77)	(178)	(119)

* Number of joint memberships: none, one, two, three, four or more. Numbers in parentheses are number of families on which mean is based.

† Frequency husband reports work events: never, seldom, monthly, weekly, daily.

‡ Frequency of visiting work mates: never, seldom, monthly, weekly.

§ Proportion of husband's friends wife knows quite well: none, some, half, most, all.

Joint participation in organizations characterizes satisfied couples, provided it is not carried to an extreme. Similarly, it is not necessary for husband and wife to possess all friends in common or to be always on the go in visiting and entertaining. The most satisfying pattern seems to be a variety of leisure-time activities, many but not all of which are shared together. There is still room in a companionable marriage for freedom and independence as well as for sharing and togetherness. In fact, companionship in interaction with outsiders (organizational, colleague, and friendship) may reduce satisfaction when carried to extremes.

On the other hand, there is no saturation point in communicating separate experiences to each other. Such communication keeps the two partners abreast of each other's development. The fact that the partner takes time to share his thoughts and experiences is further evidence of counting. But pure vicariousness is not enough. It takes shared information plus joint activities to provide an adequate sense of companionship.

The Need to Be Understood. Companionship and shared decision-making are all very well when life goes smoothly. However, there are crises in life when what is needed is not just a companion but help in solving problems and a sympathetic ear. This is a more erratic need than the other two, important chiefly when setbacks occur, but contributing to marital satisfaction even in good times because of the memory of previous help and the secure knowledge that it is available as needed.

Table 130

Marital Satisfaction, by Husband's Therapeutic Response

Husband's Therapeutic Response	Marital Satisfaction	Number of Families
1. Help solve the problem	5.27	32
2. Sympathy	4.94	170
3. Help withdraw from situation	4.90	20
4. Advice	4.74	107
5. Passivity	4.58	96
6. Dismissal	4.31	42
7. Criticism	4.17	35
Wife never tells him	4.34	48

Table 130 shows the striking differences in marital satisfaction between marriages in which the wife's problems are understood by the husband and those in which she is unable to communicate her troubles to him or is rejected for doing so. Clearly, the most satisfaction is generated when the husband is attentive to and directly helps to solve the problems his wife faces. When this is not possible, sympathetic understanding and efforts to help the wife get out of difficult situations produce satisfaction. But husbandly passivity yields little help or promise for the wife, and critical or irresponsible reactions to the wife's difficulties tend to increase dissatisfaction. In short, when the husband responds positively, the wife's need to be understood is fulfilled. If he responds negatively or she fears that he would, her needs go begging.

Self-respect, companionship, and understanding are only a few of the needs which marriage is designed to meet. Insofar as a given marriage does so, it brings to the participants satisfaction, increased love, and lasting strength.

Children (in Moderation)

Children are a source of strength in marriage provided there are not too many of them. Children are like medicine—in proper doses they create health, but an overdose can be detrimental.

Table 131

Marital Satisfaction, by Number of Children Ever Born and by Number Presently in Family

MARITAL SATISFACTION	NUMBER OF CHILDREN					
	None	One	Two	Three	Four	Five+
By Number Ever Born	4.50	4.77	4.78	4.93	4.60	3.90
	(80)	(140)	(171)	(96)	(43)	(29)
By Number Presently in the Family	4.32	4.67	4.86	5.16	— 4.86 —	
	(164)	(132)	(147)	(76)	(37)	

Both by the number of children ever born and by the number currently living at home, three is the magic number. Above three, satisfaction declines rapidly. This is related to the fact that (1) mothers of more than three or four children often wish they didn't have so many. This is not a universal reaction but occurs often enough to impair average satisfaction. (2) There is a rare but perceptible tendency for some women who are dissatisfied with their husbands to want extra children. Having more children makes them happier personally, but doesn't make them any more satisfied with their husbands. (3) The kind of people who have large families are often those whose marriages are less satisfactory anyway. Low-status, poorly educated, immigrant women (to cite a few relevant groups) wouldn't have much more satisfactory marriages if they had fewer children—although it might help. This status handicap applies more to the older generation than to the younger, hence, the especially low-satisfaction rating of women who have born more than four children (most of whom are too old to have that many still around).

Conversely, one reason why mothers of three children are so satisfied is that this is the number most often preferred by high status women. However, there is more to this business of numbers than just selectivity. Wives with many fewer than three children often feel unfulfilled and disappointed. Usually the fault is not the husband's, yet the wife's satisfaction with the kind of marriage she has is affected. More demonstrably, "extra" children strain the ability of the husband and wife to function as an intimate pair. The extra responsibilities, extra noise, extra expense, etc. tend to come between the partners. If they are not to neglect their children's needs, they must lose touch with each other to some degree. They can't have as much companionship, enjoy as many romantic evenings, take as much time to talk to each other because of the competing demands of the children.

This is not to say that they are necessarily any less happy. This may be just what they want. Most mothers of large families say they would have the same number over again if they had their choice. Indisputably, however, in having so many children they sacrifice the husband-wife relationship in favor of the parent-child relationship. They become family-oriented instead of marriage-oriented. Only within the limits of three or perhaps four children is it possible for an ordinary husband and wife to maintain effective communication with each other. Beyond this point perhaps a few couples succeed but the majority do not.

Children, then, are a source of strength in marriage—although not in every part of it or for every couple—up to a certain point. The point of diminishing returns in this particular sample is four. For other cities or at other times the precise turning point may differ. Doubtless in every modern community, some such turning point will be found, beyond which it's hard for a husband and wife to continue to see each other "across a crowded room."

The Corrosion of Time

Wearing away at the strengths in marriage is the corrosive influence of time. Table 132 shows how the average wife's marital satisfaction ebbs with the passing decades.

Table 132

Marital Satisfaction, by Length of Marriage

	LENGTH OF MARRIAGE				
	Under 2 years	3–9 years	10–19 years	20–29 years	30+ years
Marital satisfaction	5.36	5.02	4.77	4.20	4.10
Number of families	33	174	180	81	88

The first few years of marriage are a honeymoon period which continues the romance of courtship. With the birth of the first baby, satisfaction with the standard of living and companionship decline. In subsequent years, love and understanding sag, too. If children do not come, their absence is an alternative source of dissatisfaction.

These trends do not involve all couples, but affect a very large proportion of the total. In the first two years of marriage, 52 per cent of the wives are very satisfied with their marriages, and none notably dissatisfied. Twenty years later only 6 per cent are still very satisfied, while 21 per cent are conspicuously dissatisfied. These figures suggest that a majority of wives become significantly less satisfied in later marriage than they were at the beginning.

Some of this decline involves the calming of enthusiasm into satisfaction as a result of getting used to the partner, no matter how fine he may be. Newlyweds *ought* to be enthusiastic because they are tasting new satisfactions for the first time. However, much of the decline in satisfaction reflects observable decreases in the number of things husbands and wives do with and for each other. Hence, corrosion is not too harsh a term for what happens to the average marriage in the course of time. Too many husbands and wives allow their marriages to go to seed for any milder term to be appropriate. As individuals, middle-aged husbands and wives may find satisfaction elsewhere—in friends, the husband in his work, the wife in her children—they seldom find as much in each other.

Of Time and of Children. The fate of marriage is not purely a question of time. Children can be another source of weakness or of strength, depending on how old they are and how many there are. Length of marriage, and age, and number of children are three interrelated factors embraced by the single concept of the family-life cycle (see Table 133).

Table 133

Marital Satisfaction, by Stage in Family-life Cycle

		STAGE IN FAMILY-LIFE CYCLE			
Childrearing stages:		Preschool	Preadolescent	Adolescent	Unlaunched
		5.22	4.95	4.59	3.96
		(121)	(133)	(95)	(56)
Childless stages:	Honeymoon				Postparental	Retired
	5.26				4.32	4.00
	(19)				(77)	(8)
Childless couples:		4.55	4.32	4.11	
		(9)	(28)	(9)	

At first, the arrival of children effectively offsets the corrosion of time. For one thing, marital satisfaction is heightened by the fulfilment of the universal desire to have children. Moreover, the children's impairment of the standard of living and of husband-wife companionship is offset by the increased sense of understanding and love which young mothers experience. Conversely, by the time childless couples have been married as many as four to seven years, the disappointment of hopes for children affects the wife's satisfaction so profoundly that tangible compensations like a high standard of living and continued dating companionship hardly dull the sense of tragedy.

Once the preschool stage of infantile dependency has passed (dependency of the child on its mother and of the mother on her husband in turn), declining satisfaction characterizes each succeeding stage in the family-life cycle. The only possible exception to this generalization is that there may be a second honeymoon of increased satisfaction for a brief period following the departure of the last child. Unfortunately, we cannot test this hypothesis with the present data, since we failed to ask when the launching occurred for postparental couples. Even if we knew, there are historical complexities which might confuse the picture. Parents who completed their childrearing in the 1950's were those whose child-bearing had been hampered by the Depression of the 1930's. Hence the child-bearing deficiencies concentrated in this cohort of wives artificially depress their over-all marital satisfaction.

Regardless of historical factors, it seems probable that the marriage relationship is eclipsed by other interests in the later years of child-rearing. This seems especially true of women with launchable children at home. Many families don't keep their children home past the nineteenth birthday. Their children go off to college or move into apartments with working friends or get married. It may be that having adult children at home is symptomatic of deviance. One hint in this direction is the tendency of mothers of unlaunched children to wish they had fewer children. Whether this is because they resent the child's failure to become independent or because they hold onto the oldest child to help support and care for a flock of unwanted younger siblings is not clear. Whatever the reasons, these wives have notably unsatisfactory marriages.

STRESSES AND STRENGTHS IN AMERICAN MARRIAGES

Compared to the prophecies of doom cited at the beginning of this book, contemporary marriages sparkle. Most wives are satisfied with the love, the understanding, and the standard of living provided by their husbands. Moreover, economic prosperity and medical science may improve their ability to have the number of children they would like to have.

Weak spots there are—most notably in Negro marriages and to a lesser extent in low-status quarters generally. Incompatibility creates extra stresses when couples marry with major differences in age, education, religion, etc.

Nevertheless in any marriage, strength can come from meeting the needs of the partner to be consulted, to have companionship, to be understood—in short, to be loved. Strength ordinarily comes from children, too, except in those rare cases where children were not wanted or come in excess.

American marriages are particularly satisfactory in their early years—despite the fact that most divorces occur in the same years. In the midst of rearing children, the marriage relationship tends to be subordinated. However, it may retain enough vitality to reassert itself when child-rearing is completed. Moreover, lessened enthusiasm is offset by deepened habituation in the later years.

In any case, there seems to be little evidence, from the 909 wives interviewed, that American marriage as an institution is on the verge of collapse. On the contrary, as long as men and women continue to have important needs satisfied by their partners, marriage is "here to stay."

RESEARCH METHODS AND THE USE OF EMPIRICAL EVIDENCE

CONCEPTUAL APPROACH AND THE ROLE OF EMPIRICAL DATA

Although marriage and the family are the subject of many scholarly and popular works, there has been a dearth of empirical evidence to support the contentions found therein. On the other hand, there is great need for better theoretical understanding of the family—its structure and functioning and their determinants and consequences. It is apparent that a compromise must be drawn between armchair speculation and rank empiricism. We need a theoretical framework to make sense of the available data, and at the same time we need sound empirical evidence to support the theoretical propositions. Theory without supporting data and data without any theoretical context are equally meaningless.

The current project cannot pretend to have started with a well-rounded theoretical framework. To a considerable extent, our work has been exploratory in theory as well as in reality. Nevertheless, a generalized conceptual approach played an important part in instigating this research and provided a source of direction throughout the analysis of the data and the writing of the manuscript.

Stated most broadly, this approach might be termed "social dynamic." It is akin in many respects to field theory. Our basic assumption is that any particular aspect of family life is determined by a wide variety of forces or causes. Some of these forces originate in the personalities of family members, some in the internal structure and patterns of interaction which have developed within the family over the years, and some in social, cultural, and economic characteristics of the wider community.

The term "social" applies to this approach, since we have placed more stress on social factors within the family and its environment than on other factors (while not denying that economic, cultural, or psychological variables are relevant and important). The term "dynamic" indicates a concern with the forces presently acting on the family, i.e., the dynamic causes of family behavior.

Our goal has been to understand the structure and functioning of the marital relationship, assuming that there is a close connection between them, and that they are important for the welfare of the family as a unit and of the husband and wife as individuals. While searching for causes in the present and immediate past, we have also been interested in understanding the process of historical change. Therefore, at the beginning of each chapter, we have reviewed in historical perspective the topic for that chapter. Contemporary marriage patterns are thus seen as the product of forces which have developed in the past and which can be studied empirically in the present.

In short, we are concerned with both theoretical understanding and empirical evidence. Each of the many tables presented has been selected for its relevance to the theoretical issues at hand, and interpreted with respect to its bearing on those issues. Through the constant interplay of theory and data, the search for better understanding of the dynamics of married living has proceeded.

SAMPLING

The empirical evidence presented in this book is based on interviews with 909 married women living in the Detroit area and Southeastern Michigan. Our goal was to choose these women in such a way that they would form representative cross-sections of the Detroit metropolitan area and of farm families in adjacent counties.

Sampling Procedure. The sampling design for Detroit consisted of multi-stage probability sampling. (1) A random sample of census tracts was drawn from the entire metropolitan area of Detroit and its densely populated suburbs. (2) A random sample of five or six city blocks was drawn from each tract. (3) Within each block, a random start was made and every *nth* dwelling unit selected for interviewing. Each household in the community had one chance in 900 of being selected.

When it came to picking our farm families, we deliberately chose three counties close to Detroit: Washtenaw, Lenawee, and Hillsdale. We wanted to find farm families which read the same newpapers, listen to the same radio stations, and watch the same TV channels as Detroiters. Thus, any differences between city and farm families would be due to the residence factor alone and not to possible regional variations. Washtenaw County is immediately west of Detroit's Wayne County and the most urbanized of the three; Lenawee lies to the southwest of Washtenaw, and Hillsdale next to Lenawee. They form a tier of counties ranging from 30 to 100 miles from downtown Detroit and decreasing in 1950 population from 135,000 to 32,000.

The farm sampling was done by dividing each county road map into mile-square blocks, 900 per county. Blocks were then chosen randomly and interviews with all the *farm* families in each block, proceeding in the sequence that the blocks had been chosen until a total of approximately 60 interviews had been secured in each county. On the average, there were five farm families per block so that our respondents typically live in a dozen of these clusters in each county.

The interviewers sent to the addresses thus selected succeeded in interviewing 85 per cent of the farm wives and 89 per cent of the city wives. The remaining 11 to 15 per cent were either never at home despite repeated visits (one-third) or refused to be interviewed (two-thirds). Fortunately, the Detroit non-respondents do not differ significantly from the respondents in race, urban vs. suburban residence, or median value of the block they live in.

Characteristics of the Samples

Ordinarily such sampling methods secure an accurate cross-section of the community, but this assumption needs to be tested by comparing our respondents with census data for the whole community. This can be done most easily for our urban data.

Sample vs. Community. The U.S. Census of 1950 occurred five years earlier than our sampling, so some changes may have occurred in the interim. The Census Bureau's definition of the Detroit metropolitan area is somewhat larger than that used by the Detroit Area Study. The Census index of occupations includes teenage workers, whereas ours is limited to adults of 21 or more years. Despite these problems in the comparability of data, Table A1 suggests that our sampling procedure succeeded in giving us a workable cross-section of the entire community. We assume that our farm sampling did also.

Community vs. Nation. How typical is Detroit of the United States as a whole?

In some ways it is highly typical. For instance, among the ten largest cities of the United States, Detroit's percentage of people moving from

Table A 1

Comparisons between the 1955 Sample and the 1950 U.S. Census of the Detroit Metropolitan Area*

Characteristic	1955 Sample†	1950 Census
Persons per dwelling unit		
1 person	8%	6%
2 persons	26	28
3 persons	21	24
4 persons	21	20
5 persons	14	12
6 or more persons	10	11
Total	100	101
Occupation of employed persons		
Professional	10%	9%
Managerial	9	9
Clerical and sales	19	22
Skilled and foremen	19	19
Semi-skilled	27	27
Service	11	9
Unskilled	4	5
Not ascertained	1	1
Total	100	101
Education of adult females (age 25 or more)		
6 years or less	14%	16%
7–8 years	21	24
9–12 years	55	49
13 or more years	10	11
Total	100	100
Age of adult females‡		
21–29	22%	26%
30–39	29	25
40–49	20	20
50–59	14	15
60 or more	15	14
Total	100	100
Number of cases (by age)	1,060	1,016,838

* The 1955 sample covers only the tracted part (86 per cent) of the Census' Standard Metropolitan Area.

† These data include one-person households and broken families in addition to the 731 married couples living together who are the focus of this book. Comparable data for married couples are unavailable from the Census reports. We are indebted to Dr. Harry Sharp and the staff of the Detroit Area Study for much of the data presented in this Appendix.

‡ The first age category for the Census is "20–29."

one address to another in 1949–50 was closest to the national average (17 per cent).

However, there are other ways in which the fact that Detroit is a big, northern, industrial city make it somewhat different. For instance, the 1955 average total family income of $6,500 in Detroit was almost $1,500 higher than the national average. This relatively high figure reflects the un- usually large proportion of skilled and semi-skilled workers in Detroit's labor force (the largest proportion of any big city in the nation). Most other cities have more unskilled workers with correspondingly lower wages.

Such differences in income and occupation mean that statistics about family life in the United States as a whole would seldom be identical with those for Detroit. Even so, we suspect that the differences are not great enough to change the over-all picture, only the details.

Detroit also has almost twice as many Negro families (16 per cent) as the national proportion. However, the Negro families have been ex- cluded from our tables except where comparisons are made between the total rural and urban samples of 178 and 731 families respectively, or where comparisons are made between Negro and white families as such. The reason for excluding Negroes from the bulk of the tables is that early analysis showed substantial differences between Negroes and whites, not only in the level of marital interaction, but sometimes even in the direction of the relationship between variables. As a result, the published cross-tabulations normally consist of the 616 white families in our urban sample, minus whatever cases were not ascertained (there were no Negroes in our farm sample).

A cross-section of the whole nation would be a better basis for de- scribing "the American family." In the absence of such national informa- tion, data from Detroit can contribute greatly to understanding how American families function. This understanding is aided by the fact that Detroit is a melting pot like other Amercan cities. Only a fourth of the Detroit husbands were actually born there, whereas another fourth came from elsewhere in the Middle West, 22 per cent from the South, 9 per cent from the East, and 16 per cent from outside the United States.

The crucial question, however, is not how typical Detroit is of the nation, but whether such differences as those between working wives and housewives are the same in Detroit as elsewhere. In general, it seems safe to assume that comparisons between subgroups in the Detroit popu- lation show how similar circumstances affect family living anywhere in the United States. Research elsewhere will prove whether this assumption is correct.

One question about American families which cannot be answered directly is whether and how family patterns differ in the various regions of the country. Even our southern-born families are no longer living in a southern atmosphere. And of westerners we have none (people seem to move only to California, not from it!) Further studies need to be made to find out whether such things as southern hospitality, northern industriousness, and western informality are unrealistic stereotypes or real differences which affect family living.

What were the main characteristics of the families we studied? Thirty-three per cent of the city wives and 47 per cent of the farm wives had no children living at home at the time of the study, but only 14 per cent and 12 per cent had never borne any children. These figures reflect the fact that farm wives in southeastern Michigan are appreciably older than city wives (typically in their late forties and late thirties respectively). The typical (median) husband and wife have had some high school education but did not finish high school. Twenty-four per cent of the city wives are employed outside the home, but only 9 per cent of the farm wives.

The urban wives are 36 per cent Catholic and 3 per cent Jewish, while only 10 per cent of the farm wives are Catholic and none Jewish. The farm families are heavily British, German, and Scandinavian in ancestry. The city families are more often Polish, Italian, or Negro. Only 22 per cent of the farm husbands are immigrants or first generation Americans, compared to 40 per cent of the city husbands.

These figures show large differences between the city and farm families on almost every demographic characteristic. They make comparison between city and farm families complex. But they are the same differences that exist between city and farm people in most parts of the United States. So our groups are not unusual in this respect.

PROBLEMS IN INTERVIEWING AMERICAN WIVES

It may seem strange that in a study of marriage only one partner should be interviewed. However, other studies show that husbands and wives usually agree sufficiently to make it possible to rely on one partner's responses. There are undoubtedly individual cases where the husband would give a different picture from the wife's, but such differences tend to get lost in the shuffle when large numbers of cases are considered.

Wives in general probably look at marriage somewhat differently from husbands. For example, wives may prize companionship outside the home more, while husbands stress companionship in bed. Hence, it should be remembered that this is a wife's-eye view of marriage. But we assume that in comparisons between groups of wives—as between middle-class wives and working-class wives—the sex bias cancels out and the differences which emerge are real differences between families.

The selection of wives instead of husbands to represent the family is largely a matter of convenience. Wives are so much more easily located at home that a larger sample can be secured by concentrating on them.

Once the choice has been made of whom to interview, many problems remain in devising an interview schedule which will secure the desired information. Should the respondent be allowed to describe her family in her own terms, or should she be confined to preconceived answers more easily quantified and comparable for all respondents? We used some questions of both types (see Appendix B). In areas where we were unsure of the dimensions of family life (such as the topics couples disagree about and the ways couples cope with a "bad day"), we felt it was important to allow the respondent full freedom in answering. Hence, the questions were left open-ended and the answers recorded verbatim by the interviewers. For a majority of the questions, however, exploratory retesting made it possible to offer a choice among predetermined answer categories. At times, these answers formed rating scales, providing quantitative measures of some variables. Such structured questions were naturally easier to analyze, but not always easier to interpret. With the variety of questions asked, we felt confident that we were tapping many of the complexities of marriage, despite the fact that many of the individual questions were rigidly simplified.

Each interview took about an hour. The interviewers were carefully trained and supervised to guarantee uniform work. All the farm interviews and one-third of the city interviews were taken by professional interviewers—the remainder by graduate students participating in the Detroit Area Study as a training project. Interviews were conducted in the home, preferably in private, but sometimes surrounded by interested children, the husband, or other relatives.

The presence of other family members sometimes presented severe problems. For instance, one wife was being pretested while feeding her baby about 9:30 in the morning. Soon her husband, a shiftworker, wandered into the livingroom in his pajamas. He made a running series of critical and sarcastic remarks about the questions and his wife's answers, yet made no effort to terminate the interview. Only when the question of total family income arose did he react more strongly, jumping from his chair with clenched fists to yell, "You get the hell out of here!" The interviewer left.

Fortunately, no episode as serious as this arose during the regular interviewing, and seldom was the presence of others seriously disruptive. In fact, most of the wives were so interested in the research that they were willing to talk about their families even under the most difficult circumstances. Most members of the "audience" found the interviewing equally interesting and, with a little explanation, co-operated in allowing the wife to answer questions freely. Resistance was less of a problem for our "personal" questions about family troubles and feelings than for the standard stratification questions on ethnic background, income, and occupation.

DATA ANALYSIS AND STATISTICAL SIGNIFICANCE

Although we have been seriously concerned with theory, our research is largely exploratory rather than definitive in its use of the data. The primary task was the generation and development of hypotheses rather than the rigorous testing of hypotheses set forth *a priori*. For this reason, in the "mining" of the vast amount of data provided by the interviews, we attempted neither to relate every variable to every other one, nor to present rigorous evidence in support of a few well-formulated hypotheses.

The analysis was guided by general theoretical notions and implicit hypotheses, and by an exploratory process in which one finding leads to curiosity about associated empirical relationships. At all times, however, relationships which might potentially contribute to theoretical understanding were investigated. Thus, some statistically significant relationships were ignored because of their trivial nature or lack of theoretical interest, while other empirical trends which fall short of the usual criteria of statistical significance have been discussed because of their crucial role in theoretical exploration. Thus, a number of important areas of family life have been explored rather intensively, generating many hypotheses. The large number of tables published indicate the available empirical support for these hypotheses or tentative generalizations and interpretations. They also enable the reader to consider alternative explanations of the data. Beyond this, we have often speculated about relevant factors for which we have no data; such ruminating is part of the process of theorizing-and-researching which gradually enlarges our understanding of the dynamics of human behavior. At all such points, this project calls urgently for further research.

Sampling Error and Statistical Significance

We have stressed the importance of a sound empirical base for theory. It is appropriate, therefore, to consider the possibility of error in the data presented and, thus, the chances of drawing incorrect inferences from the tables. There are several sources of error, each of which might lead to wrong conclusions: inaccurate or misleading answers from respondents, mistakes in recording and processing the data, loss of information through non-response, etc.

Reporting errors were kept at a minimum by careful training of interviewers, by attempting to get the confidence of the respondents so that they answered the questions to the best of their ability, and by checking the interviews for inconsistencies.

A Detroit Area Study report points out that "there is no way to determine exactly how great reporting errors are, but repeated samples of the Detroit area population will give some indication of their extent. A comparison between this year's results and the results of the past years shows that the fluctuation between sample years is small for those variables which may be expected to change slowly (e.g., age composition). Since such comparisons could be made only with demographic and socio-economic data, however, the effect of reporting errors on attitudinal and behavioral data cannot be checked specifically. Nonetheless, there is little reason to expect that these data are affected significantly."

We have already pointed out that the non-respondents differ little from the respondents in the few ascertainable characteristics. Neither the non-response nor the reporting errors can be calculated in a mathematical sense, however. These errors must therefore be distinguished from the usually calculable "sampling errors" in a random sampling design.

Sampling Errors. Due to the fact that the data are based on interviews from a small fraction of the total population, there is an additional source of error. The distribution of families selected for a sample is expected to differ by some unknown amount from that of the population from which it was drawn. If we draw two random samples from the same population, one may contain by chance an over-representation of highly educated families, while the second may have too many low-income families. Thus, the values (e.g., means or percentages) produced by a sample survey are simply estimates of the exact values which would be obtained by interviewing the entire population.

Table A 2

Approximate Sampling Error of Percentages*

SAMPLE SIZE	SAMPLING ERROR FOR REPORTED PERCENTAGES			
	5 or 95%	10 or 90%	20 or 80%	30% to 70%
50	—	—	12	16
75	—	7	10	13
100	—	7	9	11
150	4	5	7	9
200	3	5	6	8
300	3	4	5	6
400	2	3	4	6
731	2	3	4	5

* Chances are 95 in 100 that the community value lies within the sample value, plus or minus the number of percentage points shown in this table.

The sampling error is a measure of the chance variation of a sample statistic from the corresponding value in the total population. The sampling errors calculated for the present sample may be used to determine how far on either side of the sample values the central population values can be expected to lie 95 times out of 100. Sampling error varies with the size of the sample and with the degree of variance in the characteristic measured. These two factors are combined in producing Table A2, which is a generalized table of sampling errors for this study.

To illustrate the use of Table A2, consider the percentage of the full sample of 731 families where both partners belong to three or more types of organizations (13 per cent, see Table 66).

Table A2 shows that the sampling error for an *N* of 731 and a reported percentage of around 10 per cent is 3 per cent. This means that there are 95 chances in 100 that the figure of the total Detroit population lies within the limits of 13 per cent plus or minus 3 per cent. That is, there are only 5 chances in 100 that fewer than 10 per cent or more than 16 per cent of the Detroit area couples belong to this many kinds of organizations. The table shows that sampling error decreases as the percentages approach 0 or 100 and as the size of subgroups increases.

It is even more important to know whether differences in percentages between two subsamples are significant—that is, whether the differences would be likely to be found in repeated samplings of the population or in surveying the total population. Again, the size of the groups being compared and the obtained percentages must be considered in estimating the sampling errors of differences.

For purposes of economy and simplicity, detailed tests of significance are not presented in the tables in the main part of the book. To aid the interested reader in estimating the statistical significance of differences of percentages and of means, tables of approximate sampling error are offered here. Table A3 presents the approximate sampling error of differences between percentages for two subsamples.

To illustrate the use of this table, let us examine the differences in the wife's mobility role in blue-collar and white-collar families (Table 31). Twenty-one per cent of the 160 high-white-collar wives, but only 2 per cent of the 167 high-blue-collar wives take a collaborative role. Since Table A3 shows that a difference of 11 per cent would be significant with groups of size 100, and of 8 per cent with groups of size 200, when the variable is conservatively taken as varying around a central figure of 20 per cent, we know that the difference shown in Table 31 is significant. This means that the 19 per cent difference in Table 31 would arise fewer than 5 times in 100 merely because of chance fluctuations.

Most of the tables in this book deal with means rather than with percentages. Table A4 presents the approximate sampling errors of differences between means for several key variables. Since sampling error differs for samples of various sizes, each part of this table presents a

Table A 3

Approximate Sampling Error of Differences in Percentages*

Size of Subgroup	75	100	200	350	500
	FOR PROPORTIONS FROM 30% TO 70%				
75	15	14	13	12	12
100		13	12	11	10
200			10	9	8
350				7	7
500					6
	FOR PROPORTIONS AROUND 20% OR 80%				
75	13	13	11	10	10
100		11	10	9	9
200			8	7	7
350				6	6
500					5
	FOR PROPORTIONS AROUND 10% OR 90%				
75	10	10	8	8	8
100		9	8	7	7
200			6	6	6
350				5	5
500					4
	FOR PROPORTIONS AROUND 5% OR 95%				
200			5	4	4
350				4	3
500					3

* Minimum differences required for significance in comparisons of percentages from two different sub-groups (95 per cent probability).

matrix for comparing sub-samples ranging in size from 25 to 200. Two estimates are given for each cell in the matrix, the smaller indicating the approximate minimum difference required for significance at the .05 level; and the larger, the corresponding difference for the .025 level of significance.

To illustrate the use of Table A4, we shall examine the hypothesis that the husband's power decreases when the wife works outside the home (Table 13). In order to hold constant the extent of the husband's work participation, a comparison of the effects of the wife's employment can be made independently in families where the husband works overtime and where he works a normal forty-hour week. For overtime husbands, the mean power is 5.62 when the wife stays home (195 cases), but only 4.50 when she goes to work too (44 cases). The difference of 1.12 far exceeds the minimum difference of .64 required for significance at the .025 level, for samples of about 200 and about 50 respectively.

Table A 4
Approximate Sampling Error of Differences between Means for Selected Variables*

Size of Subgroup	25	50	100	200
	HUSBAND'S POWER (CHAPTER II)			
25	.98–1.18	.85–1.01	.77–.92	.72–.86
50		.69–.82	.59–.70	.54–.64
100			.48–.57	.42–.50
200				.34–.41
	TASK PERFORMANCE (CHAPTER III)			
25	1.06–1.27	.92–1.10	.83–.99	.78–.93
50		.74–.89	.63–.76	.58–.69
100			.52–.62	.45–.54
200				.37–.44
	PREFERRED NUMBER OF CHILDREN (CHAPTER V)			
25	.65–.78	.56–.68	.51–.61	.48–.57
50		.46–.55	.39–.47	.36–.43
100			.32–.38	.28–.33
200				.23–.27
	INFORMATIVE COMPANIONSHIP (CHAPTER VI)			
25	.97–1.16	.84–1.00	.76–.90	.71–.85
50		.68–.81	.58–.69	.53–.64
100			.47–.57	.41–.49
200				.33–.40
	THERAPEUTIC UTILIZATION OF HUSBAND (CHAPTER VII)			
25	.59–.71	.51–.61	.46–.55	.43–.52
50		.42–.50	.35–.42	.32–.39
100			.29–.35	.25–.30
200				.21–.25
	SATISFACTION WITH LOVE (CHAPTER VIII)			
25	.44–.52	.38–.45	.34–.41	.32–.38
50		.31–.37	.26–.31	.24–.29
100			.21–.25	.19–.22
200				.05–.06
	MARITAL SATISFACTION INDEX (CHAPTER IX)			
25	.50–.60	.43–.52	.39–.47	.37–.44
50		.35–.42	.30–.36	.27–.33
100			.24–.29	.21–.25
200				.17–.21

* The two figures in each cell represent the minimum difference between means, for significance at the .05 and .025 levels respectively, in comparisons of subgroups of the sizes indicated in the margins.

Hence, the chances are less than 2.5 in 100 that the obtained difference stems simply from errors in sampling. The comparison for families in which the husband works a normal week yields a similar level of statistical significance, and the hypothesis is again supported.

Since the sampling error varies somewhat from one variable to another, it is important to consult the appropriate part of Table A4, as well as to consider the number of cases in each subsample when testing comparisons.

While the estimation of error due to chance is an important way of evaluating empirical evidence, this alone should not rule the inferences which can be drawn from it. As the probability of random error decreases, our confidence in the evidence increases, but any particular cut-off point such as .05 or .025 is inevitably arbitrary. Modest evidence based on "non-significant" trends may lead to new insights and understandings which would be lost if a strict rule of statistical significance were followed. Moreover, relationships which may be non-significant when taken one at a time acquire greater weight when they form consistent patterns in a variety of contexts. In an exploratory, hypothesis-generating study such as this, promising leads deserve to be followed even if they fail to meet rigorous statistical tests.

It is also important to extend theoretical interpretation of the data as far as possible. At many points in this book, we have ventured into explanatory interpretations which go beyond the available data. We have tried to alert the reader to this when we have done so.

The generation of new hypotheses and explanations requires interpretation as well as inspection of the evidence. Only in this way can a nice balance be achieved between our twin goals of empirical investigation and theory-building.

A STUDY OF THE URBAN FAMILY

SCHEDULE OF QUESTIONS*

29. Aside from visiting, what kinds of things do you do in your spare time, like going to movies, watching T.V., window shopping, and so forth?

32. About how often do you folks get together outside of work with any of the people you or your husband work with?

(Card I)
(1) Every day
(2) Almost every day
(3) Once or twice a week
(4) A few times a month
(5) Once a month
(6) A few times a year
(7) Less often
(8) Never

35. About how many of your husband's friends are men that you personally know quite well?

(Card III)
(1) All

(2) Most
(3) About half
(4) Some
(5) None

38. People have different ideas about children and families, of course. As things are now, what do you think is the ideal number of children for the average American family?

39. One way in which some couples spend their time is in clubs and organizations. Please look at this list and tell me which of these kinds of organizations you or your husband belong to, if any.

(*if necessary*) 39a. Do you and he belong to the same club?

(Card V)
Labor unions
A church
Church-connected groups
Fraternal organizations or lodges
Veteran's organizations
Business or civic groups
Parent-Teachers Associations

* Questions not used in this book have been omitted.

Neighborhood clubs or community centers

Organizations of people of the same nationality background

Sports teams

Professional groups

Political clubs or organizations

Neighborhood improvement associations

Women's clubs

Charitable and welfare organizations

(*if wife belongs to other than church*) 40. Apart from the church, how often have you attended meetings of any of these groups in the last three months?

41. Some families buy most things ready-made, while others make things for themselves. How many of the cakes, cookies, and pies you eat are baked at home? (Card III)

42. How many of the canned and frozen foods you eat are put up at home? (Card III)

43. How many of the vegetables you eat in the summer are raised by your family? (Card III)

44. How many of the dresses you (and your daughters) have were made at home? (Card III)

45. We would like to know how you and your husband divide up some of the family jobs. Here is a list of different ways of dividing up jobs. Now who does the grocery shopping?

(Card VI)
(1) Husband always
(2) Husband more than wife
(3) Husband and wife exactly the same
(4) Wife more than husband
(5) Wife always

46. Who gets your husband's breakfast on work days? (Card VI)

47. Who does the evening dishes? (Card VI)

48. Who straightens up the living-room when company is coming? (Card VI)

49. Who mows the lawn? (Card VI)

50. Who shovels the sidewalk? (Card VI)

51. Who repairs things around the house? (Card VI)

52. Who keeps track of the money and the bills? (Card VI)

53. Families keep track of the money and the bills in many different ways. In some, the husband handles it all, and in others the wife does. How did you happen to work it out the way you do in your family?

54. In every family somebody has to decide such things as where the family will live and so on. Many couples talk such things over first, but the *final* decision often has to be made by the husband or the wife. For instance, who usually makes the final decision about what car to get? (Card VI)

55. . . . about whether or not to buy some life insurance? (Card VI)

56. . . . about what house or apartment to take? (Card VI)

57. Who usually makes the final decision about what job your husband should take? (Card VI)

58. . . . about whether or not *you* should go to work or quit work? (Card VI)

59. . . . about how much money your family can afford to spend per week on food? (Card VI)

60. . . . about what doctor to have when someone is sick? (Card VI)

61. . . . and, about where to go on a vacation? (Card VI)

62. Of course, most couples differ sometimes over some things. When you and your husband differ about something, do you usually give in and do it your husband's way, or does he usually come around to your point of view?

63. It would help us to know what some of the things are that couples disagree about. Since you were married, what are the main things that you and your husband have sometimes disagreed about?

64. Would you say that disagreements come up in your household *more often, about the same*, or *less often* than in other families you know?

65. Also, would you say that, as compared to most families you know, you here feel *less close* to each other, *about the same*, or *closer* than other families do?

66. Thinking of marriage in general, which one of the five things on this next card would you say is the most valuable part of marriage?

(Card VII)
1. The chance to have children.
2. The standard of living—the kind of house, clothes, car and so forth.
3. The husband's understanding of the wife's problems and feelings.
4. The husband's expression of love and affection for the wife.
5. Companionship in doing things together with the husband.

67. Which would you say is the next most valuable? (Card VII)

68. Which would you say is the third most valuable? (Card VII)

69. Every wife has some days when things go so badly that she gets pretty tense and upset. After you've had a bad day, what do you do to get it out of your system?

70. When you've had a bad day, do you tell your husband about your troubles: *always, usually, about half the time, seldom*, or *never*?

71. Why is that?

(*if ever tells husband*) 72. When you do tell him about your troubles, what does he say or do?

73. After he's done that, do you usually feel *much better, a little better, about the same*, or *worse*?

74. We are also interested in the changing size of American families. To begin with, how many children have you had altogether?

(*if any*) 75. What are their ages?

76. Is this your first marriage?

(*if no*) 77. How many years were you married to your first husband?

78. Did your first marriage end by death or divorce?

79. How long have you been married (to your present husband)?

(*wife under 45 years old—if wife 45 or older, skip to Q. 90.*)

80. Do you expect to have any (more) children?

(*if yes, in doubt, don't know*) (*if no, skip to Q 86.*)

81. Counting those you have now, how many children do you *expect* to have altogether?

(*if married two years or more*)

82. Considering how things have turned out so far, how many children would you *want* to have by the time you are 45, if you could start over again?

(*if married less than two years*)

82a. We have been talking about the number of children you *expect* to have. Now, if you could choose and have just the number you *want* by the time you are 45, how many would that be?

(*if "wanted" same as expected*)
83. Why not more children?

(*if "wanted" less than expected*)
84. Why is it you want less children than you expect to have?

(*if "wanted" more than expected*)
85. Why is it you want more children than you expect to have?

(*if no to Q 80.*)

86. Considering how things have turned out so far, how many children would you want to have by the time you are 45, if you could start over again?

(*if "wanted" same as actual no.*)
87. Why not more children?

(*if "wanted" less than actual no.*)
88. Why is it you would like to have a smaller family than you now have?

(*if "wanted" more than actual no.*)
89. Why is it you aren't having the larger family?

(*wife 45 years old or older*)
90. Considering how things have turned out, how many children would you want to have if you could start over again?

(*if "wanted" same as actual no.*)
91. Why not more children?

(*if "wanted" less than actual no.*)
92. Why is it you would like to have had a smaller family?

(*if "wanted" more than actual no.*)
93. Why is it you didn't have the larger family?

(*if wife has ever had a child*)
96. What have been some of the good things about having children?
97. What things have been not so good about having children?

(*if wife has never had a child*)
98. Did you and your husband want any children by this time in your marriage?

(*if yes*) 99. How many did you want?

100. What have been some of the good things about not having any children?

101. What things have been unpleasant about not having any children?

102. Here is a card that lists some feelings you might have about certain aspects of marriage. Could you tell me the statement that best describes how you feel about each of the following? For example, how do you feel about your standard of living—the kind of house, clothes, car, and so forth?

(Card VIII)
(1) Pretty disappointed—I'm really missing out on that.
(2) It would be nice to have more.
(3) It's all right, I guess—I can't complain.
(4) Quite satisfied—I'm lucky the way it is.
(5) Enthusiastic—it couldn't be better.

103. How do you feel about the understanding you get of your problems and feelings? (Card VIII)
104. How do you feel about the love and affection you receive? (Card VIII)
105. How do you feel about the companionship in doing things together? (Card VIII)
106. When your husband comes home from work, how often does he tell you about things that happened there? (Card I)
107. Is there any kind of promotion or different type of job your husband would like to have?

(*if yes*) 108. What kind of job or promotion would he like to have?

109. What do you think his chances are of getting this?

110. Some wives feel that they help their husband get ahead in his job or work. What sorts of things would you say you have tried to do to help your husband along in his work?

CENSUS DATA

(*by observation*) 1. Race: white, Negro, other.
6. How long have you lived in the Detroit area?

(*if not entire life*) 6a. Where did you live most of your life before you came here?
6b. Where were you born?

6c. Have you ever lived on a farm?

(*if yes*) 6d. Where?

6e. Between what ages?

7. What was the highest grade of school you completed?

(*if attended college*) 7a. How many years of college did you complete?

8. What is your religious preference?

(*if Protestant*) 8a. What religious denomination is that?

9. About how often do you usually attend religious services?

12. What was your total family income in 1954, considering all sources such as rents, profits, wages, interest, and so on?

12a. How much of that was the income of the head of the family?

13. What is your occupation?

13b. What kind of business is that in?

13c. Do you work for yourself or someone else?

(*if wife is employed*) 13d. How long have you worked since you were married?

13e. How many hours do you usually work in a week?

(*if wife is not employed*) 13g. Have you ever worked outside the home since you were married?

(*if yes*) 13h. How long have you worked altogether since you were married?

13i. Do you think you might take a job sometime in the future?

(*if yes*) 13j. When would that be?

14. What was your mother's religious preference while you were growing up?

(*if Protestant*) 14a. What religious denomination is that?

(*do not ask of Negroes*)

15. The forefathers of all Americans came from outside the United States originally. What is the original nationality of your family on your father's side?

(*if wife born in U.S.*) 16. Was your father born in the United States?

(*if yes*) 16a. Was your father's father born in the United States?

17. What was your father's usual occupation while you were growing up?

Now we would like to ask a few questions about your husband.*

13c. Does he work for himself or someone else?

(*if works for self*) 13k. About how many people does he employ?

(*if works for someone else*) 13l. About how many people are employed where your husband works?

13m. Does anyone work under your husband at his job?

(*if yes*) 13n. Does anyone work under those people?

13o. Does he work under anyone?

(*if yes*) 13p. Does anyone work over his boss?

---

* Questions similar to those asked about the wife have been omitted.

LIST OF REFERENCES

Beigel, Hugo D. "Romantic Love," *American Sociological Review*, XVI (1951), 326–34.

Blood, Robert O., Jr. "The Division of Labor in City and Farm Families," *Marriage and Family Living*, XX (1958), 170–74.

Bowman, Henry A. *Marriage for Moderns*. New York: McGraw-Hill, 1960.

Burgess, Ernest W. and Harvey J. Locke. *The Family: From Institution to Companionship*. New York: American Book Company, 1953.

Buse, Donna. "An Analysis of Past and Present Employment of Wives in Relation to Division of Labor in the Family." Ann Arbor: Detroit Area Study (mimeographed), 1953.

Deutscher, Irwin. *Married Life in the Middle Years: A Study of the Urban Postparental Couple*. Kansas City, Mo.: Community Studies, Inc., 1959.

Folsom, Joseph K. *The Family and Democratic Society*. New York: John Wiley and Sons, 1943.

Foote, Nelson N. "Matching of Husband and Wife in Phases of Development," in *Transactions of the Third World Congress of Sociology*, Vol. IV. London: International Sociological Association, 1956.

Frazier, E. Franklin. *The Negro Family in the United States*. Chicago: University of Chicago Press, 1939.

Freedman, Ronald, *et al. Principles of Sociology*. New York: Henry Holt, 1956.

Glick, Paul C. "The Life Cycle of the Family," *Marriage and Family Living*, XVII (1955), 3–9.

———. *American Families*. New York: John Wiley and Sons, 1957.

Gold, Martin, and Slater, Carol. "Office, Factory, Store—and Family: A Study of Integration Setting," *American Sociological Review,* XXIII (1958), 64–74.

Goldberg, David. "Family Role Structure and Fertility." Unpublished Ph.D. dissertation, University of Michigan, 1957.

Goode, William. *After Divorce.* Glencoe, Ill.: The Free Press, 1956.

Havighurst, Robert J. "Changing Roles in the Lives of Women in Middle Years," in Irma H. Gross (ed.), *Potentialities of Women in the Middle Years.* East Lansing: Michigan State University Press, 1956.

Homans, George. *The Human Group.* New York: Harcourt, Brace, 1950.

Jaco, E. Gartley, and Belknap, Ivan. "Is a New Family Form Emerging in the Urban Fringe?" *American Sociological Review,* XVIII (1953), 551–57.

Kinsey, Alfred C., with Pomeroy, Wardell B., and Martin, Clyde E. *Sexual Behavior in the Human Male.* Philadelphia: W. B. Saunders, 1948.

Kligler, Deborah S. "The Effects of the Employment of Married Women on Husband and Wife Roles; a Study in Culture Change." Unpublished Ph.D. dissertation, Yale University, 1954.

Lansing, John B., and Kish, Leslie. "Family Life Cycle as an Independent Variable," *American Sociological Review,* XXII (1957), 512–19.

Le Masters, E. E. "Parenthood as Crisis," *Marriage and Family Living,* XIX (1957), 352–55.

Lenski, Gerhard E. "Status Crystallization: A Non-vertical Dimension of Social Status," *American Sociological Review,* XIX (1954), 405–13.

Levy, John, and Munroe, Ruth. *The Happy Family.* New York: Alfred A. Knopf, 1938.

Linton, Ralph. *The Study of Man.* New York, 1936.

Locke, Harvey J. *Predicting Adjustment in Marriage.* New York: Henry Holt, 1951.

Miller, Daniel R., and Swanson, Guy E. *The Changing American Parent: A Study in the Detroit Area.* New York: John Wiley and Sons, Inc., 1958.

Murdock, George P. *Social Structure.* New York: Macmillan, 1949.

Myrdal, Alva and Klein, Viola. *Women's Two Roles.* London: Routledge and Kegan Paul, 1956.

Neugarten, Bernice L. "Kansas City Study of Adult Life," in Irma Gross (ed.), *Potentialities of Women in the Middle Years.* East Lansing: Michigan State University Press, 1956.

Oeser, O. A., and Hammond, S. B. *Social Structure and Personality in a City.* New York: Macmillan, 1954.

Ogburn, William F. "The Changing Family," *The Family,* XIX (1938), 139–43.

————, and Nimkoff, Meyer F. *Technology and the Changing Family.* Boston: Houghton Mifflin, 1955.

Parsons, Talcott, and Bales, Robert F. *Family, Socialization and Interaction Process.* Glencoe, Ill.: The Free Press, 1955.

Riesman, David. *The Lonely Crowd.* Garden City, N.Y.: Doubleday Anchor Books, 1954.

Scheinfeld, Amram. *Women and Men.* New York: Harcourt, Brace, 1943.

Spiro, Melford E. *Kibbutz: Venture in Utopia.* Cambridge: Harvard University Press, 1956.

Stycos, J. Mayone. *Family and Fertility in Puerto Rico.* New York: Columbia University Press, 1955.

Taeuber, Conrad, and Taeuber, Irene B. *The Changing Population of the United States.* New York: John Wiley and Sons, 1958.

Whyte, William H., Jr. "The Wives of Management" and "The Corporation and the Wife," *Fortune,* October and November, 1951.

————. *The Organization Man.* Garden City, N.Y.: Doubleday Anchor Books, 1957.

Zimmerman, Carle C. *Family and Civilization.* New York: Harper and Brothers, 1948.

AUTHOR INDEX

SUBJECT INDEX

291